Foundation Sires
of the American Quarter Horse

PUBLISHED BY THE UNIVERSITY OF OKLAHOMA PRESS
IN COOPERATION WITH
THE AMERICAN QUARTER HORSE ASSOCIATION

Foundation Sires of the

American Quarter Horse

by
Robert M. Denhardt

A Digest of Known Information About the Stallions
Whose Descendants Appear in the Early Volumes of the
*Official Stud Book and Registry of the
American Quarter Horse Association*,
Together with a Brief History of the Beginnings of
the American Quarter Horse Association

By Robert Moorman Denhardt

The Quarter Horse (3 volumes, Amarillo, 1941-50)
The Horse of the Americas (Norman, 1947, 1975)
Horses of the Conquest (editor), by R. B. Cunninghame
  Graham (Norman, 1949)
Quarter Horses: A Story of Two Centuries (Norman, 1967)
*The King Ranch Quarter Horses: And Something of the
  Ranch and the Men That Bred Them* (Norman, 1970)
Foundation Sires of the American Quarter Horse (Norman,
  1976)

Library of Congress Cataloging in Publication Data

Denhardt, Robert Moorman, 1912–
  Foundation sires of the American quarter horse . . .

  "A digest of known information about the stallions whose
descendants appear in the early volumes of the Official Stud
Book and Registry of the American Quarter Horse Associa-
tion, together with a brief history of the beginnings of the
American Quarter Horse Association."
  Includes indexes.
  1. Quarter horse. 2. Horses—Stud books.
3. American Quarter Horse Association. I. Title.
SF293.03D37   636.1'3   75–40956
ISBN 978-0-8061-2947-1

DEDICATED TO HELEN MICHAELIS *whose research and notes made much of this book possible*

Contents

FOUNDATION SIRES
OF THE AMERICAN QUARTER HORSE

I

Introduction

It has been my pleasure to prepare for the American Quarter Horse Association pedigrees of the stallions used as foundation sires of the modern Quarter Horse. At the request of the association, I am also including the story of the founding of the modern registry and its parent organization. Obviously, the compilation of such a comprehensive registry could not have been accomplished in the last two years had not most of the information been available in my files, which included those of the late Helen Michaelis. It was only necessary to go through the files, gather the information, and then rearrange it so that it had some uniformity to make the material easily accessible.

At first it seemed like a good idea to include the source of the information, such as newspapers, letters, word of mouth, and so forth. I also originally intended to include the opinions and names of those who disagreed. Sometimes even men of George Clegg's stature could change their mind on a pedigree. It soon became obvious that many of the listings would cover several pages each and make the references unwieldy. However, the American Quarter Horse Association now has all of my notes, and those of Helen Michaelis, so that any one with sufficient interest and time can run down such items and controversies as they deem essential.

As far as the actual formation of the stud book and registry and its parent organization are concerned, a brief history was an easy task, as I was intimately involved in all of the activity—from the first suggestions that such a registry would be worthwhile up to its actual formation and early operations. I had done all of the leg work, correspondence, and the searching for men of the right caliber and interest. There is no way I can tell the story without using the first-person pronoun. I attempted to eliminate personal opinions as much as possible, although I am sure some remain.

A couple of my articles appeared about twenty years ago in the *Quarter Horse Journal* entitled "Recollections of the First Secretary." Some of that story is retold here.

II

Organization of the American
Quarter Horse Association

My interest in Quarter Horses originally was sparked by the
legendary Steel Dust, a horse that neither I nor my friends
knew anything about at that time. It occurred in the early
1930's, while I was attending the University of California in
Berkeley. As much time as I could spare from my studies
was spent at the Tarantula Ranch of Paul Albert, located
just over the hills from Berkeley, north of the then small
town of Lafayette. An interesting group of horsemen were
attracted by Paul Albert, and the bull (horse?) sessions went
on far into the nights. Among those attending with some
regularity were individuals who would make their mark in
the horse world, or were doing so then. Paul Albert was just
starting the *Western Horseman* magazine, and we all wrote
for him for fun. Dane Coolidge was a western writer of some
note. Father Rivard, a "horsey" padre if there ever was one,
wrote under the pseudonym Don Alfredo. Francis Haines,
who was a graduate history student with me, later went to
Idaho to teach and was instrumental in the organization of
the Appaloosa Horse Association. Dick Halliday created the
first Palomino Horse Association, and Luis Ortega became
one of the premier rawhide workers in America. His romals,
hackamores, quirts, and bridles are works of art and col-
lectors' items.

None of us knew anything substantial about Steel Dust,
but all had heard interesting references to Steel Dust horses.
In 1937, I accepted a teaching assignment at Texas A & M.
Before I left the group at Tarantula Ranch, I promised I

5

would write an article on Steel Dust after I arrived in Texas and had done some research.

On my way to Texas, I went by Jack and Dan Casement's ranch on the Unaweep, near Whitewater, Colorado. They were the only ones I knew at that time who were familiar with Steel Dust horses. As time went on I found more and more ranchers across the western states who had similar strains of horses, tracing back to common sires such as Steel Dust, Traveler, Peter McCue, or Joe Bailey. They would generally be called after some well-known sire, like Steel Dust or Billy. Before long I knew the oldest and best breeders, such as Coke Roberds, Ott Adams, George Clegg, Dan Casement, Billy Anson (through his wife and records), and Coke Blake. These men had begun breeding Quarter Horses during the last half of the nineteenth century and—except for Billy Anson—were, despite their age, still raising Quarter Horses. The notes, pictures, correspondence, and other materials I obtained while visiting these great breeders are all in the possession of the American Quarter Horse Association today.

Some of the ranchers I visited in the western states during the late 1930's showed interest in a registry such as I was proposing. Since I was living and teaching in Texas at the time, it was only natural that these westerners formed the basis of the original group.

It should be mentioned that during this time I met Helen and Maxie Michaelis. They were living mostly on their Mexican ranch, although they were for a while south of Alpine in the Big Bend Country. Helen was collecting all the information she could on Quarter Horses. They attended the early meetings of the association, but did not become active in association business until she became secretary in 1942. I got the greatest help from two men, Jack Hutchins and Lee Underwood, both oilmen and ranchers. Jack lived at El Campo, Texas, and Lee at Wichita Falls, Texas.

The original constitution and by-laws I drew up with the

assistance of Wayne Dinsmore, who then was the secretary of the National Horse and Mule Association. Wayne told me that the Percheron's constitution and by-laws had been through the courts and were basically sound, and suggested I use them as a framework. This I did, altering as necessary to fit our proposed organization. The secretary in the Department of Agricultural Economics of Texas A & M typed out the letters that were sent out to some thirty-five active breeders in Texas, Oklahoma, Kansas, Colorado, Wyoming, New Mexico, and Arizona telling them about our plans for a Quarter Horse registry. We were to meet at the Fort Worth Fat Stock Show in March of 1939. Duwain Hughes, of San Angelo, offered to host the get-together at the Fort Worth Club. Too many important individuals failed to come to this meeting, so—except for a lot of talk—nothing was done.

The next year I wrote more people, sending out sixty letters in all. I also telephoned most of the key individuals, including the Casements, Bob Kleberg, Ernest Browning, Hugh Bennett, Bert Benear, and the Michaelises. Others I saw personally, such as Jack Hutchins and Lee Underwood, George Clegg, L. B. Wardlaw, Bill Warren, and Jim Hall. Jim and his wife, Anne Burnett Hall, invited all of the Quarter Horse breeders to a buffet supper at their home on the evening preceding the meeting.

Jack Hutchins, Lee Underwood, Bill Warren, and I had spent considerable time deciding just how to organize. This was the procedure agreed upon: we decided on a non-profit stock-holding association, incorporated under the laws of Texas; then we selected Bill to be the first chairman; afterwards we would hold a meeting of the stock holders, and they would decide on the officers and other business. We hoped this method would eliminate a lot of discussion by people who were not willing to join and financially support the new organization.

The problems of starting a registry were not taken lightly. We knew we had to build in some sort of safety factor that

ARIZONA
   J. E. Browning, Wilcox
   W. D. Wear, Wilcox
CALIFORNIA
   Frank Logan, Monterey
COLORADO
   J. Casement, Sweetwater
   Coke Roberds, Hayden
   Marshall Peavy, Steamboat Springs

KANSAS
   Dan Casement, Manhattan
OKLAHOMA
   B. B. Van Vacter, Carter
   Joe Hough, Idabel
TEXAS
   Raymond Dickson, Houston
   Jack Hutchins, Pierce
   Lee Underwood, Wichita Falls

College Station, Texas

An Open Letter to Quarter-Horse Breeders:

For several years a group of men have been working toward a quarter-horse Registry and Studbook, and at this time the following proposals are being sent out to a number of Western quarter-horse breeders. The need is felt to obtain the opinion and advice of those men who will later make the Registry a success by their support and cooperation.

Of utmost importance at this time is the formation of some definite and practical classification for registration. A few breeders in six of the Western states have been personally contacted and the following suggested entry qualifications gathered. The greater the simplicity, the more the chance of success. This should not be interpreted to mean the acceptance of other than Quarter-horses. Once firmly established the standards can be raised. Your reactions and suggestions are required at this time.

Suggested original requirements for registration:
   1. Speed: a. Ability to run the quarter in under ___ seconds, or
             b. Ability to run and turn around stakes set ___ ft.
               apart in under ___ seconds.
   2. Size: Over 14.1, under 15.3; over 950 and under 1250.
   3. Color: Solid (No painted or spotted horses)
   4. Individuality. (Purpose--to eliminate horses which definitely lack quarter-horse conformation.)

No comments are being made at present on the above proposals. Your personal reactions as to the implications and workability of each is desired. If any meet with your disapproval suggest a better. Constructive criticism is the only type which can help the committee.

Sincerely yours,

R Denhardt

Robert M. Denhardt
for the Committee

d/e

The first draft of an exploratory letter sent out early in 1938 when the author was kindling interest in an organization for Quarter Horse breeders. Added in his handwriting for the final typing were the names of Albert K. Mitchell of New Mexico and Duwain Hughes and John Burns of Texas.

8

would insure that only real Quarter Horses were registered. Jack Hutchins, Lee Underwood, and I spent many hours on this problem before the association was officially organized. We knew those safeguards had to be in the original constitution and by-laws that were to be presented to the first meeting for adoption. We worked out descriptions of certain Quarter Horse qualities revolving around conformation, performance, and bloodlines.

We all knew that we could walk into a corral containing five Thoroughbreds and five Quarter Horses and have no difficulty in picking out the Quarter Horses, but, we wondered, would future breeders and judges and inspectors be able to do so? To help them in this process of recognizing good Quarter Horse conformation as compared with that of other breeds, we drew up a description of the ideal Quarter Horse. It was as follows:

HEAD: The head of a Quarter Horse reflects alert intelligence. This is due to his short, broad head, topped by little "fox ears" and by his wide-set kind eyes and large, sensitive nostrils over a shallow, firm mouth. Well developed jaws give the impression of great strength.

NECK: The head of a Quarter Horse joins the neck at a near forty-five degree angle, with a distinct space between jaw-bone and neck muscle. The medium length, slightly arched, full neck then blends into sloping shoulders.

SHOULDERS: The Quarter Horse's unusually good saddle back is created by his medium high but sharp withers extending well back and combining with his deep sloping shoulders so that the saddle is held in proper position for balanced action.

CHEST AND FORELEGS: The Quarter Horse is deep and broad chested, as indicated by his great heart girth and his wide-set heavy forelegs which blend into his shoulders. The smooth joints and very short cannons are set on clean fetlocks and the medium length pasterns are supported by sound feet. The powerfully muscled forearm tapers to the knee whether viewed from front or side.

BACK: The short saddle back of the Quarter Horse is characterized by being close coupled and especially full and powerful across the kidney. The barrel is formed by deep, well sprung ribs back to the hip joints, and the under line comes back straight to the flank.

REAR QUARTERS: The rear quarters are broad, deep, and heavy, viewed from either side or rear, and are muscled so they are full through the thigh, stifle, gaskin, and down to the hock. The hind leg is muscled inside and out, the whole indicating the great driving power the Quarter Horse possesses. When viewed from the rear, there is great width extending evenly from top of thigh to bottom of the stifle and gaskin. The hocks are wide, deep, straight, and clean.

BONE, LEGS, AND FEET: The flat, clean, flinty bones are free from fleshiness and puffs but still show a world of substance. The foot is well rounded and roomy, with an especially deep, open heel.

STANCE: The Quarter Horse normally stands perfectly at ease with his legs well under him; this explains his ability to move quickly in any direction.

ACTION: The Quarter Horse is very collected in his action and turns or stops with noticeable ease and balance, with his hocks always well under him.

We hoped with this guideline the future officials, who had not grown up with Quarter Horses, would be able to tell one in any company. We wanted 99 per cent of all horses registered to have this conformation.

We also knew that occasionally a good performing Quarter Horse did not have perfect conformation. We also acknowledged that occasionally a horse might not have good Quarter Horse bloodlines, but still would have satisfactory Quarter Horse conformation and be able to perform like a Quarter Horse. For these few exceptions (and some would be great ones like Peter McCue—who had poor Quarter Horse conformation), we agreed to provide a loophole so truly great horses could always gain entry. We would require 99 per cent of the registered horses to have conformation, bloodlines, and performance, but would make an occasional exception in the case of a great animal that had only two of the three requirements of the breed. In other words, we would have registered Peter McCue because he had Quarter Horse performance and Quarter Horse bloodlines, even if he did not sport ideal conformation. Our idea of Quarter Horse performance was the ability to be a better than average cow horse. Performance in the cow horse was generally to be determined by its ability to cut or to rope. A horse's speed at 200 or 300 yards was an acceptable determination of performance if the Quarter Horse had never been trained in cattle work.

The Quarter Horse bloodlines did not seem too difficult at the time, probably because no one was putting on the pressure to get his horse registered. We expected the horses to trace, for the most part, back to Little Joe, Peter McCue, Joe Bailey, and a few other well-known stallions. We assumed that most outside blood would be Thoroughbred from remount horses such as Uncle Jimmy Gray or from ranch stallions of undetermined breeding. We would try to get as many pureblooded animals as possible, but as long as they carried a minimum of 50 per cent Quarter Horse blood, we would consider registering them if the other requirements of conformation and performance were present.

We did not think we would ever be anything but a modest registry. We doubted if there were over 300 horses of the type we wanted to be registered in Texas, and probably less than a thousand in the country. This small number was not a problem because we were at the time trying to preserve a nearly extinct line of horses, not to provide the riding public with an all-round horse. We knew he was the ideal cow horse, but even cow ponies seemed to be in little demand in the 1930's. We were right in many ways, but we misjudged what the future would hold for the Quarter Horse.

The second meeting was held on the evening of March 15,

11

1940. About seventy-five men and women attended, and about half of those present were active and would be members of a Quarter Horse association. Bill Warren called the meeting to order as planned. He called on me to read the proposed charter and to explain the purpose and procedure to be followed. I pointed out that under the charter that Jack Hutchins and I obtained in Austin some weeks before, the shareholders were to have complete control of the organization, each share equal to one vote. This meant that only shareholders could vote for officers or adopt a constitution or work out methods of registration. After I sat down, Dan Casement, whose knowledge and integrity were widely recognized among cattlemen, rose and said that disposal of stock to form active members was the logical first step before any business was conducted, and that the procedure I suggested should be followed.

The chairman then requested subscription for the stock, and thirty-three breeders, representing six states and Mexico, purchased stock in the new organization. The chairman then adjourned the meeting and reconvened the group as the first meeting of the American Quarter Horse Association. The first motion made and passed was that everyone present be allowed to enter into the discussions, even though only members (those owning stock) could vote. The second business was to call upon me to read the constitution and by-laws, which were adopted as read. Then a board of directors and officers were elected: Bill Warren became president; Jack Hutchins, first vice president; Lee Underwood, second vice president; Jim Hall, treasurer; and I was elected secretary. We were also elected directors, as were twenty other ranchers who were all from Texas except for Bert Benear of Tulsa, Oklahoma; Ernest Browning of Willcox, Arizona; Dan Casement of Manhattan, Kansas; Jack Casement of Whitewater, Colorado; Helen Michaelis of Coahuila, Mexico; Marshall Peavy of Clark, Colorado; T. B. Ricks of Scotia, California,

THE STATE OF TEXAS

COUNTY OF TARRANT

KNOW ALL MEN BY THESE PRESENTS:

That we, J. F. HUTCHINS, a citizen of Wharton County, Texas, W. B. WARREN, a citizen of Harris County, Texas, and ROBERT M. DENHARDT, a citizen of Brazos County, Texas, do hereby voluntarily associate ourselves together for the purpose of forming a corporation under the terms and conditions hereinafter set out, as follows:

1.

The name of this corporation is THE AMERICAN QUARTER HORSE ASSOCIATION.

2.

The purpose for which it is formed is the support of a non-profit educational undertaking; namely, the carrying on of any and all appropriate educational activities designed to increase knowledge of, and promote the use of such knowledge, with respect to the history, pedigree, record, breeding, exhibiting, publicity, sale, and improvement of the Quarter Horse breed of horses in America, as authorized by Article 1302, Section 102, Vernon's R.C.S., 1925.

3.

The place where the business of the corporation is to be transacted is at Fort Worth, in Tarrant County, Texas.

4.

The term for which it is to exist is fifty (50) years.

5.

The number of directors shall be twenty-three (23), and their names and postoffice addresses are as follows:

Name	Postoffice Address
Mrs. M. G. Michaelis, Jr.,	Eagle Pass, Texas,
J. F. Hutchins,	Pierce, Texas,

The original incorporation papers obtained for the AQHA.

13

George Clegg,	Alice, Texas,
Jack Casement,	Whitewater, Colorado,
R. L. Underwood,	Wichita Falls, Texas,
Bert Benear,	Tulsa, Oklahoma,
J. E. Browning,	Wilcox, Arizona,
J. Goodwin Hall,	Fort Worth, Texas,
Marshall Peaby,	Clark, Colorado,
L. B. Wardlaw,	Del Rio, Texas,
Ray Canada,	Eagle, Texas,
W. B. Warren,	Hockley, Texas,
Raymond Dickson,	Houston, Texas,
Tom Hogg,	Houston, Texas,
Jim Minnick,	Crowell, Texas,
W. B. Mitchell,	Marfa, Texas,
Cameron Duncan,	Freer, Texas,
J. D. Cowsert,	Junction, Texas,
Robert C. East,	Kingsville, Texas,
T. B. Ricks,	Scotia, California,
Dwain E. Hughes,	San Angelo, Texas,
W. D. Wear, Jr.,	Wilcox, Arizona,
E. W. Brown, Jr.,	Orange, Texas.

6.

The amount of capital stock is Eight Thousand Dollars
($8,000.00) divided into eight hundred (800) shares of the par
value of Ten Dollars ($10.00) each, all of which capital stock
has been subscribed and all paid in in cash as per affidavit
attached hereto,

IN TESTIMONY WHEREOF we hereunto sign our
names this 15ᵗʰ day of April, 1940.

W B Warren

Robert M Denhardt

J F Hutchins

THE STATE OF TEXAS   }
COUNTY OF HARRIS

    BEFORE ME, the undersigned authority, on this day per-
sonally appeared J.F. HUTCHINS, known to me to be the person
whose name is subscribed to the foregoing instrument, and acknowledged to me that he executed the same for the purposes and
consideration therein expressed.
    GIVEN UNDER my hand and seal of office this 15ᵗʰ day
1940.

Thelma Abbott
Notary Public in and for Harris
County, Texas.

THE STATE OF TEXAS   }
COUNTY OF HARRIS

    BEFORE ME, the undersigned authority, on this day per-
sonally appeared ROBERT M. DENHARDT, known to me to be the
person whose name is subscribed to the foregoing instrument,
acknowledged to me that he executed the same for the pur-
consideration therein expressed.
    GIVEN UNDER my hand and seal of office this 15ᵗʰ day
1940.

Thelma Abbott
Notary Public in and for Harris
County, Texas.

THE STATE OF TEXAS   }
COUNTY OF HARRIS

    BEFORE ME, the undersigned authority, on this day
personally appeared W. B. WARREN, known to me to be the person whose name is subscribed to the foregoing instrument,
and acknowledged to me that he executed the same for the purposes and consideration therein expressed.
    GIVEN UNDER my hand and seal of office this 15ᵗʰ
April, 1940.

Thelma Abbott
Notary Public in and for Harris
County, Texas.

and W. D. Wear of Willcox, Arizona. The directors then authorized the secretary, under the direction of the executive committee, to commence registrations. The meeting adjourned.

There had been some general guidelines covering registration in article VII, sections 5 through 8 of the by-laws of the newly formed association. These included the requirements that there must be a pedigree as accurate as could be furnished; that pictures of the front, rear, and each side of the animals be provided; that none should be registered except straight colors, including grays, roans, and duns; and finally, that registration should be based on "Quarter Horse bloodlines, Quarter Horse conformation, and Quarter Horse performance." In any case, these few signposts were all that were there to lead us over the rugged trail ahead.

The executive committee was composed of the president, the two vice presidents, the secretary, and the treasurer. All were from Texas so we could get together easily. Air travel was not common in 1940.

The first president of the association was Bill Warren of Hockley, Texas, a rancher and Quarter Horse breeder, and it was at his ranch that the first inspections and registrations were made. Bill Warren had been interested in horses since his childhood, and because his family were all ranchers he had plenty of opportunity to indulge in his weakness for horses. Short speed always interested him, both as a calf roper and as a matched race enthusiast. By the time the organization was formed, he had a well-developed breeding program, and was using Billy stallions, whose blood is still sought. His sires included Pancho, Cucuracha, and Alazan.

Jack F. Hutchins of the Shanghai Pierce Estate was elected first vice president. His good-humored and down-to-earth counsel had guided the formation of the organization and, until his untimely death a few years later, he was to be its most influential voice. He had been my constant advisor—in calling meetings, drawing up the constitution and by-laws, and any other problem that arose. When finances were needed, the sky was the limit as far as he was concerned. When the meetings became so warm that a real fire was liable to break out, he always stood up and said a few words, and they were always the right words, for order would soon appear out of the chaos.

It was typical of Jack Hutchins that he would not let us register any of his horses in the first book until everyone else who wanted to had been given a chance. That is why the last forty-four registrations in the initial stud book are his.

The second vice president was Robert Lee Underwood of Wichita Falls, Texas. Lee had been breeding Quarter Horses for many years before the organization of the association. It was on his ranch that I first saw large numbers of good, Quarter-type mares. In those days, pedigrees meant very little and conformation everything. He has been especially successful with regard to his mares. One key is found in the sign that he used to always have on his corral fence—"Good Horses Like Good Men Have Good Mothers."

Lee Underwood was extremely helpful in the early organizational work and was always willing to drop whatever he was doing to lend a hand. I well remember calling him on the phone one June day in the late 1930's when I was going through Wichita Falls. He asked what I was doing and I told him I was heading into Colorado to run down something more tangible about Peter McCue and to visit a friend on the Unaweep—Jack Casement. I said all I planned to do was to see, ride, and talk Quarter Horses for twelve hours a day. He said if he could have two things, he'd come with me. I asked him what they were. He said he would need fifteen hours a day to talk Quarter Horses and fifteen minutes to get ready. Needless to say, I agreed to both, and perhaps he underestimated the time he needed for both. He was with me for one month, and we visited horsemen and talked short-horses all through north Texas, northeast New Mexico and Colorado. The high point of the trip was spending several days with Coke Roberds, that grand old man of the Quarter Horse world. It was a trip that neither of us will forget. We were putting together puzzles that all make sense now, but in the 1930's many ranchers didn't know the pedigree of their own horse for more than one or two generations back. It was great to find that the better Steel Dust stallions all seemed to go back to a few noble sires like Traveler, Peter McCue, Weatherford Joe Bailey, and Old Fred—it did not matter what state we were in or what ranch we were on. These were facts that even the older breeders did not know in those days, because no common records were being kept, and nobody had been interested enough before this to travel around, accumulate, and publish the information. The better, older breeders knew the breeding of their own sires' top line, but they had no way to know that similar blood was being used by other breeders in other states.

James Goodwin Hall was elected the first, and only, single-officeholding treasurer of the AQHA. Jim, an easterner, had been a horseman all his life. He became interested in the unusual similarity of the horses on the Burnett Estates. He was told that they were Quarter Horses, and so he decided to find out more about them. He wrote an excellent historical chapter on Colonial Quarter Horses for the first volume of *The Quarter Horse.* Most of the Burnett ranch horses traced either to Weatherford Joe Bailey or to Peter McCue. Their early stallions were Joe Hancock, Rainy Day, Gold Rush, and Roan Hancock. All of their mares were pasture bred and run by number only. Jim did his best to separate and present for the first volume the best Burnett horses. He also made some extremely valuable films—in color—of the early Quarter Horse stallions and mares.

There is one more man that must be mentioned specifically, even though he was not an official member of the executive committee. That man is James H. Minnick. He had been chosen as our first inspector. His influence on type in the modern Quarter Horse has been without parallel, and even though his ideas were certainly the minority-opinion in the early years, his influence was persistent, and grew as time passed.

Jim Minnick had had a colorful life. Born on a west Texas ranch in the late 1800's, he made his living on and from horses all his life. He ran one of the earliest dude ranches; for a short time was World Champion steer roper; took Will Rogers, his life-long friend, on Will's first trip to New York; sold polo ponies and played on Long Island; was considered one of the most under-handicapped polo players ever to play a chucker; reached his ambition to own 1000 head of horses when he was only twenty-seven; jockeyed Quarter Horses as a young man and matched them when he was a little older; bought horses for the army; and was probably the greatest judge of stock horses and using horses that ever lived. Needless to say, he knew horses like no other man I have ever met. He could sense weakness in a horse while another person was looking for it. It would be impossible to guess the number of horses he handled. Since he spent so much time playing polo, it is not surprising to find that he preferred some Thoroughbred blood in his horses. He often called himself a half-breed man to distinguish himself from a bulldog man.

I traveled thousands of miles with him looking at Quarter Horses in ten or twelve states. I can never remember three nights going by without stopping to visit one of his friends, who were legion. As far as I know, although he judged hundreds of horse shows and inspected thousands of horses, he never made an enemy.

These, then, were the men—Bill Warren, Jack Hutchins, Lee Underwood, Jim Hall, Jim Minnick, and myself—who were responsible for the beginning of the AQHA operations. Fortunately, we were not granted much foresight or we might not have been so cheerful in our jobs. Since the trail before us looked smooth and straight, we loosened the cinch and gave the old pony his head, full of ignorance and good intentions.

When the first executive committee began to discuss the problem of registration seriously, it became clear almost from the start that there were two schools of thought—those who wanted lenient registration and those who wanted it strict. I recall the meeting especially well, when we thought we had reached an ideal compromise. This meeting was held on the ranch of Lee Underwood on the Jacksboro highway not far from Windthorst, Texas, in April or May of 1940. It was primarily for the executive committee, Bill Warren, Jack Hutchins, Lee Underwood, Jim Hall, and myself. Jim Minnick, the inspector who was involved in our decisions, was also there.

We all arrived early and as it was the first visit Jack and Bill had made to Lee's ranch, we spent much of the first day looking at Lee's horses. After supper we began to work and continued far into the night and most of the next day. There is not any point in telling about our discussion in any detail, but briefly it was agreed that there were probably not too many honest-to-goodness Steel Dust Quarter Horses left alive. There were, however, quite a number that had Quarter Horse blood. It was agreed it was probably necessary to register some of these latter horses. Those not full-blooded should be bred only to the clean-blooded, heavily muscled, tight-twisted Steel Dusts of the approved type. If they were not, their offspring had little chance of being Quarter Horses. We agreed a man might successfully use part-blooded mares if he had a good enough stallion. If he did not, he would not be producing the horse we were trying to perpetuate and planned to register.

At first some of us had been hesitant to accept the idea that any but dyed-in-the-wool Steeldusts should be registered under any circumstances. Jim Minnick pointed out to us that it would be very expensive for the association to send an inspector out on the road. He wondered if we did not need to register some of the lowbred horses to stay solvent. Bill Warren said that it would be difficult for many breeders to stay in business if they could not use their grade mares for breeding. At first Lee Underwood, Jack Hutchins, and I were opposed to the idea, but after Jim Hall, Jim Minnick, and Bill Warren had pointed out the practical aspects of the situation, we agreed to compromise to a certain extent the original and professed aim of the association. We agreed at the time because we thought it would be only a temporary measure. Time was to show that the momentum, once started, could not be stopped.

The compromise provided for a letter to be placed after each horse's registration number. All bona fide Quarter Horses were to be registered with an "A" after their number to show that the animal was of the approved type. Those whose bloodlines and conformation indicated about one-fourth outside blood were to be registered with a "B" after their number. Those who were definitely borderline in conformation, or who had only half Quarter Horse blood, were to be registered as "C" horses. Our intention was to limit all "other blood" to Thoroughbred, although in practice this rule proved to be elastic.

Thus, when the first horses were registered, they all had a letter inscribed after the number. The inspector would recommend the horse and the appropriate letter. The horse would next be checked by the secretary for bloodlines, and then the executive committee would get together and review the application. They based their decision on bloodlines as presented by the secretary, conformation as described by the inspector and as shown in the four pictures, and performance and way of going on the basis of the inspector's report.

The categories "A," "B," and "C," which allowed other than the old-time Billy Steeldusts to be registered, made it possible for us to reach a compromise and settled the greatest problem that confronted us in our first year's work. As was later to become apparent, it also dictated the type of

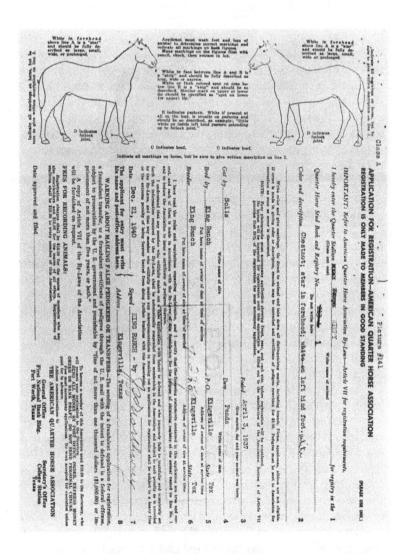

Wempe's registration papers. Note that he was originally registered Wimpy and assigned number 213A. His name was later changed to Wempe at the request of Bob Kleberg. Later, when he won the Fort Worth Quarter Horse Show, he was granted the number 1 registration.

organization the AQHA would become in the future. Had it not been for that decision (to register good horses of near Quarter-type), it is extremely doubtful if the association could have reached its present size or its international importance.

We tried to select judges for the early shows who would place the correct type of Quarter Horse, for not everyone was acquainted with the Billy Steeldusts in those days. We felt it was a part of our duty to see that a common type was placed as unbrokenly as possible at all of those early shows. A little later, in 1945, the association officials were being criticized for so instructing judges. Most of the criticism arose from owners of horses placed by the judges who were not selected by the association. Some judges were even selected just because they were members of the AQHA, and a share of stock was all that was required for membership. Some of these judges were good, but some were not. Those who were not had two common failings, even when they knew a good sound horse. They would either select a "C" type or they would select mutton withered, lard-type chunks. Neither were good Quarter Horses and the public rightfully was confused. The "C" type has become the generally approved type today, so there is no longer the confusion. This is far from the aim of the original group, but it represents the will of the majority of today's members.

Now to get back to the first registrations. The executive committee knew exactly what they were looking for, and Bill Warren's ranch was to be the test tube. The Quarter Horse, as far as we were concerned, was characterized mainly by the following features (if one or more was missing, we were inclined to be suspicious)—fox ears, bulging jaws, loaded forearms, deep heart, tremendous britches, long for his height—14 to 14–3—, small feet, ample bone, kind eye. When I say we, here, I mean the executive committee. Jim Minnick was a little more open-minded.

At this first registration, the complete executive commit-

23

tee attended: Bill Warren, Jack Hutchins, Lee Underwood, Jim Hall, Jim Minnick and myself. That evening Mrs. Warren served us a wonderful dinner, and we were still talking until almost daylight the next morning. Believe me there was plenty to go over for we had to iron out all the rough spots in our registration procedure. For the first time we were getting the breeder's point of view. Jim Minnick and I were especially interested, for we were to continue registering, but without the benefit of the whole committee.

From Bill's ranch Jim and I drove to Kingsville to register Bob Kleberg's King Ranch horses. We were awakened the next morning about 6 a.m. by a Mexican servant putting hot coffee on the nightstand by our beds. If a more satisfactory way has been devised to let you know it's time to get up, I don't know what it is. Soon we were downstairs eating breakfast and before we were through Bob Kleberg and his daughter, Helenita, came in from their home immediately behind the main house. We didn't linger over the coffee, but went right out to see the horses. Dr. J. K. Northway and Larry Cavasas had been up earlier because everyone was expecting us, and the horses were waiting. First we took a quick look at his Thoroughbreds. Among the stallions we saw was Chicaro, who was to exert a heavy influence on Quarter Horse breeding, although we did not suspect it at the time. Most of that day was spent running around the ranch from *manada* to *manada* looking at the stallions and mares. Since most of the stallions were still out with the mares, it was a most interesting day.

Before we left the King Ranch, several days later, we had registered eight or nine stallions and a little over one hundred mares. These included two daughters of Little Joe (Ada Jones and Lady of the Lake), the Old Sorrel (generally called at that time George Clegg), and Wimpy, who later was given registration No. 1 as a reward for winning the purple ribbon at our first big Fort Worth show.

Two of the greatest difficulties that arose, especially

where unbroken range-bred mares were concerned, were the problems of obtaining the four necessary pictures and deciding the performance qualification. The association bought a camera, and while I was traveling with Jim he appointed me official photographer. As he pointed out, many of the ranchers would not even try to register their mares if they had to buy and operate one of those "infernal contraptions." To hire it done was much too expensive. Unfortunately, before many months had gone by, the picture requirement was voted out at a directors' meeting. It was too bad in some ways, since these pictures provided almost foolproof identification and would have given the association a clear picture of any changes the years might bring to the Quarter Horse. We also watched the range mares move about, and if their bloodlines and their conformation were adequate, and they moved true, we accepted them.

We circled about Texas until the Stamford show. Bill, Rudy, and Swede Swenson decided to go all out and, with the assistance of Frank Reeves of the *Fort Worth Star Telegram*, wide publicity was given to this, the first official Quarter Horse show ever held by the AQHA. Since the annual cowboys' reunion held every Fourth of July at Stamford included a rodeo attended by many ranchers, it seemed an ideal setting for our first show. I was especially eager because Lee Underwood and I had been carrying on a friendly rivalry about the merits of our respective stallions, Dexter and Del Rio Joe. Del Rio Joe stood over Dexter that day.

When the first official AQHA Quarter Horse show at Stamford, Texas, was over, Jim Minnick headed for Oklahoma and I went to Sulphur Springs to complete some unfinished business. When I left I had a full-fledged partner who has been with me ever since. Jim and I were to meet several weeks later in Albuquerque, New Mexico. The place and time was rather vague, as he had only said, "I'll see you at the Spanish-named hotel on August 20th." I had found too many ranches and horses that were "about forty miles north" of such and such a town, to worry about a little lack of exactness. From Albuquerque, we were going to continue our registrations.

We were soon in Albuquerque, looking for Jim's hotel with the Spanish name. There was just one difficulty, it seemed every hotel in town had a Spanish name. Sarah and I solved the difficulty by registering at the Alvarado Hotel and waiting for Jim to find us. He and Peggy showed up the next afternoon. They had spent the night at the Franciscan, which was the Spanish name he had had in mind.

That night we called Milo Burlingame, one of the owners of Peter McCue, and invited him to have dinner with us at the hotel. The five of us talked horses far into the next morning, and from the information I obtained that night I was able to fill in many vacant places in my gathering of notes on Peter McCue.

After our pleasant evening with Milo Burlingame, we headed north early the next morning, passing Santa Fe, Taos, Eagles Nest, and stopping finally at Cimarron to visit Ed Springer on his famous CS Ranch. We spent the night talking horses and most of the next day looking at them. In front of his fireplace, Ed told us about his many horses, especially about Little Joe, the great stallion he owned during World War I. We already knew a little about New Mexico's Little Joe from our friend Dan Casement, who was a partner of Ed's in the horse business in 1923-24.

From the CS Ranch, we drove to Watrous, New Mexico, to the home of another friend of Jim's—J. W. Shoemaker. He, too, had a lovely ranch and was soon to have the reputation of being one of the greatest producers of golden palomino Quarter Horses that has ever lived. He concentrated on Plaudit, Old Fred, and Peter McCue breeding. From Watrous we drove on into Raton where we arrived just in time to see two unknowns fight to win a purse race, Question

Mark and Shue Fly, with Question Mark getting into the winner's circle.

Leaving Raton, the next day we headed for the Unaweep Canyon ranch of Jack Casement, near Whitewater, Colorado. Jack's great stallion Red Dog was then in his prime and I had the pleasure of riding him most of one day, helping Jack with his cattle work and inspecting his horses. Naturally Jim and I were inspecting horses for registration at all our stops, not just those mentioned here.

We stayed a couple of days with Jack, Xenia, and their two beautifully mannered little girls, Sandra and Julie. From there we headed for Hayden and Steamboat Springs to visit Coke Roberds and Marshall Peavy. Our visit with Coke was especially productive as he had pictures, stallion advertisements, and a delightful fund of Quarter Horse stories. He was one individual, however, that we could not talk into registering any horses. We then visited Marshall Peavy and went on up to Quentin Semotan and over to Meeker to visit Dell Owens.

When we left Marshall Peavy's for the last time, we split up. Jim and Peggy went back to New Mexico to inspect horses at the ranches of Baca, Hepler, Mitchell, Sears, Thompson, and Zurrick. Sarah and I headed for California, primarily for the trip, but we missed very few Quarter Horse ranches. We especially enjoyed visits with Dee Wilder, Forest Homer, and Bill Lamkin. On the way back we went through Arizona and stopped in to see Ernest Browning and Billy Byrne at Willcox, and then on up the way to renew our acquaintances with Tony at W. D. Wears.

Our next stop was at the Quarter Horse office in Fort Worth. The office force that first year consisted of only myself and Pearl Buck, as fine a secretary as anyone could have wished for. I had a lot of correspondence to catch up with and Jim Minnick was shipping in application blanks faster than I could process them. In those days we did not have a good file of horses built up from which we could check pedigrees. Most of the bloodlines were in my head and on notes scribbled in the field. It was not until Helen Michaelis was elected secretary that a tentative cross-reference filing system was established. It should be remembered that all horses to be registered had to be "of recognized Quarter Horse blood," and I, and later Helen, had to do the recognizing. This registry contains most of the horses on which we had information.

I had to move the office from Fort Worth to College Station when college started in September. I was extremely fortunate that our first office in Fort Worth joined the offices of Jim Hall (and the 6666's). Since he was so close, Jim could settle any immediate problems that occurred while I was gone.

I was personally responsible for only two more major projects that first year. The first was compiling and printing the first stud book and registry, and the other was the collecting and editing of volume 1 of *The Quarter Horse. The Quarter Horse* was a collection of all the articles on Quarter Horses I could find that seemed worthwhile. Volumes 2 and 3 followed at intervals of five years. They are long out of print at this time.

Three important Quarter Horse shows occupied much of my time. First was the Kingsville show. Jim Minnick judged it and Macanudo was grand champion, a horse of which Bob Kleberg was very proud. The Tucson show was a much tighter affair with more good horses in all classes. A surprising number of Quarter Horse officials attended this show. Lee Underwood, Jack Hutchins, Jim Hall, and Jim Minnick (the judge) were all there. Bill Warren was the only member of the executive committee unable to attend. There were several honorary vice presidents there, including Dan Casement, Jack Kinney, Albert Mitchell, and Guy Troutman. Among the directors present were Ernest Browning, Jack Casement, George Clegg (in charge of the King Ranch horses), Raymond Dickson, Duwain Hughes, Marshall Peavy, Helen and Maxie Michaelis, and W. D. Wear, to mention a few.

Little Joe Jr., then owned by Larry Baumer of Utopia, Texas, was named champion Quarter Horse stallion at Tucson. Mel Haskell, who was ramroding the show, also had at that time a classification for a model cow-horse type, and another Quarter Horse, Peppy, the good King Ranch horse, was picked for this. Margie, owned by Marshall Peavy, was champion mare.

It was at this Tucson show that the ability of Melville H. Haskell first came to the attention of a number of important Quarter Horse breeders. It was not to be many years until he was to become one of the most influential men in the organization. Some of the early breeders were a little fearful of his frank preference for racing Quarter Horses and his use of Thoroughbred blood. However, it should be said to his credit that he never tried to force his opinions on other breeders nor did he, when he later became a director, ever use his position to place racing above other performance classifications.

Our first annual meeting was held at the Blackstone Hotel in Fort Worth on March 13, 1941. For the sake of brevity, only the highlights will be mentioned. Bill Warren was unable to attend but the same officers were reelected. Jim Minnick and I had approved about 1000 horses in the field, but they were not all processed and registered. We definitely eliminated the ABC classification at this meeting. The reason for this will appear later. Some wanted to open the permanent stud book, but this was successfully postponed. The real fireworks came during and after the Quarter Horse show held at the old Fort Worth Coliseum.

It is rather easy to look back now and see what caused the trouble, although I do not think anyone foresaw it at the time. Basically, the issue had been present from the first. It came to the surface briefly at the meeting where we compromised with ABC registration. The compromise only put the lid on the kettle, but it was boiling just out of sight. It all came to this: was the more leggy, Thoroughbred-type eligible for complete registration, or should we be strict and permanently register only the old Steel Dust Quarter Horses. Although we did not realize it at the time, those of us who wanted to go down the straight and narrow path were "gone goslings." A terrific market for Quarter Horses had suddenly appeared. Out-of-state buyers were flocking into Texas and buying anything with a number. Most of them had never seen a Quarter Horse and could hardly be expected to know one. It was a horse raisers paradise. Most breeders put tremendous pressure on the directors and officers to register any horse that had any kind of Quarter Horse blood, regardless of how remote that blood was or how lacking in Quarter Horse conformation the animal might be.

When Jim Minnick placed Margie—as champion mare at the Fort Worth show—the same mare he put up at Tucson (and who was still in racing shape) he struck the match that set off the first pyrotechnic display. The association was to have several more, and each always seemed the worst possible. Margie was a top mare, but definitely a racing type at that time, showing all the leggy characteristics of the Thoroughbred and concealing most of her Steel Dust features. That night, Jim and Anne Hall threw a big party for the Quarter Horse crowd, and the problem was thoroughly discussed. The second floor meeting of most of the directors that night spelled the doom of the ABC classification. As a result, no horse ever appeared in the stud book with an A, B, or C after his number, and Steel Dust conformation was no longer a basic requirement for registration.

What happened was this. Margie was definitely class C. Since originally class B and C horses were only to be registered to furnish breeding stock (and not because they were good Quarter Horse specimens), some felt she should not have been placed champion. Naturally, those who had agreed under protest to allow the registration of B and C horses were upset. However, in the future they were all to be considered equal: A, B, and C. It was the will of the majority, and as such was justified.

So far, in this rather informal history, the growth of the American Quarter Horse Association has been followed from its beginnings to the end of its first active year, which culminated with the first annual stockholders meeting held in Fort Worth during the Fat Stock Show in March of 1941. It was really the only satisfactory meeting we had during the early years. Subsequent annual meetings proved to be too big and unwieldy. The directors were unable to distribute stock (which represented a membership) rapidly enough to satisfy everyone.

Before the first organizational meeting, Jack Hutchins, Bill Warren, and I had decided to make the proposed association a stockholding company, and to incorporate it as a nonprofit business in accordance with the laws of the state of Texas. The capital stock was set at $8,000, consisting of 800 shares of $10 each. Certificates were to be issued to shareholders, thereby making him or her an active member of the association. All of the stock had to be subscribed before the charter would be issued, so Jack, Bill, and I owned the AQHA for a short time. When we organized in 1940, everyone who came was asked to buy a share. Several individuals, to take the burden off our backs, bought as many as 50 shares, others were satisfied in risking $10. We were soon frantically buying back all extra shares of stock so that anxious breeders could become members. At the first annual meeting in 1941, the capital stock was raised from $8,000 to $10,000. Before too long it was again increased to $12,500, and all issues were limited to one share.

Our registrations were sustaining the association, and the increase in capital stock was not to obtain operating funds but to satisfy demands for membership. This demand, the size of which was entirely unforeseen and unexpected, arose

31

from several factors. First, a rapidly increasing interest in the Quarter Horse; second, all the business of the association was carried on by directors elected by stockholders; and third (undoubtedly not the least important), stockholders could register their mares for $10 instead of the $15 it cost nonstockholders. Their interest and their votes were welcome but, as the stock spread, many holders were unable to attend the annual meetings and consequently it became difficult to get a quorum present so that a legal meeting could be held. This problem increased until finally it was necessary to change to a membership association, and all of the stock was purchased by the association and retired. Now memberships and quorums were no longer limited by Texas law.

There were two interesting developments in 1941. The Quarter Horse Camp Meeting Association of America had been organized at Stamford, Texas, by a group known as the Quarter Stud Horse Cavaliers. Actually they were for the most part directors and stockholders of the AQHA who were interested in short racing. Jim Hall was the president and was responsible for the regular bulletins that were issued for a time. The biggest and best races sponsored by the group were put on at Eagle Pass, Texas, where Helen Michaelis was actively supervising the Fort Duncan races.

At the same time, another group in Tucson, Arizona, was doing the same thing, but with the added advantage of legalized racing and betting. The Southern Arizona Horse Breeders Association, under the active direction of Melville H. Haskell and with the assistance of Rukin Jelks, Clancy Wollard, Bob Locke, and Joe Flieger were starting what was to make Tucson the short-racing capital of the world.

The races were held from 1941 to 1943 at Bob Locke's Hacienda Moltacqua track. They were then moved to the Rillito track on Rukin Jelk's ranch. They tied their feature races in with the annual Tucson Livestock Show, and held what they called (and soon made) the World's Champion Quarter Horse speed trials. It was here that Clabber, Shue

Fly, Joe Reed II, Red Man, Nobodies Friend, Painted Joe, Blueberry Hill, Little Joe Jr., Pay Dirt, Rosalita, 803 Babe, Bartender, Noo Music, Golden Slippers, Idleen, and Jeep gained fame. Arizona, with its regularly scheduled race meets, soon won a place of prominence and came to over-shadow the Quarter Horse Camp Meeting Association in Texas. Only two large regular race meets developed in Texas. They were in Eagle Pass and the neighboring border town of Del Rio, although tracks at Sequin, San Antonio, Richmond, Skidmore, El Paso, San Angelo, and many other places saw regular, unscheduled racing.

Busy with registrations, I did not do a great deal more in 1941. Both the *Stud Book* and *The Quarter Horse* were pub-lished in that year, although I had completed most of the work on them in the later part of 1940. In Colorado, some of the more enthusiastic men organized the first active co-operating Quarter Horse association, although Oklahoma later became the first state to receive official recognition as an Exhibitors group chartered by the AQHA. Quarter Horse breeders in Colorado, headed by Jack Casement, Marshall Peavy, and Hugh Bennett organized a Colorado Short Horse Men's Racing Association on September 12, 1942, and their first futurity was scheduled for the state fair at Pueblo in 1943. Later, they reorganized as the Rocky Mountain Quar-ter Horse Association, which extended into southern Wyo-ming, and became affiliated with the AQHA.

In the spring of 1941 I was informed that I had received a Rockefeller Fellowship (General Education Board) to con-tinue my studies of the arrival and spread of the Spanish horse in America. This meant that a new secretary must be found before September, when I had to leave for Berkeley and the University of California. An idea I had had in the back of my head for a long time now came to the front. I had been in correspondence with the Quarter Horse breeders all across the country for a number of years and knew per-sonally practically every breeder and enthusiast of importance. Beginning in 1938, I began to receive letters from a woman or girl, I didn't know which, signed Helen Michaelis and postmarked either Eagle Pass, Texas, or Coahuila, Mexico. I can remember the first note I ever received from her. I had written an article for the *Cattleman* on Quarter Horses. In it, I apparently mentioned Little Joe, and after his name I put the roman numeral III. In my research, I had found two other Billy horses carrying the name Little Joe, and since I discovered him last, I called him Little Joe III. Helen wrote me a post card asking which Little Joe was number III, because she wanted to keep her records straight and in accordance with mine. I answered, and our corresponding friendship began. I did not personally meet Helen until 1940 when the organizational meeting of the AQHA was called. Here, she was at all times frank and open in her comments, and obviously possessed a great fund of knowledge about horses, especially Quarter Horses. Helen was the only woman who exerted any appreciable influence on the growth and development of the modern Quarter Horse during the formative years. At that first organizational meeting, her ability was recognized and she was made a director of the new organization. It wasn't done as a chivalrous gesture to a lady, but rather in the cold realization that she had much to offer the Quarter Horse.

In any case, when I received the fellowship and knew that my position as secretary would have to be terminated, the selection of a successor was all-important. It was not a new thought because the college had given me a limited time to serve in any case, but it was suddenly pressing. The job had peculiar requirements. There was one essential requirement that no other breed organization secretary had to have, and that was a knowledge of Quarter Horse bloodlines. It was necessary because the constitution and by-laws said that one of the requirements for registration was Quarter Horse bloodlines. This requirement may seem simple now, but remember that, unlike today, there were no books available in 1940–41, and only a few articles had ever been written. You could list them all on one hand, and they contained very little pedigree information. Only one or two articles, by Dan Casement and myself, contained any reference to living Quarter Horses. There were some who knew what satisfactory Quarter Horse bloodlines were, such as George Clegg, Ott Adams, Coke Roberds, Bob Kleberg, and Dan Casement. There were also a few others who knew the horses in their particular area pretty well, like O. W. Cardwell, J. E. Browning, Marshall Peavy, John Williams, or Forest Homer. None of them, however, would have been the least interested in devoting ten or fifteen hours a day, seven days a week at a token salary to become the secretary of a new, small breed registry. They were all business men, established in their own communities. The job needed someone with a missionary's zeal and a love of Quarter Horses gained through personal experience with no interest in cash reward. The only person who really qualified and might accept was Helen Michaelis. No one else had the ability, time, energy, and courage. She had all of these and more. Her success was due to her attitude in dealing with breeders—when talking with her you soon forgot that she was a woman. She all but gave up her family and private life to serve the association, and from then, March 20, 1942, until July 6, 1946, when she mailed in her resignation, she devoted the majority of her waking hours to the Quarter Horse. As Max Michaelis, her husband, once said to me at a Quarter Horse show, "You fellows got a secretary, but I lost the best damn ranch manager and companion a man ever had."

The second annual meeting held in Fort Worth in March of 1942 occurred after Pearl Harbor, and World War II was in full swing. I had been sent to South America, where I was reporting for the Combined Food Board through the Department of State. Although not present, I followed the actions of the association closely. Frank Roberts, acting as my assistant, was running the office, and had been doing so since I left for California in September. My secretary, who had been with the AQHA office since it opened, was still working for the association. The new officers elected were Jack Hutchins, president; Dan D. Casement and Lee Underwood, vice presidents; Jim Hall, treasurer; and, of course, Helen Michaelis, secretary.

Although everything looked peaceful, the next four years were to be troubled ones. The tremendous increase in popularity of the Quarter Horse, the restrictions on travel for inspectors during the war, and the creation of a rival organization all made for great changes in the original routines. Already the association had been moving away from the limited aims and ideas of its founders. Nothing that has grown as rapidly as the American Quarter Horse Association could be free from growing pains, and no democratic organization can remain static. It was too much to expect that the original pattern and designs would not change with the growth and years. The association had been conceived, born, and nurtured during its first few years by ranchers and allied spirits, whose main objective was to perpetuate what they saw as the greatest little cow horse the world had known, while acknowledging that this same stocky pony had a real turn of speed at short distances.

By January of 1943 there were almost 2,000 registered horses, and almost half that many more pending in the files. There were fifty-five inspectors in eight states, busy as beavers. There were members wanting service in sixteen states. The simple fact was that there were not that many authentic Steel Dust Quarter Horses of the type envisioned by the founders. However, there were many honest, enthusiastic breeders who admired the Quarter Horse, and wanted to raise them. Their voices could not be ignored, and the AQHA was on its way to making the American Quarter Horse the most popular in the world.

III

Obtaining the Pedigrees

Every breed organization must start someplace, with some animals. Generally the type of animal is already set, and certain bloodlines have become popular. This was true with the American Quarter Horse. However, when a registry is just starting, little exact information is known about the pedigrees of most of the horses beyond a generation or two. Interested individuals collect as much of this information as possible, before and just after the breed association is organized. By doing this, the breeder can find out which bloodlines are contributing the most to the new breed.

There are always a few individuals who take the time to dig for such pedigrees. It involves a lot of traveling, writing of letters, interviewing, and general detective work. Training in history, including research methods and evaluation of evidence, is most helpful in separating facts from fiction.

It is really surprising how hard facts are to come by; that is, facts in a scientific sense. This is especially true when one is trying to trace a horse whose pedigree has been handed down by word of mouth. It is normally complicated by an uncle, a brother, a wife or sister, who recalls granddad giving the same facts differently. This explains why the same writer (or different writers) may give different details concerning the same horse. More evidence has caused him to change his opinion.

One of the best of the early day Quarter Horse historians was Helen Michaelis. A chapter on her can be found in my book *Quarter Horses, A Story of Two Centuries*. Her research contributed so much to this work that I seriously considered making her the coauthor. However, she passed away, and I decided to dedicate the work to her and not make her responsible for something over which she had no control. Helen Michaelis and I were friends for thirty years and worked closely both as friends with a mutual hobby and as officers of the American Quarter Horse Association. Both of us served as secretary and director of the registry during its formative years.

When I visited her in the hospital shortly before her death in 1965, she asked that I have her collection of Quarter Horse materials. These papers (with my own) form the nucleus for this work, and are now in the hands of the American Quarter Horse Association.

No attempt has been made to list all of the information available on every unregistered Quarter Horse sire. Some, like Peter McCue, could easily have a book written about them, and others, like Steel Dust, already have one. Wayne Gard did an excellent job on Steel Dust in his book *Fabulous Quarter Horse Steel Dust* (New York, 1958). On the other hand, some legendary stallions are so nebulous that perhaps only a one-time owner is known, or just several offspring. Certainly, some stallions appear that should have been omitted, and others are omitted that should have been included.

The following information is given for each stallion if it was available to the author: name, dates, physical characteristics, pedigree, breeder, owners, and occasionally a few pertinent facts of some other nature. When well-known horses are listed, such as Little Joe, only vital statistics will be given. However, additional data may occasionally appear for some stallions who have not had very much publicity.

Unfortunately, little data are available for a great many stallions. All horses are listed alphabetically. Although a few early studs, such as imported Janus (1746–80) appear, most of the animals were foaled after the Civil War. The aim of the work is to furnish the serious breeder with the available information on the vital statistics of the sires appearing in the bloodlines of their registered horses. Due to the nature of this work, there will be errors, and there will be people who have always been told a different set of facts. All I can say is that the following reflects the serious research done by Helen Michaelis and me over a period of almost a half century.

IV

Key For Finding Horses

Horses are listed alphabetically by first names; for example, *Peter McCue*, not McCue, Peter.

Owner's name, if commonly used, is found after the name; for example, *Whip*, Blackburn's, not Blackburn's Whip.

The adjectives young, old, big, little are found after the name; for example, *Joe, Little*, not Little Joe.

Color is considered part of the name; for example, *Blue Eyes*, not Eyes, Blue.

A commonly used secondary name appears in parenthesis; for example, *King (Possum)*; and secondary names are cross-referenced, for example, *Possum,* see *King.*

The major difficulties in establishing correct pedigrees are due to the fact the same horse may have had different names at different times or places, or because two or more horses had the same name and lived at the same time. Careful study must be made of all available dates, owners, sires, dams, and locations where the stallion stood in order to get the right horse and pedigree. Spelling is inconsistent in the old records. If a question mark appears, I doubt the validity of the given fact or, as a result of other known data I consider more valid, I have myself made a correction or addition to the facts originally obtained.

V

Foundation Sire Registry

A

ABE FRANK JR. Abe Frank Jr. was foaled in 1916 or before and was sired by the Thoroughbred Abe Frank and out of a Trammell mare. He was owned by the Sims Ranch of Snyder, Texas, and was occasionally referred to as Little Abe Frank.

ACE. Ace was born a few years before 1936. He was sired by Chicaro and out of an Ace of Hearts mare. He was bred by John Dial of Goliad, Texas, who sold him to Benevides Volpe. Volpe sold him to Gen. Miguel Acosta who took him to Mexico in 1936.

ACE, LITTLE. Little Ace was foaled in 1918 and died in 1930(?). He was by Ace of Hearts and out of a Copeland mare. He was bred by W. J. "Will" Copeland of Pettus, Texas, and later was owned by Frank Jones of Marfa, Texas. He was sometimes called Little Ace of Hearts and sometimes the Copeland Horse.

ACE OF DIAMONDS. Ace of Diamonds was foaled in 1920 and lived until 1943. He was a sorrel, stood 14-2 hands and weighed 1050 pounds. He was by Johnny by Cotton Eyed Joe by Peter McCue and out of a Saski mare named Sun Dial. He was bred by Jack Saski of Cuero, Texas, raised and raced by his son, John "Shorty" Saski of Victoria. Other owners were Louis Koutech of Hallettsville, Ed Hajek of Shiner, and Anton Jahn of Hallettsville.

In his prime Ace of Diamonds was almost unbeatable at 300 yards. Saski started racing him when he was two years old. Although he ran as far as 3/8, his best distance was between 300 and 440 yards. His record was 220 yards in 12 seconds, 300 yards in 16, and 440 in 23. John Dial's Plain Jane was one of the few horses that beat him.

In 1925, Saski sold Ace of Diamonds to Louis Koutech of Hallettsville. Koutech stood him to any mare that came along. Eventually, he sold the stallion to Ed Hajek who used him a few years and then sold him. He then dropped out of sight until Hajek stumbled on to him again in 1939. At that time, he was an old horse owned by a Negro at Gonzales. Ed Hajek bought him for ten dollars. He worked on his teeth and got him back into shape. When John Saski saw him, he wanted him back, so Ed gave him to Saski. Saski later sold him to Anton Jahn in 1940. Emil Hajek, brother of Ed, borrowed the old horse in 1940 and bred him to a Little Dick mare. The resulting foal was the bay race mare Miss South St. Marys.

ACE OF HEARTS. Ace of Hearts was foaled in 1904 and died in 1917(?). He stood 14-2 hands high and weighed, in good flesh, 1000 pounds and was a sorrel. He was by the Dunderstadt Horse by Sykes' Rondo and out of Queen by Dedier. He was bred by Luke Neal of Gillett, Texas, and owned by Will Copeland of Pettus, Texas, and by John Kenedy of Sarita, Texas.

George Clegg, who knew the horse, was responsible for much of the confusion concerning his breeding and his breeder. George originally told both Helen Michaelis and me that he was by Cuadro by Old Billy, but later changed his mind about that pedigree. Queen was a mare purchased by Luke Neal of Gillett, Texas, from a Louisiana race horse man. Will Copeland bought Ace when he was six years old. His best-known race was held at Alice, Texas, when he was matched against Little Joe, Clegg's horse, for a quarter of a mile. Ace won the race and about bankrupt Alice. This was in 1908.

ACE OF HEARTS, ALDWELL'S. All that is known about this horse was that Lee Aldwell of San Angelo bought him in Sheffield, Texas. Aldwell was a breeder of polo horses and an associate of William Anson of Christoval, Texas, whose ranch he leased for a time.

ACE OF HEARTS, JONES'. This Ace of Hearts was sired by Little Ace and bred by Frank Jones of Marfa, Texas. He was owned by W. B. Mitchell of Marfa.

ACE OF HEARTS, SCHAFFER'S. This bay stallion was foaled in 1931 and bred by Dick Schaffer of Pampa, Texas. His sire was Glen Wilkins by John Wilkins by Peter McCue. His dam was one-half Thoroughbred. Schaffer sold him to Sam Wattley of Pampa, Texas.

ACE OF HEARTS II, SAENZ'S. Ace of Hearts II was foaled in 1918(?) and died in 1942(?). He also was sorrel. He was by Ace of Hearts and out of a Saenz mare by Hickory Bill. He was bred by Anastacio Saenz of Rios, Texas, who sold him to Bill Warren of Hockley, Texas, first president of the AQHA.

A. D. REED. A. D. Reed was foaled in 1916; he was a dark bay. He was by Peter McCue and out of Good Enough by Tom Campbell. He was bred by A. D. Hurley of Canute, Oklahoma, and died in the ownership of Filiburto Gallegos in New Mexico in 1935. A. D. Reed was registered by the Jockey Club as: "DR. B. H. 1916. By Speedy Ball, Dam Swing Corners by *Tithonus" (*American Stud Book*, Vol. XII, 594).

A. D. REED II (UTE CREEK REED). A. D. Reed II was a brown stallion foaled in 1935, sired by A. D. Reed and out of a mare by Little Mike. He was bred by Eloisa Gallegos of

Gallegos, New Mexico, and owned by P. G. Newkirk of Clinton, Oklahoma.

AEOLUS. A gray stallion foaled in the 1760's, sired by Old Peacock, a famous Colonial Quarter Horse by *Janus and out of a *Janus mare. His second dam was by *Jolly Roger. He was bred and owned by George Davison in Virginia.

AGATE. Agate was a dun stallion sired by Shiek and out of a Fresno mare. He was bred by the Matador Land and Cattle Company of Channing, Texas, and later owned by Floyd Bull of Lefors, Texas.

AGUARDIENTE. Aguardiente was a sorrel stallion foaled about 1920. He was by Pancho Villa and out of a Hickory Bill mare. He was bred by E. L. Armstrong of Hebbronville, Texas, and owned by Louis Yeager of Hebbronville, Ossie S. Harper of Piedras Negras, Coahuila, Mexico, and Albert Harper of Zapata, Texas.

ALAMO. Alamo was foaled sometime around 1925. He was by Uncle Jimmy Gray, a Thoroughbred Remount Horse sired by Bonnie Joe (TB). Alamo's dam was Baby Bess of unknown breeding. Alamo was bred by Jessie James of Somerset, Texas, and later owned by Jess D. Perkins of San Antonio, Texas. James raced Alamo and Perkins used him as a roping horse.

ALASCO. Alasco was foaled in about 1820. He was by Tiger by Cook's Whip (Kentucky Whip) by imported Whip and out of Clay's mare by imported Speculator. His second dam was the C.A.Q.R.M. Blue Sow. He was bred and owned by Dr. Bryan of Kentucky.

ALBERT. Albert was foaled in 1918 and lived until 1939. He was by Hickory Bill by Peter McCue and out of Mary Bill by John Gardner by Traveler. He was bred by George Clegg of Alice, Texas, who sold him to John J. O'Brien of Refugio,

Texas, who later sold him to Frank Rooke of Woodsboro, Texas.

ALEX. Alex was foaled about 1914. He was a sorrel with a blaze and stockings. He was by Ben by John Crowder and his dam, according to Sproul A. Morriss, was a Parker mare sired by Yellow Jacket. M. P. Leonard said Alex was called "Ellick," and that his sire, Ben, was a full brother of Pleas Walters. He was bred by William Parker of Knox City, Texas, and apparently was raced at one time by the White brothers at Brady, Texas.

ALEX GARDNER. This stallion was foaled in 1890(?) and was sired by Anthony by Billy and out of Artie by Billy. Artie was out of Paisana. Alex Gardner was bred by William B. Fleming of Belmont, Texas. Fleming had sold several horses to a Mr. Jack Hardy from Mississippi, among them the race horse Pink Reed. Hardy allowed Pink Reed to become foundered (laminitis) and so he came back to Texas looking for another race horse. Fleming told him Alex Gardner could outrun any living horse except Pink Reed, so Hardy took Alex to Mississippi and when he beat the horse he was supposed to, Hardy bought Alex Gardner.

ALP, LITTLE. This sorrel stallion was foaled about 1875, and he was sired by Oregon Charlie. He weighed about 1050 pounds and stood 14-2 hands. For a time, he stood at stud about fifteen miles north of Merced, California, by T. C. Dean of Merced.

ANDY, LITTLE. Little Andy was by Little Jack by Anthony by Old Billy and out of a Fleming mare. He was bred by Fred Matthies of Seguin, Texas.

ANTHONY. Anthony was foaled in 1856 and was a dark brown stallion. He was by Billy by Shiloh and out of Paisana by Brown Dick. He was bred by W. B. Fleming of Belmont,

Texas. Anthony only ran one race in his life, at Austin. W. E. Jones borrowed Anthony from Fleming and took him to Medina where he eventually died. Among his better known gets were Billy Dibrell, Alex Gardner, Little John Moore, Fashion, Lemonade, and Pink Reed.

ANTI PRO. Anti Pro was foaled in 1891 and was sired by Shelby by Tom Driver and out of Jenny Capps. He was bred by Shelby Stanfield of Thorp Spring, Texas, and later owned by Pid Hart of Cleburne, Texas, and then by John Plott of Sepe Springs. E. A. Whiteside told Helen Michaelis that Anti Pro was raised near Cleburne and that he was owned by Pid Hart. John Plott said that Anti Pro was a full brother of the stallion Pid Hart and could outrun him for 440 yards.

APACHE. Apache was foaled in 1930 and was by the Remount Horse Royal Ford and out of a Yellow Wolf mare. He was bred and owned by W. T. Waggoner of Fort Worth.

APACHE KID (WOLF or LUCKY). Dee Wilder said that Apache Kid was a one-eyed sorrel stallion sometimes known as Wolf or Lucky, and that he was sired by Guinea Pig by Possum. He was bred by Jim Kennedy of Bonita, Arizona, and was raised by Willis Gardner who sold him to the Getzwiller Ranch in 1930.

ARCHER, THE. This bay stallion was foaled in 1927. He was sired by Cannon Shot (TB) and out of Alice (Mlle. Denise) by Arch Oldham by Gallantry (TB). Our reference has his sire Arch Oldham as being by Brown King, which seems unlikely. He was bred and owned by the U.S. Remount of Fort Robinson, Nebraska.

ARCHIE. Archie, a bay stallion foaled in 1891, was sired by Pid Hart and out of Mayflower by Bill Garner. He was raced under the ownership of J. B. Gililand. His dam, Mayflower, was owned by Lee McCameron of Baird, Texas. His racing record can be found in *Goodwin's Turf Guide*.

46

ARCH OLDHAM. Arch Oldham was a bay stallion with no white markings. He was foaled in 1902. He was sired by Gallantry (TB) and out of Pearl Barnes, a quarter mare. He was bred by O. G. Parke of Kyle, Texas. He was registered with the Jockey Club for racing purposes only. He was a full brother to Buster Jones. He was put into training by B. C. Bimbury and raced extensively up to one-half mile, and was supposed to be the fastest half-mile horse raised in Texas. He was taken to Brewster County in 1914 and in 1920 was still serving mares. He died in the hands of Grover King of Sanderson.

ARCH OLDHAM JR. This stallion, foaled around 1906, was by Arch Oldham and out of a Rondo mare. He was bred by Crawford Sykes of Nixon, Texas, and purchased by William Anson of Christoval, Texas. Anson raced this stallion some.

ARIEL, LITTLE. This bay stallion was by John Crowder by Old Billy and out of Marge. He was bred in Texas and raced in Denver in 1891 by H. S. King.

ARIZONA JIMMY GRAY, see Uncle Jimmy Gray, Siminoff's.

AURY. Aury was by the Red Dutchman by Lock's Rondo by Whalebone and out of a mare by Brown Dick by Old Billy by Shiloh.

 B

BABE RUTH. Babe Ruth was a bay horse foaled in 1938. He was by Flying Bob and out of Beauty. His second dam was a mare by Dedier. He was foaled in Louisiana and brought to Texas by J. F. Hutchins in 1943.

BABRAM, GOODE'S OLD. Babram, F.A.Q.R.H., was foaled in 1766 and died twenty years later. He was bred by John Goode Sr. of Mecklenburg County, Virginia. He was sired by *Janus and his dam was also a *Janus. Edgar calls him one of the best Quarter Racers in America of his day. In running a Quarter race with Jupiter over the Lewis Path's, he fell and broke his neck. He was kept both as a race horse and as a covering horse. Babram is found in both Edgar and in *ASB*.

BACCHUS, CONE'S. Cone's Bacchus was foaled in 1825 and his sire was Bacchus by Sir Archy. His dam was Crazy Jane by *Merryfield. He was foaled in North Carolina, and had been bred by Lester Cone of Ohio. He is sometimes referred to as Ohio Bacchus. Cone, a race horse man, was shot on a race track according to Forester.

BACCHUS, COX'S. This roan horse, who stood 14-2 hands, was foaled in 1796. He was by Old Bacchus by Old Babram and out of a mare also by Babram. He was bred by John Cox of North Carolina.

BACCHUS, LITTLE. Little Bacchus, C.A.Q.R.H., was a blood bay stallion, 14 hands high, foaled in 1778. He was bred by William Mills of Granville County, North Carolina, and later sold to John Dickinson of the same county. He was sired by F.A.Q.R.H. Old Bacchus and his dam was by Apollo.

BACCHUS, OLD. This F.A.Q.R.H. was a blood bay stallion foaled in 1774. He died in 1789. He was sired by Old Babram and out of a *Janus mare. He was bred by John Potter of Granville County, North Carolina. He was, according to Edgar, exceedingly well formed and very heavily made for his height, which was 14-2 hands. He is listed in both Edgar and in the *ASB*.

BADGER (GREY BADGER). Badger was foaled in 1912 and was an iron-gray stallion. He was by Peter McCue and out of Mazie Marie by Tom Campbell. He was bred by Johnny Parvell of Elk City, Oklahoma, and owned by Reed Armstrong and Roy Cockran of Foss, Oklahoma, and by Billy Montgomery of Reydon, Oklahoma. Badger was more famous for running than for breeding. His dam also produced Roger Mills and Older. Badger is only known to have been bred to two mares, one was Nettie Stinson and the other Nellie Trammell. His most famous son, Midnight, was out of Nellie Trammell who was by Pid Hart. Armstrong raced Badger under the name of Grey Badger. He was also known, at one time, as Midnight.

BAILEY (BUCK). Bailey was foaled around 1913 or 1914 and he was a dun horse. He was by Old Joe Bailey by Eureka by Shelby. His dam was thought to be a range mare. Tony Hazelwood told Lee Underwood that Bailey was by Old Joe Bailey and that Waggoners got him at Weatherford. The Waggoners apparently only got four colt crops from him. They lost him when he broke a hip and had to be destroyed. Paul Waggoner told Helen Michaelis it was his opinion that Bailey was bought "on the yard" in Fort Worth.

BALL. This dark chestnut stallion was foaled in 1774. He was by *Janus and his dam was also. Ball was bred by Thomas Hunter of Edgecombe County, North Carolina. Edgar describes him as a beautiful dark chestnut with a snip on his nose and one white hind foot. He was 14-2½ hands in height and exceedingly well formed. Although Edgar says he won large sums of money, he doesn't list him as a Quarter Horse, but other authorities do. He was sometimes referred to as Bandy Ball.

BALLEYMOONEY. Balleymooney was foaled in 1914 on the Unaweep Canyon Ranch of Dan Casement, near Whitewater, Colorado. He was a sorrel with a sox on his left rear pastern. Balleymooney was by Concho Colonel by Jim Ned and out of Little Judge by Little Steve by Pony Pete. He was bred by Dan D. Casement, who owned him throughout his life. Balleymooney was taken to Manhattan, Kansas, as a two-year-old and remained there until 1932, when he was returned to the place of his birth. On the Unaweep that year, he was bred to eight mares, and got Duece, Red Dog, Frosty, Red Cloud, Billey Byrne, and one unnamed colt that went to Bill Horton of Buffalo, Wyoming.

BALLY. Bally was a sorrel stallion foaled in 1925. He was bred by J. E. Browning of Willcox, Arizona, and was sired by Possum (King) who was by Traveler. Browning sold him to W. D. Wear of Willcox, who in turn sold him to John Taylor of Chowchilla, California. Bally was registered #7356 in the NQHBA. He was a bulldog type and one of Possum's last colts. He went to California in 1928.

BANDY BALL, see BALL.

BAREFIELD HORSE. This stallion was foaled in 1909 and was sorrel. He was by Little Joe by Traveler and out of a sorrel Clegg mare. He was bred by George Clegg and later sold to John Barefield of Alfred, Texas. Barefield bought this young stallion from George Clegg, along with four mares, and then drove them home. On the road, the stallion bred the mares. Barefield gelded him when he got him home. One of the resulting offspring was Juanita, the great race mare that Ed Fields of Richmond, Texas, owned for many years.

BARLOW. This Barlow was a bay stallion by Cold Deck and was foaled in 1884. In 1890, he was raced by the Garrett brothers, and in 1891 by J. W. Smith. *Goodwin's Turf Guide* gives detailed records of his track career.

BARLOW. This stallion was foaled in the late 1800's. He was owned by Nitz Reid of Silverton, Texas, who had him when he died in 1910 or 1911. He was by Lock's Rondo.

BARNEY. Barney was foaled in 1884, sired by Lock's Rondo and out of Mollie by Steel Dust.

BARNEY, CARDWELL'S. This Barney was a dun stallion by Sam King by Hondo and out of a Cardwell dun mare. He was bred by O. W. Cardwell of Junction, Texas, and owned by Felix Watson of Junction.

BARNEY G. Barney G was by Old Joe Bailey by Eureka. His dam is unknown, as is his breeder. He stood in Hunt County, Texas.

BARNEY, GARNER'S. This Barney was by Danger by Barney Owens and out of the McKinney black mare by Bill Garner. He was bred and owned by J. T. (Joe) McKinney of Willcox, Arizona.

BARNEY, KANE'S. This Barney was by Ribbon by Big Apple by Joe Collins and out of an unnamed Joe Kane Quarter mare. He was bred by Joe Kane of Nogales, Arizona, and owned by G. W. Page and Dan Misenhimer of Willcox, Arizona.

BARNEY L. This bay stallion was foaled in 1926. He was by Barney Lucas by Traveler and his dam was Daisy Lucas by Barney Lucas. He was bred and owned by D. W. (Webb) Christian of Big Spring, Texas.

BARNEY LUCAS. Barney Lucas was foaled in 1910. He was a bay stallion sired by Traveler and out of Annie May. He was bred by Webb Christian of Big Spring, Texas, and owned by Dick Gray of Gorman, Texas. Some said he was by Cunningham's Traveler by Traveler.

BARNEY McCOY. This bay stallion was foaled in 1910. He was by Floyd K (TB) and out of Bridget McCue by Peter McCue. He was bred and owned by Harry Stuart of Lewiston, Illinois.

BARNEY OWENS. Barney Owens was foaled in 1870 or soon thereafter. He was not as large as his famous son, Dan Tucker, but he stood 14-3½ and weighed 1200 pounds. Barney Owens was sired by Cold Deck by Billy by Shiloh and out of Nettie Overton. John Hedgepeff of Joplin, Missouri, bred Barney Owens; Bill Cassity broke him; and he was owned and raced at one time by James Owen of Berlin, Illinois, who then sold him to Sam Watkins of Petersburg, Illinois. Watkins later sold him to Thomas Trammell of Sweetwater, Texas, who at the same time bought Barney's son, Dan Tucker.

BARNEY OWENS, YOUNG. Young Barney Owens was by Barney Owens by Old Cold Deck by Billy and out of a Trammell mare. He was bred by Walter Trammell of Sweetwater, Texas, and owned by John T. Sims Jr. of Snyder, Texas.

BARNEY, WALLING'S. This Barney was by Grover by Barney Owens and out of a JHC mare. He was bred and owned by W. P. (Pres) Walling of Robert Lee, Texas.

BASIL PRINCE. Basil Prince was a sorrel and he was born in 1912. He was by Hickory Bill by Peter McCue and out of Hattie W by Hi Henry. He was bred by George Clegg of Alice, Texas, and owned later by Jap Bishop and then by Frank Jones, both of Marfa. Frank Jones said he was sometimes called Jap and Bishop's Hickory Bill.

BAY BILLY SUNDAY. This Billy Sunday was foaled in 1908 and was by Peter McCue and out of a Thoroughbred mare named Tern. He was bred by Samuel Watkins of Petersburg, Illinois, and owned by Ed and Bill Moore of Mobeetie, Texas.

BAY BROWN. Bay Brown was by Little Joe by Traveler and out of an Adams' mare. He was bred by Ott Adams of Alfred, Texas, and owned by Reynaldo Flores of Laredo, Texas.

BAY COLD DECK. This Cold Deck was foaled in 1881 and he was by Hamburg Dick by Fort Stock Dick and his dam was by Printer. He was bred and owned by Bill Owens of Smithville, Missouri.

BAY JIMMY GRAY. Bay Jimmy Gray was sired by Uncle Jimmy Gray by Bonnie Joe (TB) and owned by Whitehead and Wardlaw of Del Rio, Texas. His dam was a ranch mare whose pedigree is unknown.

BAY PRINTER. Bay Printer was foaled in 1853. He was sired by Gray Eagle by Woodpecker by Bertrand and out of Blinkey (Mary Porter) by Muckle John by Muckle John by Sir Archy. His second dam was by Old Printer. He was bred by Webb Ross of Scott County, Kentucky, and later stood in Kansas. He was a full brother of Flying Dutchman, Sweet Owen, and Viley.

BELL PUNCH. This stallion lived from 1882 until 1896 and was bay in color. He stood 15 hands and weighed 1000 pounds. He was bred by Tom Martin of Kyle, Texas, and owned by W. W. Haupt of Kyle. W. W. Lock, who raced against Haupt, claimed Bell Punch "never sired anything that could run fast enough to get hot," and that "Rondo beat Bell Punch like passing a post."

BEN. Ben was a sorrel stallion. He is believed to have been bred by Emmett Butler of Kenedy, Texas, in about 1902. He was by John Crowder and out of Dutch and was a full brother of Pleas Walters and Hondo. John Crowder was by Billy and out of Paisana. He was owned by Dorman McBride of Kenedy, Texas, and E. E. Morriss of Rocksprings, Texas. He was a blaze-faced sorrel with stockings.

BEN BOLT. Ben Bolt was foaled in 1908 and died in 1928. He was a bay that stood 15 hands and weighed 1200 pounds. He was occasionally called Rondo. He was by Aguinaldo by Lone Man by Lock's Rondo and he was out of Lizzie. Ben Bolt was bred by Gil Kuykendall of Buda, Texas. Ben Bolt was later owned by J. Seidensticker of Kerrville, M. G.

Michaelis Jr. of Kyle, and Frank Auerbach of Columbus, Texas. He was generally raced under the name of Rondo.

BEN BURTON, LITTLE. This stallion was foaled about 1880. He was by Old Ben Burton by Barney (Blind) by Steel Dust. His dam was an Oklahoma racing mare. He was owned by W. Lewis of Kirkland, Texas.

J. C. Terrell of Kirkland, Texas, said, "Some of the boys found a fast filly up in Oklahoma and stole her and brought her to Texas and bred her to Ben. When the colt was one year old, he weighed 1050 pounds and ran the quarter in 24 seconds without a rider against one of the Wolf colts with a rider and was 50 yards ahead." Mr. Terrell further stated that after Mr. Lewis died the boys sold Little Ben to Burke Burnett for $250 in 1891.

BEN BURTON, OLD. This stallion was foaled in the late 1800's. He was by Blind Barney by Steel Dust and his dam was by Brown Dick.

BEN HUR. This sorrel stallion was foaled in 1921. He stood a trifle over 15 hands and weighed 1200 pounds. He was sired by Rainy Day by Lone Star and out of Nettie Jacket by Yellow Jacket. He became one of the best-known Quarter Horse sires in Arizona. He was bred by Eugene J. Schott of Riomedina, Texas. Other owners were Jap Bishop of Marfa, Texas, and then Dave Parker of Sonoita, Arizona, and later by Parker's sons, Bud and Dink. Ben Hur ran a quarter in 22.5 seconds from an open gate.

BEN, LITTLE. This Little Ben was a bay stallion that was foaled in 1920(?) and died in 1939. He was by Old Joe Bailey by Eureka and out of Nell by Old Ben Burton. He was bred by Dick Baker of Weatherford, Texas. He burned to death in a barn near Bridgeport about 1939.

BEN, LITTLE. This chestnut stallion was by Ben Hur by Rainy Day and out of Donna by Barney by Danger. He was bred by Roy Sorrills of Nogales, Arizona, and owned by several other men in Arizona.

BEN, LITTLE, see BEN BURTON.

BERRYESSA. This chestnut colt was foaled in 1876. He was sired by Oregon Charlie and he was out of Jennie Gibbons. He was a half brother of Brick and Little Alp. He was owned by John Adams of Woodland, California.

BERTRAND. Bertrand was a bay stallion foaled in 1821 and was sired by Sir Archy by *Diomed. Wallace, in his *American Stud Book*, says Bertrand was as good in the stud as he was on the track. He died in the ownerships of Lindsey and Hutchcraft in Kentucky in 1838. Several sons in Virginia, Kentucky, South Carolina, and Pennsylvania scattered the blood of this popular stallion. He was owned at one time by Col. Wm. Buford of Kentucky.

BILL AUSTIN. This bay stallion was foaled in 1831 and was bred by Col. John Crowell of Alabama and owned later by Messrs. J. M. Henderson and D. Myers of Mabington, Georgia. He was by Bertrand and out of a Timoleon mare. He is in the *American Stud Book*.

BILL FLEMING, BOULDIN'S. Bill Fleming was a brown stallion foaled in 1930. He was bred by Clayton Bouldin of Belmont, Texas. He was sired by Thad Bronson's paint stud who was by Jimmy Elder and out of a mare by Doc Odem. The dam of Bill Fleming was a sorrel mare named Patsie, who was by Paul Murray and out of Patsie Keith by Billy Dibrell. Bill Fleming was being used to head sheep when Dink Parker of Sonoita, Arizona, bought him according to Ed Echols. He outran Jimmie Allred in a famous match race. Parker sold him to Bill Hall of Oakland, California.

BILL GARNER. Bill Garner was foaled in 1870 and bred by E. Shelby Stanfield of Thorp Spring, Texas. He was by Steel

Dust and out of one of Stanfield's race mares. R. H. Norton, an early-day Quarter Horse breeder from Quanah, Texas, considered Bill Garner the fastest and best sire of note. Bill Garner was raced during most of the 1870's.

BILLIE GRAY. Billie Gray was a bay stallion sired by Uncle Jimmy Gray by Bonnie Joe (TB) and out of a Little Joe mare. He was bred by Bob Sutton of Cotulla, Texas, and owned by J. W. House of Cameron, Texas. He was occasionally called Billy.

BILLIE SUNDAY. This chestnut stallion was foaled in 1921 and was by Tom Sunday (TB) and out of Bay Orphie by The Senator. He was bred and owned by the 7-11 Ranch, Hot Springs, South Dakota.

BILLY ANSON, FOSTER'S. This Billy Anson was foaled in 1923(?), and was a bay stallion bred by Billy Anson of Christoval, Texas. He was later owned by Allen Foster of Sterling City and then by Earl Barley of Sterling City. He was sired by Harmon Baker by Peter McCue and out of Annie Hathorne by Jim Ned.

BILLY ANSON SORREL. This Billy Anson was foaled in 1920(?). He was bred by Billy Anson of Christoval, Texas, and owned all of his life by Albert K. Mitchell of Albert, New Mexico. He was by Harmon Baker by Peter McCue and out of an Anson mare.

BILLY ANSON, WHITEHEAD AND WARDLAW'S. This Billy Anson is either a three-quarter or full brother to Foster's Billy Anson. He was foaled in 1925(?) and was by Harmon Baker and out of a Jim Ned mare. He was bred by Billy Anson of Christoval, Texas, and owned by Whitehead and Wardlaw of Del Rio, Texas.

BILLY BARLOW. Billy Barlow was a bay stallion foaled in 1886 by Old Cold Deck by Old Billy. His dam and breeder are unknown, but he was raced and stood by J. Turner of Illinois.

BILLY BARTLETT. Billy Bartlett was a chestnut stallion foaled in 1902, bred by Alex Gardner of San Angelo, Texas, and later owned by Pres Walling, Steve Sterett, and Gray Bankers of San Angelo. He was sired by Traveler and out of Dot by Traveler.

BILLY CAVINESS. There is considerable confusion surrounding this bay stallion foaled toward the close of the nineteenth century. He was foaled in Texas, and his sire was Box Billy or Brown Dick, who may have been the same horse. In any case, Brown Dick (and/or Box Billy) was sired by Billy. At one time or another, he was owned by Bob Caviness of La Plata, New Mexico, and by Kirk Williams of Mancos, Colorado. In *Goodwin's Turf Guide of 1902*, Billy Caviness is referred to as Tom Cavendish. He was the sire of Silver Dick, who was foaled in 1897. He was sometimes known as Billy Cavanous.

BILLY COWEY. Billy Cowey was foaled in 1907, and was a sorrel bred by Crawford Sykes of Nixon, Texas. He was by Arch Oldham and out of a Rondo mare. He was first purchased by Earl Cowey of Nixon and then by Allen Moody of Rocksprings, Texas.

BILLY DAWSON. Billy Dawson was foaled in 1927 and was a beautiful bay stallion. He was bred by Joe Parker of Gorman, Texas, and was sired by Barney Lucas by Traveler and out of Alline D by Withers.

BILLY DIBRELL (BILLY DRIBBLE). This Billy was a black stallion foaled in 1880(?) who was owned by Anthony W. Dibrell of Guadalupe County, Texas, and later owned by R. T. Nixon. He was sired by Anthony by Old Billy. He was bred by Billy Fleming of Belmont, Texas, and is often referred to as Billy Dribble.

57

BILLY FLEMING, DUNMAN'S. Billy Fleming was foaled in 1884 and was bred by Jim Brown of Giddings, Texas, and later owned by R. L. Dunman of Coleman, Texas. He was sired by Old Billy by Shiloh and out of Gray Alice by Steel Dust. He was the sire of the noted race horse Procter.

BILLY GARDNER. Billy Gardner was by Three Finger Jack by Traveler and out of a mare by Brown Billy. He was taken to Arizona to race about 1914 by Mayburn Gardner, along with his brothers Fuzzy, Blue Eyes, Big Jim, Pancho, Danger, Chief, and Wild Cat. Fred Mickel of Cottonwood, Arizona, obtained Billy from Gardner and raced him all through Arizona, New Mexico, Utah, and California.

BILLY MANGUM. Billy Mangum was foaled in 1913 and was a sorrel stallion bred by William Nack of Cuero, Texas. He was sired by Cotton Eyed Joe (Nack's) by Peter McCue and out of Babe Ruth by Sykes' Rondo by McCoy Billy.

BILLY MASON. Billy Mason was foaled in 1895 and was a brown stallion bred by Thomas Watkins of Petersburg, Illinois. He was later purchased by John Dwell, Walden and Sweet, and G. A. Haleman, all of Wyoming. Billy Mason was sired by Oliver Twist (TB) and was out of Miss Rhoder by Willie Renfro. Billy Mason was registered in the appendix of the *American Stud Book* (Vol. VII, 1226). His dam traced to Harry Bluff, sire of Steel Dust. In his first race in 1897, he ran second to Peter McCue.

BILLY, McCOY'S. McCoy's Billy was by Old Billy by Shiloh and his dam was a running mare owned by Billy Fleming. His best-known get was Sykes' Rondo. He was owned by Mr. McCoy of Central, Texas.

BILLY McCUE. Billy McCue was foaled in 1917 and died in 1936. He was a sorrel stallion with a streak and two sox behind. He stood 15 hands and weighed 1200 pounds. He was by Jack McCue by Peter McCue and out of Sorrel Alice by Chickasha Bob. He was bred by S. B. "Blain" Barnes of Tulia, Texas, and later owned by Newt Grey and Jim Vaughn of Plainview, Texas. Sometime later, Jim Cox of Plainview got him and he was sold to the JA Ranch at Palo Duro, Texas. Billy was known by several names. Barnes called him Billy, Cox called him Keeno or Keno McKeu. He was also referred to as Blain Barnes after his breeder, Narrow Heel Benny, the Cox Horse, and the Renfro Horse. Barnes sold him in 1927 to Newt Grey. Jim Cox owned him in 1932 when the JA's bought him. Will Stead bred several mares to Billy before he started out for Palo Duro. He broke his leg enroute to the JA's, so they never got to use him, although they had a son of Billy they called J. A. McCue.

BILLY, NIXON'S. This sorrel stallion was foaled in 1921. He was sired by Little King by Possum by Traveler and out of a Nixon mare by Rebel by Nixon's Joe Bailey. He was bred by Dr. J. W. Nixon of Hondo, Texas, and owned by J. C. Davis of Leesville, Texas, and later by Ed Dickinson of Gonzales, Texas.

BILLY, OLD. Billy was born about the time of the Civil War. His first owner was supposed to have kept him chained to a tree while he was away fighting in the Confederate army. Billy became famous while owned by William Fleming of Belmont, Texas. Billy was by Shiloh and out of the mare Ram Cat, who was by Steel Dust. He is often referred to as Old Billy to distinguish him from the many other horses by the same name. Occasionally he was referred to as Billy Boy and as Billy Fleming. Some of his best known gets include Anthony, John Crowder, Joe Collins, Whalebone, Pancho, and Yellow Wolf.

BILLY SMOOT. Billy Smoot was a sorrel stallion of unknown breeding. Raymond Hollingsworth said that from what he could find out, Billy Smoot was by Bob Wade. He was owned in succession by Dick Carson of Clayton, New

Mexico; Hill Barrow of Texline, Texas; and then T. E. Mitchell of Albert, New Mexico. Merle Paul said Billy Smoot was by Sykes' Rondo. Albert Mitchell always contended that they did not know the breeding of Billy Smoot.

BILLY SUNDAY. Billy Sunday was a sorrel stallion foaled in 1916 and registered by the Jockey Club under the name of Huyler (see *American Stud Book* Vol. XII, 55). He was bred by John Wilkins of San Antonio, Texas, and later was owned by J. E. Parke of Kyle, Graves Peeler, and Ott Adams of Alice, Texas. Ott Adams had the registration papers for Huyler and a letter from John Wilkins dated December 17, 1919, in which he stated "the sorrel colt Huyler is by Horace H, a very fast horse ½ mile. I bought him from F. Newman and gave $1000 for him. The dam of Huyler was Belle of Oakford, nicknamed Carrie Nation. I believe she was the fastest ¼ horse I ever saw."

BILLY SUNDAY, ROBERDS'. This stallion was by Roman Gold by Old Nick by Old Fred and out of a Roberds' Quarter mare. He was bred by Coke T. Roberds of Hayden, Colorado, and owned by Bob Dunn of Toponas, Colorado, and by Leonard Horn of Wolcott, Colorado.

BILLY THE KID, see OKLAHOMA SHY.

BILLY THE TOUGH. Billy the Tough was foaled in 1927 and was by A. D. Reed and out of Betsy. He was bred by Kenneth Montgomery of Reydon, Oklahoma. He showed good speed and, in order to race him more successfully, he was gelded before he was four years old. He sired only two small crops of colts. One report gave his dam as having been sired by Kid Welder.

BILLY, TIM PAGE'S, see WONDER WORLD.

BILLY WHITE. Billy White was foaled in 1898 and was sired by Billy Caviness and out of Fanny White. He was bred by Kirk Williams of Mancos, Colorado. John Taylor of Moab, Utah, said that Billy White was raised by Charles Johnson of Mancos. Billy White was injured by a barb wire and as a result was used only as a stallion. His dam, according to Ed Kerby, was raised by George White of Mancos.

BINKLY HORSE, see PANCHO VILLA.

BISCUIT, OLD. Old Biscuit was a sorrel stallion foaled in about 1926. He was by the RO Sykes by Peter McCue and out of an RO mare. He was bred and owned by the Greene Cattle Company of Cananea, Sonora, Mexico. He was not one of the Steel Dust studs bought by the ranch in 1916.

BLACK BALL. Black Ball was a black stallion foaled in 1888 and sired by Missouri Rondo by Missouri Mike. His dam's name was Nan. He was bred and owned by Alex Chote of Lockwood, Missouri, and his best son was Old Fred. Nan was a Standardbred mare.

BLACK BEAR. This black stallion was foaled in 1926 and was by A. M. White who was by Everett (TB). His dam was a dun mare of Yellow Jacket breeding. He was bred by Eugene J. Schott of Riomedina, Texas, and owned by Rube Williams of Llano, Jack Bridger of Glen Rose, and John Garner of Girvin, all in Texas. He was registered in the *American Stud Book.*

BLACK BOB, see CHICKASHA BOB, YOUNG.

BLACK DASH, see DASH.

BLACK GOLD. Black Gold was a black horse foaled in 1921 who died in 1928 after a New Orleans race, when he ran the last furlong with a broken leg and was shot afterward. He was by Black Tony (TB) and out of Useeit by Bonnie Joe (TB). Several writers, including Quentin Reynolds, claim Useeit was not a Thoroughbred, but a Quarter mare. Black Gold won the Kentucky Derby in 1924.

BLACK JACK. A black stallion by Harmon Baker Jr. by Harmon Baker and out of a Wheat Quarter mare. Bred by Gus Wheat of Sonora, Texas, and owned by Therrill Rose of Del Rio, Texas.

BLACK JIM. Black Jim was foaled in 1922. He was by Uncle Jimmy Gray by Bonnie Joe (TB) and his dam was a Haby Quarter mare. He was bred by Martin Haby of Riomedina, Texas.

BLACK SNAKE. This celebrated Quarter running horse was bred and owned by a black man, Hugh Snelling of Granville County, North Carolina. He was a black horse foaled in 1788 by *Obscurity and out of Harlot by Old Bacchus.

BLACK STREAK. This was a brown stallion foaled in 1924. He was by Uncle Jimmy Gray by Bonnie Joe (TB) and out of Katy Flyer by Paul Murray. He was bred by F. G. Senne of Hondo, Texas.

BLACK WHIP, BOWMAN'S. Black Whip was foaled in 1822, he was black and sired by Cook's (Edgar also lists him as Blackburn's) Whip by *Whip. Imported Whip, who was foaled in 1749, was a bay horse imported by Mr. Durand. Imported Whip was by Old Saltram. Black Whip's dam was by Shark. His breeder is unknown, but he was owned by Wilson Bowman of Bardstown, Kentucky.

BLEVIN'S LITTLE TOM, see TOM, BLEVIN'S LITTLE.

BLIND BARNEY. Blind Barney was by Steel Dust by Harry Bluff and out of Mary. His breeder is uncertain but he was owned by Thomas Trammell of Sweetwater, Texas. He was one of the foundation sires used on Trammell and Newman mares. He was used during the 1880's.

BLUE BOAR. Blue Boar was foaled in 1774. His sire was *Janus and his dam was by *Fearnought. He was bred by

Wyllie Jones of Halifax Town, North Carolina. Edgar claims he was "the fleetest horse of his day for Quarter racing." He is listed in the *ASB*.

BLUE DICK. Blue Dick was a brown stallion foaled in 1883 by Wade Hampton and out of Bettie Worth. He died in 1889.

BLUE EYES. This Blue Eyes by Sykes' Rondo was foaled about 1890. He was bred by Sykes and Mangum of Nixon, Texas, and owned by Dow and Will Shely of Alfred, Texas. This was the Shely's first stallion of note. His dam was May Mangum. He was a well-known race horse.

BLUE EYES. Blue Eyes by Possum was foaled about 1910. Mayburn Gardner sold him to Fred Mickel of Cottonwood, Arizona, who later sold him to Whitey Montgomery of Rimrock, Arizona.

BLUE JACKET. Blue Jacket was foaled May 15, 1888; he stood 15 hands and weighed 1050 pounds. He was by Lock's Rondo and out of Mary Lee by Joe Lee. He was sold and taken to Mexico City.

BOANERGES, ACKLEY'S. He was by Boanerges by Printer and his dam is unknown. He was bred by Hyson Ackley.

BOANERGES, GREENSTREET'S. Boanerges was foaled in 1854(?). He was by Owens' Boanerges and out of Greenstreet's mare.

BOANERGES, LOWREY'S. This Boanerges was by Ackley's Boanerges and out of Jenny Crassom, second dam by Fenton's Weasel. He was bred and owned by Edward Lowrey of Norwich, New York.

BOANERGES, ORIGINAL. Boanerges was by Old Printer by Atkinson's Janus. Breeder and owner unknown. He was foaled in 1822(?) and died in 1844(?).

BOANERGES, OWENS'. This Boanerges was probably foaled in 1848, and he was sired by Lowrey's Boanerges by Ackley's Boanerges and out of a Printer mare. He was reportedly bred by Bill Owens of Smithville, Missouri.

BOBBIE LOWE. This bay stallion was foaled in 1909. He was by Eureka by Shelby and out of Suzie McWhorter by Old Ben Burton. He was bred by Webb Christian of Big Spring, Texas, and owned by W. T. Waggoner of Fort Worth, Texas.

BOB H. Bob H was a bay stallion foaled in 1916 who died in 1924(?). He was by Old Fred by Black Ball and out of Queen Litze (TB). He was bred by Si Dawson of Hayden, Colorado, and owned by Coke Roberds.

BOB, LITTLE, see CHICKASHA BOB, YOUNG.

BOB PETERS, OLD. This roan stallion was foaled in 1884 and died in the early 1900's. He was by Pony Pete by Barney Owens and was bred by Smith Kellum of Cheyenne, Oklahoma.

BOB PETERS, YOUNG. He was by Old Bob Peters and his dam a Kellum Quarter mare. He was bred by Smith Kellum of Cheyenne, Oklahoma, and raced by Reed Armstrong of Elk City, Oklahoma. Until defeated by Hermus at Texola, Oklahoma, in the early 1900's, he was thought to be unbeatable.

BOB S. Bob S was foaled in 1886 and was sired by Sam Harper and out of an unknown mare. He was owned and raced by L. C. Ball.

BOB WADE. Bob Wade was a bay gelding foaled in 1886. He was registered in the Jockey Club for racing purposes, and his sire is given as Roan Dick. Helen Michaelis said more likely he was bred by Billy Fleming and was by Old Billy. He is listed here because occasionally one finds a pedigree showing a horse sired by Bob Wade. He was never bred, but ran short races all over the West and had few rivals on the straightaway. *Goodwin's Turf Guide* covers his races in 1890-94. There were several other stallions named Bob Wade, after this famous Quarter miler. See under Roan Dick.

BONNIE JOE (DR. ROSE). Bonnie Joe was foaled in 1924, and was a bay stallion by Little Joe and out of Genevieve. He was bred by Ott Adams of Alice, Texas. He was later owned by Joe Bridge, O. W. Cardwell, Dr. Fred Rose, Raymond Dickson, and Hal Mangum. Raymond Dickson got the horse from Dr. Rose and named him after the doctor. Ott Adams said he originally named him Bonnie J.

BOOGER RED. Booger Red was by Old Fred by Black Ball and out of a gray Dawson mare. He was bred by Bruce Dawson of Hayden, Colorado, and owned by Don Taylor of Moab, Utah.

BOOGER RED. This stallion was foaled in 1905(?) and was by Rancocas (TB) and out of a Barney Owens mare. He was bred by Jim Newman of Sweetwater, Texas, and after changing hands several times ended up in the ownership of Bryant Turner of Colorado Springs, Colorado.

BOWIE, see BUIE.

BOWLAWAY. Bowlaway was a dark chestnut stallion listed by Edgar as a celebrated American Quarter running horse. He was by Young Monkey and out of a mare by Liberty. He was a capitol racer and won immense sums of money. He stood 14 hands, 2 inches. He is listed in the *ASB*.

BOY, BIG. A. J. Kennedy of Albuquerque, New Mexico, said this stallion was by Rainy Day, but others say he was by the Thoroughbred Don Movari and out of a Quarter mare. Big Boy sired Jack Dempsey. It is possible that his sire, given as Don Movari, was Dominus Arvi (1904) by *Kismet.

BOY, LITTLE. This bay stallion was foaled in 1923. He was by Uncle Jimmy Gray by Bonnie Joe (TB). His dam was Nancy Brown by Nixon's Joe Bailey. He was bred by Bert Bendele of Riomedina, Texas.

BRICK. Brick was a chestnut stallion foaled in California in 1871. He was sired by Oregon Charlie and his dam was by Pilgrim. His second dam was Choctaw's Sister by Obe Jennings. He was owned by John Adams of Woodland, California, and was the sire of Adams' two well-known running mares, Pearl and Ita.

BRIMMER, ALSUP'S. Alsup's Brimmer was one of a large number of Brimmers, all related, that lived in Virginia, Kentucky, and Tennessee during the nineteenth century. Edgar lists eight, Wallace six, and Bruce eight. Bruce enters all of his in the appendix, showing he does not consider them to be pure Thoroughbred. The original Brimmer belonged to John Goode of Powhatan County, Virginia. The Alsup horse was by a son taken to Tennessee.

BRIMMER, GOODE'S. This bay stallion is listed by Edgar as a celebrated running horse. He was got by Harris' Eclipse by *Fearnought and out of Polly Flaxen by *Jolly Roger. He was foaled about the time of the outbreak of the Revolutionary War. He was bred by Captain Thomas Turpin of Powhatan County, Virginia, and owned most of his life by John C. Goode of Mecklenburg County, Virginia. This is the original Brimmer.

BRIMMER, TENNESSEE. By Club Foot by *Janus and out of Doll Pearson by Old Pearson. This horse was probably bred in North Carolina, but stood in Tennessee most of his life and is probably the fountainhead of the Alsup's Quarter Horses.

BROKE SHOULDER (BROKEN SHOULDERED, BROKE SHOULDERED STUD). Broke Shoulder was a bay stallion foaled in 1931, he was by George Alice and out of an O'Connor mare and was bred by the Southerland Brothers of Eagle Lake, Texas. He was owned by many people including Ira Wood of Dilley, Texas; Cavin Woodward and George Cowder, both of Pearsall, Texas; Keith Underhill of Pontotoc, Oklahoma; Frank Bounds of Madill, Oklahoma; Glen Lowry; and George R. Jones of Oklahoma City. According to the AQHA stud book, #7250, Broken Shoulder was by Ace of Diamonds.

BRONCHO. This chestnut stallion was foaled in 1886 and was by Joe Hooker and out of Lady Winston. He was bred by Theodore Winter of Woodland, California.

BROTHER, LITTLE. Little Brother was foaled about 1915 and he was sired by Possum by Traveler and out of a Jim Kennedy mare. He was bred by Jim Kennedy of Bonita, Arizona, and owned later by Joe Herridge and Bill Cassidy of Fairfax, Oklahoma.

BROTHER II, LITTLE. This stallion was by Little Brother by Possum and out of a mare by Gold Digger. He was bred by Joe Herridge of Fairfax, Oklahoma.

BROWN BILLY (HIPPED BILLY, BROWN HIPPED BILLY). Brown Billy was foaled in 1893 and was by Pancho, who was by Billy. He was bred by Alex Gardner who gave Brown Billy to his brother, Pete Gardner, of Big Foot, Texas.

BROWN DICK. Brown Dick was a brown horse foaled in 1887 by Cold Deck by Steel Dust by Harry Bluff and out of Louise. His racing record is in *Goodwin's Turf Guide 1894-96*.

BROWN JUG. Brown Jug was foaled in 1906(?) and was by Jim Ned by Pancho. He was under 15 hands and weighed 1125. He was bred by William Anson of Christoval, Texas. Anson sold him to the Corrallitos Ranch in Mexico. He was stolen from the ranch by Pancho Villa and became his personal mount for a number of years.

BUCK, see BAILEY.

BUCK. Buck was by Joe Bailey of Weatherford. He was bred by Jack Tindall of Eastland, Texas. He was purchased by Bus Whiteside, who later sold him to the Waggoner Ranch at Electra, Texas.

BUCK, LITTLE. Little Buck was a bay stallion foaled in 1890. He was by Buck Walton (TB) and out of Maud, a Quarter mare raised by Jim Garrett. He was bred by John R. Nasworthy of San Angelo, Texas.

BUCK, OLD. This stallion was by the Montgomery horse and out of a mare by Shiek. He was bred in Colorado and owned by Arzon Mills of Clark, Colorado.

BUCK SHOT. Buck Shot was by Joe Collins and foaled in the 1890's. He was used extensively by the McGonigal family of the Midland, Texas, area.

BUCK SORREL. This sorrel stallion was foaled in 1780 and was by Twigg by *Janus and out of a mare by *Jolly Rogers. He was bred and owned by Jacob Bugg of Mecklenburg County, Virginia.

BUCK THOMAS. Buck Thomas was a sorrel stallion foaled in 1921. He was sired by Peter McCue and out of Stockings by Old Fred. He was bred by Coke Roberds of Hayden, Colorado, and sold to W. T. Waggoner of Electra, Texas, in 1927. While on the Waggoner Ranch, he sired most of his well-known progeny such as Bill Thomas and Red Buck. A full brother by the same name set several track records as a race horse, but he was a gelding.

BUDDY. This Buddy was by Canadian by Yellow Jacket and out of an unknown dam. He was bred by Bud Bennett of Dumas, Texas, and later owned by Tom Record of Dumas. His sire, Canadian, was also referred to as the Bud Bennett Grullo and as the Bud Bennett Horse.

BUDDY. This Buddy was a bay stallion foaled in or around 1930, dying in 1950. He was by Charley by Zantanon and out of Three O'Clock by Cameron by Texas Chief. He was bred by C. Manuel Benevides of Laredo, Texas, and owned by Amador Garcia of Loredo and by Tito Harper of Piedras Negras, Coahuila, Mexico. Buddy had a streak and one white rear foot.

BUIE (BOWIE). Buie was by *Janus and out of an imported mare. He was bred by Mr. Buie of Virginia. He was owned in 1787 by John Park and David Berclay of Jefferson City, Tennessee. Bruce lists him, but not Edgar.

BULGER. Bulger was bred by Alex Gardner of San Angelo, Texas, and owned by Jim Kennedy of Bonita, Arizona. Kennedy also owned Possum. He was by Traveler and out of an old gray Billy mare.

BULLET. Bullet was by Paul El by Hickory Bill and out of an Adams' mare who was by Billy Sunday. He was bred by Ott Adams of Alfred, Texas, and owned by Jim Adams of Alice, Texas.

BUMBLE BEE. This bay stallion, foaled in 1934, was by King Plaudit (TB) and out of Queen by Ashton (TB). He was bred and owned by the Lindauer brothers of Grand Valley, Colorado.

BUNCOM CHROMO. This bay stallion was foaled in 1889 in Marshall, Missouri, and was by Cold Deck by Billy. He was owned by Bill Owens of Smithville, Missouri.

BUNTON HORSE. This bay stallion was foaled in 1906(?). He was by Little Rondo by Lock's Rondo and out of a Bunton mare. He was bred by J. Ashley Bunton of Uvalde, Texas, and owned by F. C. Stockley of Montell, Texas.

BURTON BROWN. This bay stallion, foaled in 1926, was by Barney Lucas by Traveler and out of Nellie Tamsit by Palm

Reader. He was bred by "Webb" Christian of Big Spring, Texas, and owned by W. T. Waggoner of Fort Worth, Texas.

BUSTER. Buster was by Little Rondo by Lock's Rondo and out of Shely's Lulu Mc. He was bred and owned by Dow and Will Shely of Alfred, Texas.

BUTLER HORSE, see WARRIOR.

BUTLER RED. Butler Red was a sorrel foaled in 1926. He was by Booger by Rancocas (TB) and out of a Senator mare. He was bred in Colorado and owned by Riley Van Dyne of Fort Garland, Colorado.

BUTTON, see GOLD BUTTON.

C

CADD (CADDO). Cadd was foaled in 1888 and was by Steel Dust and out of a mare by Sam Harper. He was raced extensively and his record is in *Goodwin's Turf Guide*.

CAMDEN. A chestnut stallion by *Janus and out of the great brood mare Polly Flaxen by *Jolly Rogers. He was bred and owned by Captain Turpin of Powhatan County, Virginia. He was a full brother of Fleetwood and a half (maternal) brother of Goode's Brimmer.

CANALES, see CIRILDO.

CAP. Cap was foaled in 1914 and was sired by Tom Glover; his dam was Dutchie. Tom Glover's dam was Rondo, although which Rondo is not known for sure, as several sons of the original Sykes' Rondo were called Rondo also. Cap was bred by Dolph Peril of Kerrville who sold him to R. N. Cowsert in 1917.

CAPTAIN JOE (JOE GARDNER, GATES HORSE). Captain Joe was a sorrel horse by Traveler and out of Mamie Crowder who was by John Crowder. He was bred by Will Shely of Alfred, Texas, and then owned by Ott Adams of Alfred, Texas. Later he was obtained by Jack Gates who lived on a ranch south of San Antonio.

CAVINESS, see BILLY CAVINESS.

CELER, HENDRICK'S. Edgar says that this stallion was a running Quarter Horse. He was a sorrel and was bred about 1786(?). He was by Mead's Celer and his dam was by Cooper's Janus. Edgar says that Cooper's Janus "was a full bred Janus horse having eight crosses of Old Janus in him." He then adds that Celer was unquestionably the swiftest quarter-mile race horse in the United States of his day. He was bred by Mr. Obed Hendrick of Halifax County, Virginia. He is listed in Edgar and the *ASB*.

CELER, MEAD'S OLD. Celer was a sorrel stallion foaled in 1776 who was by *Janus and out of Brandon by *Aristotle by the Cullen Arabian. He was the foundation horse for the Celer Quarter Horse family. He was bred by Everard Mead of Amelia County, Virginia.

CHARLEY HOWELL. This bay stallion was foaled in 1910. He was by Peter McCue by Dan Tucker and out of Sister Ida (TB). He was bred and owned by John Wilkins of San Antonio, Texas.

CHARLEY WILSON. This sorrel stallion was foaled in 1889 and was by Buck Walton (TB) and out of a Quarter mare named Daisy. He was bred by John R. Nasworthy of San Angelo and owned by A. A. Daniels of Chicago, Illinois. He was a full brother of Captain and is listed in the appendix of the *American Stud Book*. Billy Anson said he understood Charley Wilson was never defeated when run under 600 yards. His running weight was 1205 pounds, and his stride 27 feet. He was ruled off the tracks in Chicago.

CHARLIE, JENKIN'S, see OREGON CHARLIE.

CHARLIE, OLD, see OREGON CHARLIE.

CHEROKEE. Cherokee was a sorrel Thoroughbred stallion foaled in 1824. He was by Sir Archy and out of Roxana.

CHEROKEE. According to the *American Stud Book* (Vol. II, 565), this Cherokee was a Quarter Horse stallion foaled in 1847. He died in 1872 at Council Bluffs, Iowa, at the age of 25 years. He was probably sired by a son of Cherokee by Sir Archy.

CHICKASHA BOB. Little is known about this stallion. He was probably by Pid Hart or Rocky Mountain Tom, although some refer to his sire as a Tennessee horse named Captain Sykes. He was very fast, having two races with Croton Oil and beating her both times. Warren Shoemaker of Watrous, New Mexico, said that he was owned at one time by Cliff Neafus of Newkirk, New Mexico.

CHICKASHA BOB, YOUNG. Young Chickasha Bob was a black stallion foaled about 1900. He was by Chickasha Bob by Pid Hart by Shelby and out of Maud by a Quarter Horse stallion named Billy. He was bred by J. C. "Cliff" Neafus of Newkirk, New Mexico, and owned by A. L. McMurtrey of Silverton, Texas. He was sometimes called Black Bob.

CHICKEN SMART. Chicken Smart was foaled in 1925 and was a red sorrel. He was by Belamour (TB) and out of Goldie by Big Jim. He was bred by George Doty of Afton, Oklahoma. Joe Adolph of Pawhuska bought him as a yearling and ran him short. Charley Carter and Roger Leahy of Pawhuska owned him briefly and then sold him to Barton Carter in about 1928. Carter loaned the stallion to Joe Crow of

Bartlesville for one season and Monsieur Moore bred several mares to him that year.

CHICO LINDO. Chico Lindo was by Red Cloud by Possum and out of Hollyhock by No Good by Barney Owens. He was bred and owned by Mark Dubois of Bonita, Arizona.

CHIEF. Chief was by Captain Jinks and out of an unknown mare. He was bred by George Eaton of Yakima, Washington, and owned by Charles E. Green of Manson, Washington.

CHIEF. This Chief was by Ed by Possum and owned by M. Raymal and Sons of Chihuahua, Mexico.

CHIEF. This Chief was a dun stallion foaled about 1935, and sired by Saladin by Ding Bob 269. His dam was Buckeye by Sheik. He was bred by Quentin Semotan of Clark, Colorado, and owned by Alfred Lester of Clark.

CHIEF WILKINS. This stallion was by John Wilkins by Peter McCue and out of the mare Georgie. He was bred by John Gardner of San Angelo, Texas, and owned by Bob Cunningham and Dick Godfrey, both of Menard.

CHOCOLATE. This black stallion was by Grano de Oro by Little Joe and out of an unknown mare. He was owned by the King Ranch and sometimes referred to as the Little Black Norias Horse.

CHOCOLATE. This Chocolate was by Yellow Wolf by Joe Bailey and out of a mare by Midnight by Badger. He was bred by W. T. Waggoner of Fort Worth, Texas.

CHOCOLATE DROP. This stallion was by Red Seal by Sealskin and out of a Corder mare. He was bred and owned by Monty Corder of Sanderson, Texas.

CHOCOLATE SOLDIER. Chocolate Soldier was foaled in 1932 and was by Ding Bob and out of Majesty by Dalstom

(TB). He was bred and owned by Ben Savage of Steamboat Springs, Colorado.

CHOCTAW. Choctaw was by Line Up (TB) and out of Barnes' Black Mare by Billy McCue by Jack McCue. He was bred and owned by John Burson of Silverton, Texas.

CHOCTAW. Choctaw was owned and bred in Oregon. He was by Obe Jennings by Patete's Ariel and his dam is unknown. The *ASB* (Vol. VI, 1171) shows a Choctaw—a bay horse foaled in 1881 sired by *Saxon—but this is probably not the same stallion, although a son may have gone to Oregon.

CHULO MUNDO. This bay stallion was foaled in about 1895 and was by Traveler and out of Georgie. He was bred by John Gardner of San Angelo, Texas, and owned by Dick Godfrey of Menard.

CHUNKY BILL. Chunky Bill was a brown stallion foaled in 1879. He was by Whalebone by Billy (Old) and out of Paisana by Brown Dick. He was bred by Billy Fleming of Belmont, Texas, and owned first by D. F. Fox of Live Oak County, Texas, and then by Pat Sheeran of Cotulla, Texas. His most famous race was his loss to Yellow Wolf in the middle 1880's.

CIMARRON. Cimarron was a brown stallion foaled in 1930 by Jeff Self by A. D. Reed and out of Poor Mama by Joy by Jeff. He was bred by Aubra Bowers of Allison, Texas, and later owned by Kenneth (Skip) Montgomery of Reydon, Oklahoma.

CIRILDO (CANALES HORSE). Cirildo was by Sutherland by Hickory Bill and out of a King Ranch mare. He was bred by C. Canales of Premont, Texas.

CLAMP SORREL. This stallion was by Little Joe by Traveler and out of a Dial mare. He was bred by John Dial of Goliad and owned by Jim Clamp of Brackettville, Texas. He was foaled in about 1910.

CLAY, see KELLY.

CLAY McGONIGAL (CLAY). This bay stallion was born in 1911 and was sired by Joe Collins by Billy and out of a McGonigal mare. He was bred by Clay McGonigal of Midland, Texas, and owned by Jim Harkey of Fort Stockton, Texas.

CLEGG CRIPPLED SORREL. This sorrel stallion was by Tom Thumb by Little Joe by Traveler and out of a Clegg mare sired by Cuadro by Billy. He was bred by George Clegg of Alice, Texas, who gave him to Banks Barbee and Will Lane of Wharton, Texas. He was later sold to J. D. Hudgins of Hungerford, Texas.

CLEGG CUT FOOT HORSE, see SAM WATKINS.

CLEGG DUN. A dun stallion by Randado Dun and out of a Clegg mare by Hickory Bill. He was bred by George Clegg of Alice, Texas, and owned by J. D. Hudgins of Hungerford, Texas.

CLEMENTE GARCIA (LUPITE). Clemente was by Little Joe by Traveler and out of an Adams' mare. He was bred by Ott Adams of Alice, Texas.

CLIMAX. This sorrel stallion was foaled in 1927 and was by Concho Colonel by Jim Ned by Pancho and out of Christina by Old Joe by Harmon Baker. He was bred by Dan Casement of Manhattan, Kansas, and was owned by Joe Doherty of Folsum, New Mexico. He was the last of the Colonel's get.

CLOUDIUS, MEAD'S OLD. Cloudius was foaled about 1778 and was by *Janus and out of the famous Brandon by *Aristotle. He was bred and owned by Everard Mead of Amelia County, Virginia. He was a full brother to Celer.

CLOVER. Clover was by Clover Leaf by Fleeting Time (TB) and out of a Waggoner Quarter mare. He was bred on the Waggoner Ranch and owned by Bill Cooper of Throckmorton, Texas.

CLOVER LEAF. Clover Leaf was a palomino stallion foaled in 1928. He was by Fleeting Time (TB) and his dam was a dun Spanish mare. Although this stallion may have had no Quarter blood, he contributed to the breed. He was bred by W. M. "Bill" Moore of San Saba, Texas, and owned by two early Quarter Horse breeders, W. T. Waggoner of Fort Worth and Duwain E. Hughes of Big Lake, Texas. He was a well-built horse of Quarter Horse conformation. He was a half brother of Buddy Niles, #26,752, and the sire of Van Vacter's Yankee Doodle, a well-known race horse in the late 1930's.

CLOVER WOLF. He was by Clover Leaf by Fleeting Time (TB) and out of a Yellow Wolf mare. He was bred and owned by W. T. Waggoner of Fort Worth, Texas.

CLUB FOOT. Club Foot was foaled in 1778. He was a chestnut standing 15 hands, 1 inch. He was by *Janus and out of a mare by *Fearnought. Edgar says Club Foot was an excellent quarter-mile racer. He was taken to the "Western Country" in later life. An injury caused his foot to swell to great size. He is listed by both Edgar and the *ASB*.

COALIE. This black stallion was by Abe Frank (TB) and out of a Newman mare. He was bred by J. F. Newman of Sweetwater, Texas, and owned by Jim Wilson of Alpine, Texas.

COAL OIL JOHNNY. He was foaled in 1899, and was by Peter McCue by Dan Tucker and out of Flexy by Voltigeur (TB). He was bred and owned by Elias Watkins of Petersburg, Illinois.

COCK-ROBIN. Cock-Robin is listed indirectly by Edgar. Under Napolean, he says "this last Celer mare was also the dam of the famous quarter racers, Copper-Head and Cock-Robin."

COKE T (PRINCE). This sorrel stallion was foaled in about 1920 and died in 1940. He was by Brown Dick by *Derring-Doe (TB). His dam was Stockings by Old Fred. He was bred by Coke Roberds of Hayden, Colorado, and owned by Charles Redd of La Dal, Utah, and Jack Casement, then of Whitewater, Colorado.

COLD DECK. Cold Deck was foaled in 1862, stood a scant 15 hands and was a dark sorrel. He was foaled at Carthage, Missouri, according to the generally accepted version. He was sired by Steel Dust by Harry Bluff by Short Whip.

There are several well-known Cold Decks, but this was the most famous. He was bred by Nathan Floyd of Carthage and owned by Foster (Foss) Barker of Van Buren, Arkansas. Tom Stogdon of Alba, Missouri, also owned him for a while. Coke Blake, who knew Cold Deck, and Foss Barker said he had beauty, style, speed, and elegance and was the fastest horse of his time.

COLD DECK, BERRY'S. This bay stallion was foaled in 1873 and lived until 1904. He was by Cold Deck by Steel Dust by Harry Bluff and his dam was a Red Buck mare by Grinder. He was bred by Joe Berry of Mount Vernon, Missouri, and owned by N. B. Maxwell of Wendell, Tennessee, and by S. Coke Blake of Pryor, Oklahoma.

COLD DECK, GATES'. This bay stallion was foaled about 1907 and was by Captain Joe by Traveler and out of a Gates' mare. He was bred by Jack Gates of Devine, Texas, and raced by Bud Mangum.

COLD DECK, LOCK'S. This Cold Deck was a dun stallion sired by Martin's Cold Deck by Old Billy and out of a dun Lock mare named Nellie. He was bred by W. W. Lock of Kyle, Texas, and owned by John Lock, W. W. Lock's son.

COLD DECK, MARTIN'S. This Cold Deck was by Billy by Shiloh and out of a daughter of Steel Dust called Ram Cat. He was a brown horse foaled in about 1868. He was bred by Tom Martin of Kyle, Texas, and owned by Jim Brown of Giddings, Texas, and Bill Owen of Smithville, Missouri. Tom Martin was a federal officer from Missouri who came to Texas and settled at Kyle. He was a race-horse man and a gambler of the old school. He and Jim Brown were close friends.

COLD DECK, SPRINGER'S. This Cold Deck was foaled about 1900 and his sire and dam are unknown at this time. He was purchased by Ed Springer of the CS Ranch from George Crocker and used by the CS Ranch until 1910. Many of his fillies were bred to Little Joe (Springer) and ten of them were sold to Waite Phillips of the Philmont Ranch at Cimarron.

COLD DECK, YOUNG. Young Cold Deck was a brown stallion foaled in 1888. He was by Berry's Cold Deck by Cold Deck by Steel Dust and he was out of a Bertrand mare. He was bred by N. B. Maxwell of Wendell, Tennessee, and purchased by Coke Blake of Pryor, Oklahoma, in 1896. A year later, Blake sold Young Cold Deck and bought his sire, Berry's Cold Deck, from Maxwell.

COLEY. This black stallion was foaled in 1908 and was sired by Little Jack by Anthony and out of Annie Springs by Democrat (SB). He was bred by Andrew Springs of Seguin, Texas, and owned by Doc Malear of Kingsbury, Texas; Rube Walkerwitz of Luling, Texas; Dr. J. W. Nixon of Hondo, Texas; and Fred Matthies of Seguin, Texas. He was somewhat jug-headed, stood 14½ hands high and weighed around 900 pounds.

COLONEL HUNT. This bay stallion was sired by Frogtown by *Bonnie Scotland and out of Florence. He was owned by W. R. Rogan.

COLORADO SORREL, see RED.

COLUMBUS. Columbus was by Silver Dick by Billy Caviness and out of Fannie Anderson by Billy Caviness. He was bred and owned by Kirk Williams of Mancos, Colorado.

COMET. There were several Comets and considerable confusion exists between Edgar, Bruce, and John B. Irving about these horses. However, this Comet was a black horse (described by Edgar as a skewbald) by Lee's Mark Anthony by Pardner and out of Matchless by Old *Janus. He was bred by Governor Williams of Craven County, North Carolina, and foaled in 1778. He was very small, just 14 hands and a fraction. Irving describes him as black with a blazed face, the iris of his eyes a light gray; he had four white legs, to the knees and hocks. He ran with his hind legs very wide apart, and won most of his races. He was taken into South Carolina by a Mr. Twining.

CONCHO. Concho was by Ketchum by Capitan and out of Nellie by Doc Link. He was bred and owned by W. R. Davis of Sterling City, Texas.

CONCHO CHIEF. Concho Chief was by Jack McCue by Peter McCue and out of an unknown dam. His breeder is also unknown. He was owned by Charles Clossom of Santa Fe, New Mexico.

CONCHO COLONEL. He was a sorrel stallion foaled in 1904 who died in 1927. He was by Jim Ned by Pancho by Billy and out of a Billy Anson Quarter mare. He was bred by Billy Anson of Christoval, Texas, and owned by Dan D. Casement of Manhattan, Kansas. Concho Colonel was a full brother to Brown Jug.

CONCHO KID. This bay stallion was foaled in 1927 and was by Everett (TB) and out of Concho by Harmon Baker. He was owned and bred by J. E. Renfro of Menard, Texas.

CONFIDENCE, LITTLE. This chestnut stallion was foaled in 1887. He was by Old Confidence by Walnut Bark and out of a Blasingame short mare. He was bred by Lee Blasingame of Fresno, California, and owned by W. B. Fudge of Tulare, California.

CONFIDENCE, OLD. Confidence was a sorrel foaled in 1878 and by Walnut Bark by Blevin's Little Tom. His dam was Delph. He was owned by P. D. Bozeman and L. A. Blasingame of Fresno, California. He was a famous California race horse and sire.

COPELAND HORSE, see ACE, LITTLE.

COPPER BOTTOM. Copper Bottom was foaled in 1828, a sorrel, and bred by Edward Parker of Lancaster, Pennsylvania. He was brought to Texas by Sam Houston in 1839. He was sired by Sir Archy and out of a daughter of imported Buzzard. Copper Bottom landed in New Orleans and was ridden overland to Galveston. Later he was taken to Chambers County and eventually died in Hopkins County in 1860.

CORBETT, see JOHNNY CORBETT.

COTTON. Cotton was a sorrel horse foaled in 1934 by Paul El and out of Adalina by Little Joe. He was bred by Ott Adams of Alice, Texas, and owned by John Almond of Alfred, and by Ed Peters of Alice, Texas.

COTTON EYED JOE. Cotton Eyed Joe was foaled about 1920 and died in 1936. He was a sorrel with a bald face and a glass eye. He had white on his rear feet and roan hairs in his flanks and around the root of his tail. He weighed 1050 pounds and was a typical hard-twisted Quarter Horse. He was sired by Little Joe by Traveler and out of Black Bess by Captain Sykes. He was bred by Ott Adams of Alice, Texas, and owned in order by George Clegg of Alice, Tom East of Kingsville, and W. T. Waggoner of Fort Worth, Texas.

COTTON EYED JOE, WATKINS'. The Cotton Eyed Joe by Peter McCue was foaled in 1904 and registered by the Jockey Club. His dam was Hattie W, who like Peter McCue was registered as being by the Duke of Highlands. O. W. Cardwell thought he was a better horse than Harmon Baker or Hickory Bill. He was an excellent race horse for up to one-half a mile. He may have been bred by Bill Nack of Cuero, Texas, although it seems much more likely that he was purchased from the Watkins of Petersburg, Illinois.

CRAWFORD. This stallion was foaled in 1892 and was by Traveler and his dam was a Gardner mare. He was bred by Alex Gardner of San Angelo, Texas, and owned by Jake Boone of Wilson County, Texas, and F. Crawford of Dimmitt, Texas. John Gardner's brother-in-law, Jake Boone, took Crawford back to San Angelo where he had been bred and raced him there and at Midland. He lost to 80 Grey at Midland in 1898.

CRAWFORD SYKES, ANSON'S. This brown stallion was by Arch Oldham by Gallantry (TB) and out of a Sykes' mare by Sykes' Rondo. He was bred by Crawford Sykes of Nixon, Texas, and his owners were Billy Anson of Christoval, Texas, W. P. Fisher of Marfa, Texas, and Henry T. Fletcher of Marfa, Texas. He was foaled in 1907.

This horse is sometimes confused with the Ketchum stallion of the same name. He has also been referred to as Arch Oldham Jr.

CRAWFORD SYKES, KETCHUM'S. This sorrel stallion was foaled in 1890 and died in 1915. He was by Sykes' Rondo by McCoy Billy by Billy and out of a Sykes' mare. He was bred by Crawford Sykes of Nixon, Texas, who gave him as a baby to his friend Berry Ketchum of Sheffield, Texas.

CRIPPLE. This F.A.Q.R.H. was foaled about 1765 and died in 1782. He was a dark chestnut about 14½ hands high. Edgar says he was one of the prettiest horses of his size ever seen.

He was bred by Sir Peyton Skipwith of Mecklenburg County, Virginia. He was by *Janus and his dam was by *Janus. He died in the ownership of Thomas Claiborne of Brunswick County, Virginia.

CROWDER. Crowder was a sorrel stallion foaled around 1920, and he was by Rowdy by Cheppy (TB) and out of Mary by Blue Eyes by Possum. He was bred and owned by Goodyear Farms at Litchfield Park, Arizona.

CRY BABY. Cry Baby was foaled in about 1916 and did most of his racing around 1920. He was owned by Earl Kelly. John Armstrong said Cry Baby was a full brother of Apron Face, but Earl Kelly said the colt was by Little Danger by Tom Campbell.

CUADRO. Cuadro was foaled in 1885 and was by Billy by Shiloh and out of Paisana by Brown Dick by Berkshire. He was bred by Billy Fleming of Belmont, Texas.

CUTER. This black stallion was foaled in 1935 and was by Big Nigger by Harmon Baker and his dam was Schuhart by Magician by Rainy Day. He was bred by L. B. "Cuter" Wardlaw of Del Rio and owned by Duwain E. Hughes of San Antonio.

CY, see SI.

CYCLONE. Cyclone was a sorrel stallion sired by Dan Tucker, bred by Elias Watkins of Petersburg, Illinois, and owned by Charles Rogers of Pana, Illinois.

D

DAMIT. Damit was foaled around 1900 and was by Red Rover by Billy and out of a mare by Red Rover. He was bred and owned by George Berry Ketchum of Sheffield, Texas.

DAN. Dan was a sorrel stallion foaled around 1920 and sired by Joe Bailey by Eureka by Shelby. He was out of June Bug by Harvester. He was bred by a man named Allred of Mineral Wells, Texas, and his owners were Horace Wilson of Fort Worth, Texas, Jim Nail of Albany, Texas, and Paul Hodge of Eastland, Texas. He was sometimes referred to as Dan Bailey.

DANGER. Danger was foaled around 1895 and was by Barney Owens by Cold Deck and out of Black George by Moreland by Steel Dust. He was owned by Tom Trammell of Sweetwater, Texas, and by Joe McKinney of Willcox, Arizona.

DANGER, LITTLE. This Little Danger was by Tom Campbell by Old Bob Peters. His dam was Little Pug by Bobby Beach.

DANGER, LITTLE. This brown stallion was foaled in 1894. He was by Okemo (TB) and out of Vergie by Cold Deck. His second dam was Cherokee Belle by Cherokee. He was bred and owned by S. Trowbridge of Belle Mead, New Jersey.
    H. A. Trowbridge of Wellington, Kansas, of the same family, had an older stallion sired by Cold Deck he called Little Danger.

DAN, OLD. (1850–70?) According to the *American Stud Book* (Vol. VI, 1106), Old Dan was a brother of Comet. He was owned in California and Oregon. He was by a horse called Selim. His dam, Brown's mare, was bred in Missouri and said to be of Brimmer or Printer stock. Selim was by Barnes Black Whip, his dam a son of Printer. He was sometimes called Oregon Dan.

DAN SECRES. Dan Secres was by Joe Chalmers Jr. and out of Mary Cook by Printer. He was owned by Capt. Tom Haley of Sweetwater, Texas.

DAN TUCKER. Dan Tucker was foaled in 1887 and died in 1912. He was dark brown and grew into a big horse standing over 15 hands and weighing around 1300 pounds. He was by Barney Owens by Cold Deck and out of Butt Cut by Jack Traveler by Steel Dust. He was bred by Samuel Watkins of Petersburg, Illinois, and sold to Thomas Trammell of Sweetwater, Texas. He sired Peter McCue. *Goodwin's Turf Guide* lists him as the winning sire of 1896.

DAN TUCKER, LITTLE. This stallion was sired by Silver Dick by Roan Dick and out of a Koontz mare. He was bred and owned by Mr. Koontz of Illinois.

DAPPLED JOHN. This celebrated American Quarter Running Horse was a dappled bay, well formed, about 15 hands high. He was very compact with heavy hind quarters, one white hind foot, a fine head, and a very short neck. Edgar says he was very fleet for a short distance. He was sired by Lloyd's Traveler by imported Morton's Traveler and out of a mare by *Janus. His second dam was also by *Janus. He was bred in the early 1800's.

DARK ALLEY. This black stallion was foaled in 1934 and was by Belcross (TB) and out of a Harmon Baker mare. He was bred by Hemphill and Walters of Mertzon, Texas.

DASH (BLACK DASH). Dash was a black stallion foaled in 1877 and he was by Little Jeff Davis by Shiloh and out of Caddo Maid by Joe Chalmers. He was bred and owned by Capt. Tom Haley of Sweetwater, Texas. He was one-eyed.

DAVE MACK. He was by Tubal Cain by Berry's Cold Deck and out of a Blake mare. He was bred and owned by S. Coke Blake of Pryor, Oklahoma.

DAY BOOK. This bay stallion was foaled in 1929 and was by Uncle Jimmy Gray by Bonnie Joe (TB) and out of Winsome May by Garland Jr.

DEB WALKER, see WILLIE.

DECEITFUL JIMMY. This sorrel stallion was foaled in 1922 and was by Uncle Jimmy Gray by Bonnie Joe (TB). His breeder and his dam are unknown, but he was owned by M. T. Schuhart of Cliff, Texas.

DEDIER (OLD D. J.). Little is known about this stallion who was the fountainhead of Louisiana short-horses and whose blood contributed much to the speed of the Quarter Horse in the 1920's, 1930's, and 1940's. He may have been sired by Henry Star, a Thoroughbred. He was brought into Louisiana by a traveling race-horse man. See Dewey for more information.

DEL MONTE. This stallion was foaled in 1920 and was by Little Joe by Traveler and out of Silver Queen by Warrior by Captain Sykes. He was bred by Ott Adams of Alice, Texas. He eventually went to Mexico to race and became a well-known sire.

DENVER. Denver was a sorrel stallion foaled in the early 1890's. He was by Pid Hart and out of a Campbell mare. He was bred by Charles B. Campbell of Minco, Oklahoma.

DEUCE OF HEARTS. By Ace of Hearts and out of a Traveler mare.

DEWEY. Dewey was brought into Louisiana by a race-horse man to defeat Louisiana Girl who had built up a reputation there. He was undoubtedly the Thoroughbred Dewey, a bay stallion foaled in 1899 by *Sain and out of Sister of Uncle Bob by Luke Blackburn. He was sold to the owners of Louisiana Girl after defeating her going 256 yards. The following year the same race-horse man returned with another stallion, Dedier, and beat Dewey and again sold his horse to the Cajuns. For more information see Dedier.

DEXTER. This Dexter was by Young Cold Deck by Berry's Cold Deck and out of a Blake mare. He was bred and owned by S. Coke Blake of Pryor, Oklahoma.

DEXTER. Dexter was by Joe Collins by Billy and out of a McGonigal mare. He was bred and owned by George McGonigal of Midland, Texas.

DIAMOND. He was by Red Bug by Everett (TB) and out of a Holman mare by Master Gould by First Chip (TB). He was bred by Jap Holman of Sonora, Texas, and owned by Billy Holland of Sonora.

DIAMOND DECK. Diamond Deck was foaled in 1885. He was by Old Cold Deck by Old Billy by Shiloh. He was probably bred or raised in Missouri.

DIAMOND JOE. By Peter McCue by Dan Tucker and out of Floranthe (TB). Bred and owned by Samuel Watkins of Petersburg, Illinois.

DICK DILLON. He was by Jack McCue by Peter McCue and out of Fanny by Jack McCue by Peter McCue. He was bred and owned by Charles Francis of Floyd, New Mexico.

DICK, LITTLE. This sorrel stallion was foaled in 1911 and lived until 1942. He was by Sleepy Dick by Little Rondo and out of Flora by Pilgrim (TB). He was bred by Wilson Sulden of Hallettsville, Texas, and later owned by Joe Sleffek of Hallettsville.

DINERO. Dinero was by Moss King by Big King by Little Kingfisher and out of Napanee by Barney. He was bred and owned by the Waddell brothers of Kermit, Texas.

DINK. Dink was by Ben Hur by Rainy Day by Lone Star and he was out of a Parker mare. He was alive in the 1930's. He was bred and owned by Dink Parker of Sonoita, Arizona.

DIOMED, RAGLAND'S. This Diomed was foaled in 1801 and was by *Diomed and out of Silverheels by Old Liberty by *Janus. He was bred and owned by Lipscomb Ragland of Halifax County, Virginia. Edgar says he was 15 hands and 2 inches high. He sired the dam of John Randolph.

D. J., OLD, see DEDIER.

DOBBIN. This bay stallion was foaled in 1888 and was by Famous (TB) and out of Kitty Waddle by Jack Traveler. He was bred by Samuel Watkins of Petersburg, Illinois, and owned by the Coope brothers of Illinois.

DOC. This stallion was by Possum by Traveler and out of Dottie by No Good by Barney Owens. He was bred by J. J. Kennedy of Bonita, Arizona, and owned by Doc Pardee of Phoenix, Arizona, and Chester Cooper of Roosevelt, Arizona.

DOC OLDHAM. This bay stallion was by *Gallantry (TB) and out of Lizzie by Old Kingfisher. He was a blood bay and stood 15-1 hands high and weighed 1200 pounds. He was bred by Ove Oldham of Buda, Texas.

DR. ALL GOOD. He was by Charley Wilson (TB) and out of Nina T by Barney Owens. He was bred by J. F. Newman of Sweetwater, Texas, and owned by D. F. Doak of Sweetwater, Texas.

DR. BLUE EYES. This sorrel stallion was a roan with a glass eye and some white patches on his body. He was by A. D. Reed by Peter McCue and out of Apron Face by Little Danger by Tom Campbell. He was bred and owned by Reed Armstrong of Foss, Oklahoma.

DR. GLENDENNING. This bay stallion was foaled in 1895 and was by *Tubal Cain (TB) and out of Maud, a Quarter mare. He was bred by William M. Sumners of Lineville, Iowa, and owned by F. S. Warran of Missouri.

DR. HOWARD, YOUNG, see FIRECRACKER.

DR. MACK. This bay stallion was foaled in 1903 and considerable confusion exists concerning his breeding. He was registered in the *American Stud Book* (Vol. IX, 172) as by Samavas and out of Clincher by Boot Maker. Billy Anson called him a Quarter Horse and owned one of his sons. Walter Trammell said he was registered, but that he was a shorthorse. Trammell and Newman of Sweetwater, Texas, owned him for a number of years, but he was bred by W. H. Norton of Corsicana, Texas. He died in the possession of W. T. Waggoner of Fort Worth.

DR. MACK, YOUNG (RED MACK). Young Dr. Mack was by Dr. Mack (TB?) and out of a mare by Bobbie Lowe. His second dam was a Waggoner mare. He was bred by W. T. Waggoner of Fort Worth, Texas, and owned by W. P. McFadden of Benjamin, Texas; by John T. Sims Jr. of Snyder, Texas; and by Tom Masterson of Truscott, Texas.

DR. ROSE, see BONNIE JOE.

DODGER. This sorrel stallion was foaled in 1924 and died in 1941. He was by Harmon Baker by Peter McCue and out of Froggie by Joe Collins by Billy. He was bred by Jim Harkey of Fort Stockton, Texas, and owned by Millard Smith and Foster Conger, both of Sterling City, Texas.

DODGER, LITTLE. Little Dodger was by Dodger by Harmon Baker and out of a Harkey mare of Ketchum stock. He was bred by Leigh Harkey of Sheffield, Texas, and owned later by Lee Henderson of Ozona and by Howard B. Cox of San Angelo.

DOE BELLY. This bay stallion was foaled in 1880 and was by Bobby Cromwell by Cold Deck and out of Grasshopper by Cold Deck. He was bred and owned by Joe Lewis of Hunnewell, Kansas.

DOGIE BEASLEY. This stallion was foaled around 1900 and was by Sykes' Rondo by McCoy Billy by Billy. Some reports have him by Little Joe Fleming by Sykes' Rondo. His dam was May Mangum by Anthony by Billy. He was bred by Crawford Sykes and Joe Mangum of Nixon, Texas. He was owned by Les Beasley of Junction, Texas; by Jap Holman of Sonora, Texas; and by Eli Taylor of New Mexico. He was a well-known race horse.

DO GO. This sorrel stallion was foaled in 1928 and was by Slipalong (TB) and out of Lady Mack by Joe Bailey. He was bred in Texas and owned by D. T. Taylor of Ardmore, Oklahoma.

DON TOPAZ. This palomino was foaled in 1934 and was by Golden Don D by Golden Cargile and out of Gold Sophie by Brass Button by Gonzalo. He was bred and owned by Roy C. Davis of Big Spring, Texas.

DORADO. By Traveler and out of a Shely mare. Bred by Will Shely of Alfred, Texas.

DREADNOT, GOODE'S. This F.A.Q.R.H. stallion was owned by, and probably bred by, Jacob Bugg of Mecklenburg County, Virginia. He was by Twigg and his dam by *Fearnought. He was purchased and owned for many years by John Goode, Sr. He is listed in both Edgar and the *ASB*.

DRIVER, OLD. Driver was foaled in the 1790's and was by Bellair and out of a mare by Spadille, a famous Colonial Quarter Horse. His second and third dams were by *Janus. He was sorrel and 15-1 hands high.

DROWSY HENRY (TULLOS STUD). By Alamo by Uncle Jimmy Gray and out of Tullos by Pancho Villa by Little Joe. He was bred by Emory Tullos of Charlotte, Texas, and owned by W. O. Henderson of Charlotte, Texas.

DUCK HUNTER. Duck Hunter was a sorrel stallion foaled in 1901 by Peter McCue by Dan Tucker and out of Ball by The Hero (TB). He was bred by Hugh Watkins of Oakford, Illinois, and owned by W. C. Allen of Gate, Oklahoma. He won $20,000 in a match race against Library going 440 yards in 1908. He ran the race in 22 seconds flat.

DUCK HUNTER. This sorrel stallion was foaled in 1924. He was by A. D. Reed by Peter McCue and out of Queen. He was bred and owned by John A. Harrel of Canute, Oklahoma.

DUD. By Tony by Guinea Pig by Possum and out of a Wear mare. He was bred by W. D. Wear of Willcox, Arizona, and owned by Rex Glenn of Benson, Arizona.

DUNDERSTADT HORSE. Little is known about this horse except that he was by Rondo and sired Will Copeland's Ace of Hearts. George Clegg once said that this horse was a son of Rondo and out of Queen, a mare purchased by Luke Neal of Gillett, Texas, from a Louisiana horse trader. He lived in the early 1900's.

DUENO. A palomino stallion foaled in 1935 by High Step (TB) and out of Dulcie by Sappho by Brown King by Arch Oldham. Bred and owned by Thomas B. Dibbler Estate, Santa Barbara, California.

DUKE. This sorrel stallion was by Albert by Hickory Bill and out of an O'Brien mare. He was bred by John J. O'Brien of Refugio, Texas, and owned by the O'Conner brothers of Victoria, Texas.

DUKE. This stallion was by Guinea Pig by Possum by Traveler and out of a Kennedy Quarter mare. He was bred and owned by J. J. Kennedy of Bonita, Arizona.

DUKE. He was by Ed Howell and out of a Spencer mare. He was bred by Homer Spencer of Potter Valley, California, and owned by Ed Howell of Ukiah, California.

DUKE. This stallion, foaled in 1910, was by Ignacio Chief (TB) and out of Dutch by Billy Hubbard. His breeder is unknown, but he was owned by Harry Wommer of Bayfield, Colorado.

DUN KING. By Grano de Oro by Little Joe and out of a Northington horse. Bred and owned by Mentor Northington of Egypt, Texas.

DUSTY BROWN. By Barney Owens by Cold Deck and out of a Christian Quarter mare. He was bred by Webb Christian of Big Spring, Texas, and owned by Jack Cunningham of Comanche, Texas.

DUSTY, LITTLE. This stallion was by Dusty Brown by Barney Owens and out of Peggy by Traveler. He was bred by Jack Cunningham of Comanche, Texas, and owned by William Burns of Brownwood, Texas.

DUTCH. By Billy Hubbard by Billy Caviness. He was bred by Kirk Williams of Mancos, Colorado, and owned by George Morgan of Denver.

DUTCH. This stallion was foaled in 1929 and was by Little Joe by Traveler and out of Flashlight by Sam King by Hondo. He was bred by O. W. Cardwell of Junction, Texas, and owned by R. C. Tatum of Junction, Texas, Dewitt Cowsert of Junction, and Alvario C. Canales of Premont, Texas.

DUTCH, BIG. Big Dutch was bred by Trammell and New-man of Sweetwater, Texas, according to Byrl McNeill. Big Dutch was also called Dutch. Big Dutch was the sire of the fast mare Katy Belle, and he lost his most famous race with 80 Gray at Midland, Texas, in 1898.

DUTCHMAN, OLD. Old Dutchman was foaled in 1883, and he was sired by Lock's Rondo by Whalebone by Old Billy. His dam was Mallie by Steel Dust. He was bred by Charles R. Haley of Sweetwater, Texas.

DUTCH MARTIN (YOUNG FRED). Dutch Martin was by Old Nick by Old Fred by Black Ball and out of Mary Dawson. He was bred by Earl Moye of Arvada, Wyoming, and owned by Henry Martin of Steamboat Springs, Colorado.

E

EADS HORSE, see EDES HORSE.

EAGLE, see GRAY EAGLE.

EAGLE. This palomino stallion was foaled in 1930 and was by Yellow Jacket by Little Rondo and he was out of a Waggoner mare. He was bred by W. T. Waggoner of Fort Worth, Texas, and owned by Otto Lambert of Wichita Falls, Texas.

EAGLE JR. By Eagle (TB) and out of a Quarter mare. Bred and owned by Jim Minnick of Crowell, Texas.

EAGLE, YOUNG. Young Eagle was a gray stallion bred by J. H. Minnick of Crowell, Texas. He was by Gray Eagle by Beetch's Yellow Jacket by Yellow Jacket and out of a mare by Old Joe by Harmon Baker by Peter McCue. He was bred by J. H. Minnick of Crowell, Texas.

EARL EDERIS. This sorrel stallion was foaled in 1912, and he was by Bobbie Lowe by Eureka by Shelby. His dam was Nellie Tamsit (TB). He was bred by Webb Christian of Big Spring, Texas.

EARL, LITTLE. This Little Earl was by Little Earl (Old Earl) by Missouri Mike by Printer by Cold Deck and out of a Link Willey mare. He was bred by Link Willey of Oologah, Oklahoma, and foaled sometime before 1920. Later he was owned by John Dawson of Pryor, Oklahoma.

EARL, LITTLE (OLD EARL). Little Earl was foaled on or about the year 1884. He was by Missouri Mike by Printer by Old Cold Deck and out of a Missouri short mare. He was sometimes called Old Earl. He was bred in Missouri, but taken to Oklahoma and there owned by Link Willey of Oologah and John Dawson of Pryor.

EASTER. Easter was foaled in the late 1800's and was sired by Barney Owens by Cold Deck and out of Hereford by Black George by Moreland. He was bred by the Trammells of Sweetwater, Texas, and owned by S. J. Nolen of Sweetwater.

EASTER LILL. Easter Lill was a sorrel stallion foaled in 1890. He was by Yakima Dick and was bred and owned in Oregon.

ED. Ed was by Possum by Traveler and out of an unknown dam. He was bred and owned in Arizona.

EDDIE EARL. Eddie Earl was a sorrel foaled in 1919 by Barney Lucas by Traveler and out of Overknight by Be-Knighted (TB). His second dam was a Quarter mare. He was bred and owned by Webb Christian of Big Spring, Texas.

EDDIE GRAY. This brown stallion was foaled in 1928, and he was by Uncle Jimmy Gray by Bonnie Joe (TB) and out of Miss Vassar (TB). He was bred and owned by Henry Pfefferling of San Antonio, Texas.

EDES HORSE (EADS HORSE). This sorrel stallion was by Hickory Bill by Peter McCue and out of Cherokee by Cuter. He was bred by George Clegg of Alice, Texas, and owned by Henry Edes of Hebbronville, Texas.

EDGAR UHL. Edgar Uhl was a sorrel stallion foaled in 1913. He was by Horace H (TB) and out of Carrie Nation by Peter McCue. He was bred by John Wilkins of San Antonio, Texas, and owned by the Greene Cattle Company of Cananea, Sonora, Mexico.

EIGHTY GRAY. Eighty Gray was foaled in 1891. He was a gray horse standing 14-3 hands. He was by Bill Fleming, a son of Grey Alice by Steel Dust. 80 Gray's dam was a sister of Wolf Catcher. He was bred by Mrs. Clay Mann of Mitchell County, Texas, and sold to T. A. Morrison of the same county.

ELEXA JOE. By Little Joe by Traveler and out of Elexas (½ TB). He was bred by M. A. Cowsert of Rocksprings, and owned by J. D. Cowsert of Junction, Texas.

EL GRULLO. This grullo stallion was by Little Hickory Bill by Hickory Bill and out of an Yturria mare by the O'Conner Roan. He was owned by William Young of Raymondville, Texas.

EL REY. El Rey was by Traveler and out of Black Bess by Warrior by Captain Sykes. His second dam was Jenny by Sykes' Rondo. He was bred by George Clegg of Alice, Texas, and owned by Ott Adams of Alfred, Texas. Later, he was owned by T. T. East of Kingsville, W. T. Waggoner of Fort Worth, and Raymond Dickson of Houston, Texas.

EL VENADO (BENADO). By Right Royal (TB) and out of a King Ranch Quarter mare. Bred and owned by the King Ranch of Kingsville, Texas.

EL ZARCO. By Cotton Eyed Joe by Little Joe. Bred at Beeville, Texas, and owned by A. A. Martinez of Hebbronville, Texas.

EUREKA. Eureka was foaled in about 1890 and was by Shelby by Tom Driver by Steel Dust. His dam was Jennie

Capps by Dash by Little Jeff Davis. He was bred by E. Shelby Stanfield of Thorp Spring, Texas, and owned by Bob Couts of Weatherford, Texas.

F

FABRICIUS, HAYNES'. This bay stallion, sired by *Janus and out of a mare by *Partner, was bred and owned by Herbert Haynes of North Carolina. He was a blood bay, stood 15 hands, and was foaled about 1776.

FAITHFUL. This palomino stallion was by Old Nick by Old Fred and his dam was by The Senator by Leadville (TB). He was bred by Coke Roberds of Hayden, Colorado, and owned by Robert Scholl of Parshall, Colorado.

FALACY. Falacy was a sorrel stallion foaled in 1924. He was sired by Booger Red by Rancocas (TB) and out of Felestin. He was bred and owned by D. Bryant Turner of Colorado Springs, Colorado.

FARO. Faro was by Ben Hur by Rainy Day. He was bred in Arizona and owned by M. Raynal and Sons of Chihuahua, Mexico.

FEAR ME. This stallion was a roan foaled in 1914. He was by Tom Campbell by Old Bob Peters and out of Stockings. He was bred by Dan C. Armstrong of Doxey, Oklahoma, and owned by Reed Armstrong of Foss, Oklahoma.

FILIPE (FELIPE ANGELES). This brown stallion was foaled in 1932. He was sired by Paul El by Hickory Bill by Peter McCue and out of Little Sister by Little Joe. He was bred by Ott Adams of Alice, Texas, and owned by Bud Summers of Brownsville.

FIRECRACKER (YOUNG DR. HOWARD). Firecracker was a sorrel foaled in 1929 who died in 1940(?). He was by

Dr. Howard (TB) and out of a Harmon Baker mare. He was bred by Mrs. William Anson of Christoval, Texas, (or Lea Aldwell) and owned by Roy Headrick, Ramon L. Rasberry, and Marshall Pryor, all of Sweetwater, Texas.

FLAG OF TRUCE, OLD. This gray stallion was by Gold Finder by *Janus, and his dam was by Crawford. He was bred and owned by Col. Robert Goode of Mecklenburg County, Virginia. He was foaled in the late 1700's.

FLEETWOOD. This chestnut stallion was foaled in 1770. He was by *Janus and out of Poll Flaxen by *Jolly Roger. He was bred by Capt. Thomas Turpin of Powhatan County, Virginia. Fleetwood was a full brother of Camden and a half brother of Goode's Brimmer.

FLYING BOB. This great dark bay stallion was foaled in 1929 and died in 1946. He was by Chicaro (TB) and out of Zeringue Belle by Dedier. He was bred by Noah Zeringue of Abbeville, Louisiana, and sold late in life to V. S. Randle of Richmond, Texas.

FLYING DUTCHMAN. Flying Dutchman was a bay stallion foaled in 1845. He was sired by Gray Eagle by Woodpecker by Bertrand and out of Blinkey (Mary Porter) by Muckle John by Muckle John by Sir Archy. He was bred by Webb Ross of Scott County, Kentucky, and later owned by Frank M. Lilly of Thorp Spring, Texas. He was a full brother of Sweet Owen, Viley, and Bay Printer.

FOLSOM. This palomino stallion was foaled in 1924 and lived for twenty years. Neither his sire or dam is known, although they were reported to be Quarter Horses. He was bred at Folsom, New Mexico, and then purchased as a twelve-year-old by W. T. Waggoner of Fort Worth. Later he was owned by Ramon A. Wood of Wichita Falls, and by Les Stringer of San Angelo. Folsom, according to Ramon Wood, was 14-½ hands and weighed 1100 pounds.

FORT, LITTLE. Little Fort was occasionally called Little Fort Worth. He was foaled about 1929 and was brown. He was by Black Bob by Bob Carraway by Carey Jones. His dam was Lucinda by a son of Kid Weller. He was bred by P. L. Fuller of Snyder, Texas. Others owning this stallion were Aubra Bowers of Canadian, W. E. Britt of Wheeler, Duwain E. Hughes of San Angelo, and The Spade Ranch at Colorado City, Texas. He died in 1946 or a little later. He has been referred to as the Pi Fuller Horse.

FORTUNE. Fortune was foaled in 1915. He was by Barney Lucas by Traveler and out of Chiromancy by Palm Reader (TB). He was bred and owned by W. R. Matsler of Plainview, Texas.

FOUR FLUSH. This stallion was foaled in 1922 and was by Damit by Red Rover by Billy and out of May Baker by Harmon Baker. He was bred by Jim Harkey of Fort Stockton, Texas, and owned by Gus Duncan of Duncan, Arizona.

FOWLER HORSE, see GOLDEN GRAIN.

FOX. There were two Foxes that were influential in producing Colonial Quarter Horses. The first one was sired by Morton's Traveler and was bred by John H. Cocke. He was foaled in the 1790's. The second was by the imported Hob-or-Nob and out of a *Jolly Roger mare. His second dam was by Morton's Traveler. This Fox was bred and owned by James Golding of North Carolina and was foaled around the 1770's. Will Williams, writing to Henry William Herbert in 1856, said that *Janus, Fox, and Bald Galloway "produced the fleetest, then and since known as Quarter Horses."

FOX. By Old Fred by Black Ball and out of a Nott Spring Jones mare. Bred and owned in Colorado.

FOX. By Young Dr. Mack by Dr. Mack. Breeder unknown. Owned by the Reynolds Cattle Company of Fort Worth, Texas.

FOX, LITTLE. Little Fox was by Uncle Jimmy Gray by Bonnie Joe (TB). His dam was by Lone Star by Gold Enamel (TB). He was a bay, foaled in 1923, and bred and owned by Eugene J. Schott of Riomedina, Texas.

FRANK. By Peter McCue II by Peter McCue and out of a Roberds mare by Old Fred. He was bred by Coke Roberds of Hayden, Colorado, and owned by Robert Parsons of Weston, Colorado.

FRANK ALLEN. Frank Allen was a brown stallion foaled in 1909. He was by Palm Reader (TB) and out of Mary T by Traveler. He was bred and owned by D. W. "Webb" Christian of Big Spring, Texas.

FRANK GRAY. This black stallion was by Shiek #11 by Peter McCue and out of a Fresno 50 mare by Fresno (TB). He was bred and owned by Matador Land and Cattle Company of Channing, Texas.

FRANK GRAY. This gray stallion was by Uncle Jimmy Gray by Bonnie Joe (TB) and he was out of Flossy Brown. He was foaled in 1928 and bred and owned by Mose Franklin of San Antonio, Texas.

FRANK JOHNSON. This brown stallion was foaled in 1918 and died in the early 1920's. He was by Uncle Jimmy Gray by Bonnie Joe (TB) and out of Oklahoma. He was bred and owned by George Axley of Guthrie, Oklahoma.

FRANK NORFLEET (THE NORFLEET HORSE). This stallion was by Joe Rutledge and out of Florence Herrington. He was bred and owned by Frank Norfleet of Hale Center, Texas.

FRANK PATTON DUN (BOYD ROGERS HORSE). This dun stallion was by Yellow Jacket by Little Rondo by Lock's

Rondo and out of a Minnick polo mare. He was bred by J. H. "Jim" Minnick of Crowell, Texas, and owned by Frank Rhodes of Throckmorton, Texas; Joe Sneed of Moore County, Texas; Frank Patton of Guthrie, Texas; Boyd G. Rogers of Guthrie, Texas; and the CS Ranch at Cimarron, New Mexico.

FRED. Fred was by Brown Dick by *Derring-Doe (TB) and out of Queen by a grandson of Peter McCue. He was bred and owned by B. G. Anderson of Craig, Colorado.

FRED LITZE. Fred Litze was foaled in 1915. He was sired by Old Fred by Black Ball and out of Queen Litze (TB). He was bred and owned by Si Dawson of Hayden, Colorado.

FRED, OLD. Old Fred was a palomino who was foaled in 1894 and died in 1915. He was sired by Black Ball by Missouri Mike and his dam was a palomino mare by John Crowder. He was bred at Lockwood, Missouri, and later owned by Coke Roberds of Hayden, Colorado.

FRED, YOUNG, see DUTCH MARTIN.

FREEDOM. Freedom was a chestnut stallion foaled in 1838. He was bred in Virginia. His sire was *Emancipation (TB), and his dam a short mare sired by Wilkes Madison.

FROGTOWN. This bay stallion was foaled in 1868. He was sired by *Bonnie Scotland (TB) and died of colic on August 14, 1888. His dam was Ada Cheatham.

FUZZY. This bay stallion was foaled in 1911 and was by Three Finger Jack by Traveler, and his dam was a Gardner mare by Brown Billy by Pancho. He was bred by Mayburn Gardner of Camp Verde, Arizona. He may have been owned later by Clay McGonigal.

G

GACHO, see GOTCH.

GAGE HORSE. A sorrel stallion by a Quarter stallion owned by the West Cattle Company of Sanderson, Texas. This Quarter Horse stallion was brought from Colorado to Texas by John Zurick. The Gage Horse was foaled about 1930.

GARRICK, EATON'S. Garrick was by Meade's Celer and out of a *Janus mare. He was bred by Col. Charles R. Eaton of Granville County, North Carolina. He was a full brother of Eaton's Little Janus.

GATES HORSE, see CAPTAIN JOE.

GAUCHO, see GOTCH.

GEORGE. By Hickory Bill by Peter McCue and out of a Clegg mare. Bred by George Clegg of Alice, Texas.

GEORGE DICKINSON. This bay stallion was foaled in 1890 and was by Glen Dudley (TB) and out of Fanny Lewis. His breeder is unknown, but he was owned by P. Pointer and J. Wilkins of Oregon.

GEORGE DUKE. This brown stallion was foaled in 1927. He was by Barney Lucas by Traveler and out of Beauty Rose (TB). He was bred and owned by Dick Gray of Gorman, Texas.

GEORGE HOUSE. This sorrel stallion was foaled in 1890 and was by Black George by Moreland by Steel Dust and out of a Trammell mare. He was bred by Thomas Trammell of Sweetwater, Texas.

GEORGE MORGAN. George Morgan was a sorrel stallion sired by Texas Chief by Lock's Rondo and out of a Jeffries mare. He was bred by Joe D. Jeffries of Clarendon, Texas.

GLAD ONE. This black stallion was foaled in 1928. He was sired by Prepare Away (TB) and out of Hippie by John Wilkens by Peter McCue. He was bred and owned by J. Erwin Renfro of Mineral, Texas.

GLENWOOD SPRINGS. This dun stallion was foaled in 1932. He was by Cruzad (TB) and out of Buck by Old Fred. He was bred and owned by T. D. Jenkinson of Glenwood Springs, Colorado.

GLORY (PETERSON HORSE). Glory was foaled in 1912, and he was by Ben by John Crowder and out of Maggie. He was bred by E. E. Morris of Rocksprings, Texas, and owned by Sid Peterson of Kerrville, Texas, and R. M. Corder of Rocksprings, Texas.

GOLD BUTTON (BUTTON). Gold Button was a sorrel foaled in 1903. He was by Slip Shoulder by Missouri Mike and out of a Parker mare. He was bred by Albert "Bert" Parker of Oklahoma City, and owned by Coke Blake of Pryor, Oklahoma. He was 15 hands and weighed about 1100 pounds. Mr. Parker told Blake he raced Gold Button before he weaned him, and raced him for several years thereafter. He never lost a race or carried a rider.

GOLD COIN. This stallion was foaled in 1915 and was by The Senator by Leadville (TB). His dam was Selvy D. He was bred and owned by Alex Peterson of Elbert, Colorado.

GOLD DOLLAR. Gold Dollar was by Yellow Wolf by Old Joe Bailey and out of a Waggoner mare. He was bred by W. T. Waggoner of Fort Worth, Texas, and owned by Duard Wilson of Vernon, Texas.

GOLD DOLLAR BILLY (GOLD DOLLAR). This sorrel stallion, foaled in 1900, was by Crawford by Traveler. He was bred at Seguin, Texas, and owned by Julius Helwig of Miles, Texas, and G. B. "Berry" Ketchum of Sheffield, Texas.

GOLD DUST. By Beetch's Yellow Jacket by Yellow Jacket and out of a Deahl mare. Bred by Ed Deahl of Panhandle, Texas, and owned by H. T. Baca of Gallegos, New Mexico.

GOLD DUST. This palomino stallion was foaled in 1932 and was by Champagne by Dundee (TB) and out of a mare by Ding Bob 269. He was bred by Coke T. Roberds of Hayden, Colorado, and owned by Jack Eckstine of Ethel, Missouri.

GOLDEN ADMIRATION. This palomino stallion was foaled in 1935. He was by Golden Cargile and out of Gonzales Mary. He was bred by W. R. Davis and Sons of Sterling City, Texas, and owned by A. A. Roberson of Gunnison, Colorado.

GOLDEN AMEL. Golden Amel was a sorrel stallion foaled in 1922 by Uncle Jimmy Gray by Bonnie Joe (TB) and out of a Haby mare by Lone Star by Gold Enamel (TB). He was bred and owned by Nick Haby of Riomedina, Texas.

GOLDEN GRAIN (FOWLER HORSE). This sorrel stallion was by Sappho by Brown King by Arch Oldham and out of a Mitchell mare. He was bred by W. B. Mitchell of Marfa, Texas, and owned by T. Meade Wilson, also of Marfa.

GOLDEN LAD. This palomino stallion was foaled in 1935 and was by Plaudit by King Plaudit (TB) and out of a Phillips mare. He was bred by Waite Phillips of Cimarron, New Mexico, and owned by J. R. Cates of Tulsa, Oklahoma.

GOLDEN MAIZE. Golden Maize was a palomino stallion foaled in 1933 and sired by High Step (TB) and out of Mazie by Sappho by Brown King. He was bred by the Thomas B.

Dibbler Estate of Santa Barbara, California, and owned by Lyle Bush of Cimarron, New Mexico.

GOLDEN STREAK. This brown stallion was foaled in 1923. He was sired by Uncle Jimmy Gray by Bonnie Joe (TB) and out of a Haby mare sired by Lone Star. He was bred and owned by Nick Haby of Riomedina, Texas.

GOLD NUGGET. This stallion was by Yellow Jacket by Little Rondo and out of a Waggoner mare. He was bred and owned by W. T. Waggoner of Fort Worth, Texas.

GOLD STANDARD. This palomino stallion was by Clover Leaf by Fleeting Time (TB) and out of a Yellow Wolf mare. He was bred by W. T. Waggoner of Fort Worth, Texas, and owned by B. B. Van Vacter of Carter, Oklahoma.

GOLD WING. This brown stallion was foaled in 1935 and was by High Prince (TB) and out of Betsy Bobbie by Rex Beach. He was bred by John Dial of Goliad, Texas, and owned by Cornelius Haby of Riomedina, Texas.

GOLDY, TUG DALE'S, see ROMAN GOLD.

GOTCH. This Gotch was by the Dunderstadt Horse by Sykes' Rondo and out of a Neal mare. He was bred and owned by Luke Neal of Gillett, Texas. George Clegg said he was a half brother of Ace of Hearts.

GOTCH (GACHO). This was a bay stallion by Little Joe by Traveler and out of a Clegg Quarter mare. He was bred by George Clegg of Alice, Texas, and owned by Kyle H. Drake of Cotulla, Texas; Robert Cage of Cotulla; and by the Franklin Brothers of Tilden, Texas.

GOTCH (GAUCHO). This brown stallion was by Hickory Bill by Peter McCue and out of a Fred Raymond mare by Little Joe by Traveler. He was foaled in the 1920's. He was bred by Fred Raymond of Raymondville, Texas, and owned

103

by Grover Brady of Harlingen, Texas. There are several different stories about this horse. One version says that Jesus Pettus' father bought Gotch for Fred Raymond when Fred was a lad. George Clegg said he bred Gotch, and that Gotch was sired by Will Wright by Little Joe and out of a Hickory Bill mare. George said he sold the mare to Fred Raymond.

GRAL ORTIZ. This bay stallion was foaled in 1929 and was sired by Pride of India and out of Betsy Bobby by Rex Beach. He was bred and owned by John Dial of Goliad, Texas.

GRANO DE ORO. A bay stallion foaled in 1925 by Little Joe by Traveler and out of Della Moore by Dedier. He was bred by Ott Adams of Alfred, Texas, and owned by John Dial of Goliad, and Mentor Northington of Egypt, Texas.

GRAY DICK. This gray stallion was foaled in 1874 and was by Steel Dust by Harry Bluff, and his dam, as well as his breeder, are unknown. He was owned by a Mr. Thomason of Denton, Texas, and by J. M. "Jim" Brown of Giddings, Texas.

GRAY EAGLE (EAGLE). This gray stallion was foaled in 1835. He was by Woodpecker by Bertrand and out of an unidentified mare. He was bred and owned by Maj. H. T. Duncan of Kentucky. He died in 1863 in Delaware County, Ohio.

GRAY EAGLE (EAGLE). This gray stallion was foaled in 1930(?). He was by Beetch's Yellow Jacket by Yellow Jacket and out of a gray Quarter race mare. He was bred by Mike Beetch of Lawton, Oklahoma, and owned by the J. A. Ranch of Palo Duro, Texas. He was purchased to replace Midnight, and they used him until about 1942.

GRAY JOHN. This gray stallion was foaled in 1874 and was by Steel Dust by Harry Bluff and out of a Watson mare. He was bred by John Watson of Burnet County, Texas, and owned by Sampson Haile and Hiram Casner of Llano, Texas.

GREASER. By Hickory Jim by Dasher by Steel Dust and out of a Jackson Quarter mare. He was bred and owned by J. J. Jackson of Coleman, Texas.

GREEN HORSE, GRANT'S, see SYKES HORSE, CUSTER'S.

GREY BADGER, see BADGER.

GREY COLD DECK. This gray stallion was foaled in 1884 and was by Cold Deck by Billy. He was the sire of Nellie Miller.

GREY RABBIT (RABBIT). This gray stallion was foaled in 1885 and was by Roan Dick by Black Nick. He was owned by T. M. Nesmith and Tom Cook of Amarillo.

GREY REBEL. This gray stallion was by White Lightning and out of a mare by Brimmer. He was bred by Dudley Hunter of Tennessee and owned by Dan Hunter of Collin County, Texas. This is the horse that Coke Blake spoke so highly about. Dan Hunter was supposedly a brother or son of Dudley Hunter and he brought Grey Rebel to Texas. Grey Rebel was a half brother to Coke Blake's foundation sire, Young White Lightning. The sire of this horse, White Lightning, is the one Shelp Alsup stole in Tennessee and took to Missouri.

GREY SIS. By John Lucas by Barney Lucas and out of a Jim Ned mare. Jim Ned was by Pancho. He was bred and owned by Marcus Snyder of Hardin, Montana.

GREY TOM, see TOM CAMPBELL.

GREY WOLF. This gray stallion was by Young Cold Deck by Berry's Cold Deck and out of Gray Mag by Possum by Young White Lightning. He was bred and owned by Coke Blake of Pryor, Oklahoma.

GROVER. By Barney Owens by Cold Deck and out of a Trammell Quarter mare. He was bred and owned by Thomas Trammell of Sweetwater, Texas.

GRULLA, OLD. Old Grulla was a blue dun stallion by Yellow Jacket by Little Rondo and out of a Waggoner mare. He was later owned by a Mr. Thompson who sold him to T. T. East of Kingsville. He was also known as Thompson Dun and Old Grulla Thompson.

GUINEA PIG. This sorrel stallion was foaled in 1892 and was by Pony Pete by Barney Owen by Cold Deck and out of Cherokee Maid by Cold Deck by Billy. He was bred by Mike Smiley of Sylvan Grove, Kansas.

GUINEA PIG. This is the most famous of the Guinea Pigs. He was sorrel and foaled in 1922(?). He was by King (Possum) and out of Mamie by No Good by Barney Owens. He was bred by Jim Kennedy of Bonita, Arizona, and owned by Doc Pardee of Phoenix, Arizona, and by W. D. Wear of Willcox, Arizona.

GULLIVER. This sorrel stallion, foaled in 1885, was by Missouri Rondo by Missouri Mike. He was bred by Arron Cunningham of Comanche, Texas, and owned by Jim Jackson of Coleman, Texas, and John Gardner of San Angelo, Texas.

GUN POWDER. This stallion was a sorrel by Esquire (TB) and out of Blossom by Billie Tom. He was bred and owned by J. M. Corder of Sanderson, Texas.

GUY. This black stallion was by Fred Matthies' Horse and out of Frickie Roan. He was owned by R. D. Dulling of Gonzales, Texas, and bred by Otto Fricke of Gonzales, Texas.

H

HAIRPIN. This stallion was by the Thoroughbred Chappaqua and out of a Parker Quarter mare. He was bred and owned by W. D. Dink Parker of Sonoita, Arizona.

HAL FISHER. Hal Fisher was a brown stallion foaled in 1887. He was by Buck Walton (TB) and out of Alice by Grindstone. He was bred by John R. Nasworthy of San Angelo, Texas, and owned by O. F. Johnson.

HALIDAY. This bay stallion was foaled in 1913 and was by Bobby True by Eureka and owned by Jack "Webb" Christian of Big Spring, Texas.

HANDSOME HIRAM. This bay stallion was foaled in 1935 and was by Hiram Kelly (TB) and out of Medina Belle by Uncle Jimmy Gray by Bonnie Joe (TB). He was bred by Eugene Schott of Riomedina, Texas, and owned by J. E. White of Brady, Texas.

HANKS. Hanks was a bay stallion foaled in 1905. He was by Prince Plenty (TB) and out of Little Gift by Rancocas. He was bred and owned by Trammell and Newman of Sweetwater, Texas.

HARDTACK, HERREN'S. This bay stallion was by Henderson's Chip by First Chip (TB) and out of Babe Anson by Harmon Baker by Peter McCue. He was bred by Tom Henderson of El Dorado, Texas, and owned by Dick Herren of Fresno, California.

HARMON. This stallion was foaled in 1932. He was by One-Eyed Billy by Harmon Baker by Peter McCue and his dam was a Burris mare. He was bred and owned by J. T. "Dick" Burris of Mountain Home, Texas.

HARMON BAKER. Harmon Baker was foaled in 1907 and died in 1925. He was a brown stallion who showed some Thoroughbred blood. He was by Peter McCue by Dan Tucker and out of Nona P by Duke of Highlands (TB). He was bred by George Watkins of Petersburg, Illinois, and owned by William "Billy" Anson of Christoval, Texas. He was used some by Sam Harkey of Sheffield, Texas.

It is an established fact that many Watkins mares registered as by The Hero or Duke of Highlands were shorthorses by Dan Tucker, Barney Owens, or Peter McCue. Harmon Baker's second dam, Millie D, was a half sister of Peter McCue. Their dam, Nora M, was out of Kitty Clyde, a Quarter race mare.

Nona P, Harmon Baker's dam, like many other Watkins horses, was brought to Texas. Coke Roberds said John Wilkens of San Antonio brought Peter McCue, Nona P, and her yearling son (the gelding Buck Thomas) to Texas. This was in the fall of 1907 or spring of 1908.

Harmon Baker was a full brother of Hattie Jackson, Tot Lee, Buck Thomas (the gelding), Edee Ree, and San Antonio.

Harmon Baker was registered in the *American Stud Book* (Vol. X, 871). Helen Michaelis said that she would always believe that Harmon Baker was out of a straight Quarter mare because his Quarter Horse characteristics have been so predominant in his descendants.

HARMON BAKER JR. (HIRAM BAKER JR.). This sorrel stallion was foaled in 1920. He was by Harmon Baker by Peter McCue and out of a mare by Sam Jones by Black Nick. His second dam was by Jim Ned. He was bred by William Anson of Christoval, Texas, and owned by Duwain E. Hughes of San Angelo, Texas; by Gus Wheat of Sonora; by Roy Miller of Ozona; and by Marshall Cook of Garden City, Texas. Harmon Baker Jr. was a full brother to the Burris Horse, One-Eyed Billy.

HARMON N. This stallion was by Harmon Baker by Peter McCue and out of an Anson Quarter mare. He was bred by William "Billy" Anson of Christoval, Texas, and owned by George D. Miers of Villa Acuna, Mexico.

HARRISON (POWERS HORSE). This stallion was foaled in 1897 and was sired by R. Q. Ban (TB) and out of a Waggoner mare. He was bred by W. T. Waggoner of Fort Worth,

Texas, and owned by Joe Budine of Ada, Oklahoma, and by a Mr. Powers of the same city.

HARRY BLUFF. Little is known about this stallion who was the sire of Steel Dust. He was sired in about 1860 by Short Whip by Blackburn's Whip and out of Big Nance, who was by a grandson of Timoleon by Sir Archy.

HELL CAT. This sorrel stallion was foaled in 1935, and he was sired by Goldie II (TB) and out of Allie San (Alazan?) by Lone Star. He was bred and owned by Josephine Davenport of Center Point, Texas.

HELTER. Helter was a sorrel stallion foaled in 1927 by Everett (TB) and out of Johnnie by John Wilkins by Peter McCue. He was bred and owned by J. Renfro of Sonora, Texas.

HENRY. Henry was by Sam Watkins by Peter McCue and his dam was by Tom Thumb. He was bred by George Clegg of Alice, Texas, and owned by Artia Gomez of Alice.

HENRY, OLD. Old Henry was by Blue Eyes by Possum by Traveler and out of a Morgan mare. He was owned by Arthur Beloat of Buckeye, Arizona, and by the Goodyear Farms of Litchfield Park, Arizona.

HERMUS. This sorrel stallion was foaled in 1910 and was sired by Tom Campbell by Old Bob Peters, and he was out of Nellie Hart by Pid Hart. He was bred by the Armstrong Brothers of Elk City, Oklahoma, and owned by Earl Kelly of Las Vegas, New Mexico, and by Thurman Sears of Logan, New Mexico. Kelly and Sears bought Hermus from Reed Armstrong as a colt in 1910 and raced him until he died in Gallup, New Mexico, in 1914. His two best known colts were Star Shoot and White Socks. Kelly said he rode Hermus in a race against Bob Peters in the spring of 1913 at Texola, Oklahoma, on a bad track and won in 23 seconds. Kelly weighed 135 pounds at the time.

HICKORY BILL. This sorrel stallion was foaled in 1907 and died in 1923. He was by Peter McCue by Dan Tucker and out of Lucretia M by The Hero (TB). He was bred by Samuel Watkins of Petersburg, Illinois, and owned by George Clegg of Alice, Texas; John Kenedy of Sarita, Texas; and by the King Ranch of Kingsville, Texas. Lucretia M was out of Bird who was by Jack Traveler by Steel Dust.

HICKORY SWITCH. This bay stallion was by Hickory Bill by Peter McCue and out of a Lazarus mare (TB). He was bred by the King Ranch of Kingsville, Texas, and owned by the McGill brothers of Alice, Texas.

HI EASTLAND. This sorrel stallion was foaled in 1917 and was by Harmon Baker by Peter McCue and out of an Anson Quarter mare. He was bred by William Anson of Christoval, Texas, and owned by Hi Eastland of Sonora, Texas.

HIGHBALL. Highball was by Uncle Jimmy Gray by Bonnie Joe (TB), and the breeding of his dam is unknown. He was bred by Henry Pfefferling of San Antonio, Texas, and owned by Lester B. Gerdes of Bandera, Texas.

HI HENRY. This bay stallion was foaled in 1891 and he was by Big Henry (TB) and out of Butt Cut by Jack Traveler by Steel Dust. He was bred by Samuel Watkins of Petersburg, Illinois. He was owned by the Crosby brothers of Petersburg. It was once thought that Hi Henry was by Dan Tucker, but the Watkins family has verified that his sire was the Thoroughbred Big Henry. He won a half-mile race as a two-year-old in 54 seconds. His racing career is in *Goodwin's Turf Guide*.

HILL TOP. Hill Top was foaled in 1925 and was sired by a grandson of Sam King by Hondo and out of Loma by Sam King. He was bred by O. W. Cardwell of Junction, Texas, and sold to a Florida man.

HIPPED BILLY, see BROWN BILLY.

HIRAM BAKER, see HARMON BAKER.

HOG EYE. Hog Eye was by Red Cloud by Possum by Traveler and out of an unknown mare. He was owned by Doc Pardee of Phoenix, Arizona.

HOGUE HORSE. This sorrel stallion was by Gold Button by Slip Shoulder by Missouri Mike and out of a Blake Quarter mare. He was bred by S. Coke Blake of Pryor, Oklahoma, and owned by a Mr. Hogue of Oklahoma.

HOLMAN HORSE. This sorrel stallion was foaled in the late 1920's. He was by Red Bug by Everett (TB) and out of a Master Gould mare owned by Jap Holman. He was bred by J. S. "Jap" Holman of Sonora, Texas, and owned by Ben L. Wheat of Sonora, Texas; Dee Harrison of Del Rio, Texas; and J. W. Friend of Dryden, Texas.

HONDO. Hondo was by John Crowder by Billy and out of Dutch. He was bred by Pleas Walters of Oakville, Texas. He was a full brother to Ben and Pleas Walters. His dam, Dutch, was bred by Joe Mangum of Nixon, Texas.

HONEST DICK. This bay stallion was foaled in 1928 and he was by Barney Lucas by Traveler and out of Beauty Rose (TB). He was bred and owned by Dick Gray of Gorman, Texas.

HONEST JOHN. Honest John was a Missouri race horse of note, foaled in or about 1886. He was by Sleepy Jim (TB) and out of Sorrel Nell, a well-known short-race mare. His breeder is unknown, but he was raced by D. H. Hogg and E. Grey of Illinois.

HONEST JOHN. This horse was by Red Cloud by Possum by Traveler and out of a Hooker Quarter mare. He was an Arizona horse.

HOUSE, LITTLE. This chestnut stallion was foaled in 1934. He was by *House (TB) and out of a Farish Quarter mare.

111

He was bred by S. P. and W. S. Farish of Berclair, Texas, and later owned by L. A. Clark of Rocksprings, Texas.

HUDSON JR. This bay stallion was foaled in 1913 and was by Bobbie Lowe by Eureka by Shelby and out of Chiromaney by Palm Reader (TB). He was bred and owned by "Webb" Christian of Big Spring, Texas.

I

IDLE BOY. Idle Boy was a sorrel stallion foaled in 1891. He was by Long Tom and out of a Quarter mare named Red Bird. He was bred and owned by W. J. Miller of Sweetwater, Oklahoma. Milo Burlingame is said to have broken Idle Boy and lowered the track record for the half mile with him at Kansas City.

INTERROGATOR. This horse was sometimes called Terry and Big Steve. He was by Concho Colonel by Jim Ned by Pancho by Old Billy and his dam was Sweet by Johnny Corbett by Little Steve by Pony Pete. He was bred by Dan Casement of Manhattan, Kansas, and owned by the Eden Valley Ranch at Willits, California.

IRA. By Traveler, dam unknown. He lived in Texas.

IRON WOOD. This stallion was by Tubal Cain by Berry's Cold Deck and out of a Blake mare. He was bred and raised by S. Coke Blake of Pryor, Oklahoma.

J

JACK DEMPSEY. Jack Dempsey was foaled about 1919. He was by Big Boy by Dominus Arvi (TB) and out of Oklahoma Queen by Tom Campbell by Bob Peters. He was bred by either John A. Harrel of Canute, Oklahoma, or by a Mr. Schultz of Arizona. He was owned by Louis A. (Lude) Kirk of Gallup, New Mexico, and by J. W. Ashcroft of Ramah, New Mexico. Lou Kirk of Farmington, New Mexico, used this stallion to breed some fast horses.

JACKIE BOY. This roan stallion was foaled in 1915 and was by Barney Lucas by Traveler and out of Christine C by Palm Reader (TB). He was bred and owned by D. W. Christian of Big Spring, Texas.

JACK, LITTLE. Little Jack was foaled about 1890. He was by Anthony by Old Billy and out of Little Blaze by Old Billy. His second dam was Paisana by Brown Dick. He was bred by William B. Fleming of Belmont, Texas, and owned by Fred Matthies of Seguin, Texas. Mrs. Matthies told Helen Michaelis that Billy Fleming called this horse Little John Moore, but that Mr. Matthies called him Little Jack. He was also referred to as Jack and Jack Hardy.

JACK McCUE. This sorrel stallion was foaled in 1914 and died in 1940. He was by Peter McCue by Dan Tucker and out of Marguerite by Barlow by Lock's Rondo. He was bred by W. J. Francis of Elida, New Mexico, and owned by M. E. Andes of Portales, New Mexico. He stood 14-3 hands high and weighed 1130 pounds.

JACK McCUE II, see TEXAS JACK.

JACK O'BRIEN. Jack O'Brien was by Albert by Hickory Bill by Peter McCue and out of an O'Brien Quarter mare. He was bred and owned by John J. O'Brien of Refugio, Texas.

JACK OF DIAMONDS. This stallion was by Uncle Jimmy Gray by Bonnie Joe (TB). His dam is not known, but he was bred by Ed Pfefferling of San Antonio, Texas.

JACK OF DIAMONDS. This stallion was by Chulo Mundo by Traveler and was bred and owned by Dick Godfrey of Menard, Texas.

JACK OF DIAMONDS. This sorrel stallion was foaled in 1934 and died in 1943. He was 15-2 hands and weighed 1200 pounds. He was by Jack McCue by Peter McCue by Dan Tucker and out of Pet Kid by Serf Savin (TB). He was bred by M. E. Andes of Portales, New Mexico, and owned by Glen Chipperfield of Phoenix, Arizona.

JACK TRAVELER. This bay stallion lived from 1873 until 1891. He was by Steel Dust by Harry Bluff and out of Queen by Pilgrim (TB). He was bred by John A. (Jack) Batchler of Lancaster, Texas, and owned by A. W. Green of Hutchins, Texas, and Samuel Watkins of Petersburg, Illinois. This is probably the same horse that was raced in Texas by Green under the name Traveler. He may have been by a son of Steel Dust.

JACK WALTON. This stallion was by Yellow Boy by Yellow Jacket by Little Rondo and out of a J. A. mare. He was bred and owned by the J. A. Ranch at Palo Duro, Texas.

JAKE. Jake was by Ben Hur by Rainy Day by Lone Star and out of Georgie by W. A. He was bred by W. D. Parker of Sonoita, Arizona, and owned by Jake McClure, Roy Adams, and Arthur Beloat, all of Arizona. Roy Adams traded a roping horse to Jake McClure for the horse and then later traded Jake to Beloat for Little Bill, Carl Arnold's roping horse, a gelding.

J. A. McCUE. This horse was by Billy McCue by Jack McCue and his dam was a J. A. mare. He was bred and raised by the J. A. Ranch of Palo Duro, Texas. He was later sold to W. J. Lewis of Clarendon, Texas. He was probably foaled about 1932.

*JANUS. Imported Janus was a chestnut stallion foaled in England in 1746 who lived until 1780. He was taken to Virginia in 1752 and owned there by J. Goode Sr., a widely known breeder of short-race horses. Imported Janus was bred by a Mr. Swymmer of England and he was sired by Old Janus by the Godolphin Barb and out of a mare by Fox, who was by Clumsy. In Edgar's *Studbook*, *Janus is called a Quarter Horse and had a record of producing the fastest animals then and since known as Quarter-mile racers. He was of compact build and sired stock of similar form and ability. He is recognized as the forefather of the modern American Quarter Horse.

JANUS, ATKINSON'S. This C.A.Q.R.H. was foaled prior to 1784, and his sire and dam were by *Janus. He was bred by John Atkinson of Virginia. He is listed in the *ASB* and in Edgar.

JANUS, EDMUNTON'S. Edmunton's Janus was a bay stallion with a white streak in his face and three white feet. He was sired by Old Bellair and out of the running mare Linnet by Balwin's Friday. He was bred by William McGeehee of Person County, North Carolina, and owned by Edmundston of Halifax, Virginia. He is listed both in Edgar and in the *ASB*. Edgar says he was a "beautiful, high formed horse, and a very successful quarter of a mile racer, 14 hands 1 inch high."

JAP. This Jap was by Dogie Beasley by Sykes' Rondo. His dam was a Holman mare bred by J. S. Holman of Sonora, Texas, and owned by L. B. Cox of Ozona, Texas.

JAP HOLMAN. This brown stallion was by Brown Jug by Texas Chief and out of a Dogie Beasley mare. He too was bred by J. S. "Jap" Holman of Sonora, Texas, and owned by Ross Beasley of Junction, Texas.

JAZZ. This bay stallion was foaled in 1916 and died in 1941. He was by Harmon Baker by Peter McCue, and he was out of an Anson mare by Jim Ned by Pancho. He was bred by William Anson of Christoval, Texas, and owned by Louis

L. Farr of Barnhart, Texas, and John R. Scott of Mertzon, Texas; he was also used by Tom Elrod of Odessa, Texas.

JAZZBO, see JOE PETER.

J. D. This stallion was by Paul El by Hickory Bill by Peter McCue and out of Lady by Little Joe by Traveler. He was bred by Jim Adams of Alfred, Texas, who sold him to his brother, Ott Adams of Alfred.

JEFF (JEFF C). This gray stallion was foaled in 1885 and died in 1916. He was sired by Printer by Old Cold Deck and out of a Campbell mare. He was bred by Charles B. Campbell of Minco, Oklahoma, and owned by Charles Cronnin of Loyal, Oklahoma, and W. J. Patton of Seedey, Oklahoma. He was a great race horse and a fine sire.

JEFF SELF. Jeff Self was a bay stallion sired by A. D. Reed by Peter McCue by Dan Tucker and out of Casino by Peter McCue. He was bred by E. Alden Meek of Foss, Oklahoma, and owned by Aubra Bowers of Canadian, Texas. He was sometimes referred to as the Conner Horse and as Justus F.

JENKINS CHARLIE, see OREGON CHARLIE.

JESSE HOOVER. This bay stallion was foaled in 1908. He was by Peter McCue by Dan Tucker and out of Path Tennyson (TB). He was bred and owned by Walter C. Watkins of Oakford, Illinois.

JESSIE, OLD. Old Jessie was by Bobby Beach by Bob Wade and out of a Jenkins mare. He was bred by J. R. Jenkins of Corona, New Mexico.

JESS PARSONS (LITTLE JESS). This stallion was by Traveler and he was out of a Shely mare. He was bred by Dow Shely of Alfred, Texas, and owned by Tom E. Garrett of Devine, Texas. He was sometimes referred to as Little Jess.

JIGGS. This Jiggs was a sorrel stallion foaled in 1924 and sired by Uncle Jimmy Gray by Bonnie Joe (TB) and out of Sir Hopkins by Suffragist (TB). He was bred by E. E. Wisdom of San Antonio, Texas, and owned by Ed Pfefferling of San Antonio, Charles Armstrong of Hebbronville, the King Ranch of Kingsville, George Clegg of Alice, and Fred Barrett of Comstock, all of Texas.

Charley Armstrong obtained Jiggs from Pfefferling stables, and after breeding him a few years let the King Ranch have him. They used him briefly and then gave him to George Clegg. Clegg sold the horse and he changed hands several more times. Jiggs was registered in the *Half-Breed Stud Book* when Wisdom owned him (Vol. II, 14).

JIGGS. This Jiggs was a light palomino color, foaled about 1925. He was by Fred Litze by Old Fred and out of April Fool. He was bred by Coke T. Roberds of Hayden, Colorado, and owned by the CS Ranch of Cimarron, New Mexico.

JIM. Jim was a bay stallion by Harmon Baker by Peter McCue and out of a mare by Brother Compton. He was bred by William Anson of Christoval, Texas, and owned by L. J. Farr of Barnhart, Texas; Leroy Spires of Roscoe, Texas; and Cecel Childress of Ozona, Texas.

JIM BROWN. Jim Brown was sired by Paul El by Hickory Bill and out of Mary Brown by Hondo by John Crowder. He was bred by Ott Adams of Alfred, Texas. He was owned at one time by Juan Lamb of Alfred, Texas.

JIMMIE. Jimmie was by Runflor (TB) and out of Queen by Yellow Jacket by Little Rondo. He was bred and owned by J. A. Laning of Rocksprings, Texas.

JIMMIE BELL. This stallion was foaled in 1922. He was by Uncle Jimmy Gray by Bonnie Joe (TB) and out of a Schott Quarter mare. He was bred and owned by Eugene J. Schott of Riomedina, Texas.

117

JIMMIE GRAY JR., HABY'S. This stallion may have been a paint horse. He was by Uncle Jimmy Gray by Bonnie Joe (TB) and out of a Haby mare by A. M. White by Everett (TB). His second dam was by Lone Star. He was bred and owned by Sterle Haby of Riomedina, Texas. He was the grand sire of the running-mare Free Silver.

JIM MILLER. This chestnut stallion was foaled in 1885. He was sired by Roan Dick and out of Amanda Miller. He was reportedly bred at Butte, Montana, and later owned by J. R. Thomas of Walla Walla, Washington.

JIMMY GRAY, see UNCLE JIMMY GRAY.

JIM NED. Jim Ned was a brown stallion who was foaled in 1892 and died in 1914. He was sired by Pancho by Old Billy. His dam was a Gardner mare by Traveler. He was bred by Charles A. Gardner of San Angelo, Texas, and later owned by William Anson of Christoval, Texas. He was a full brother of Brown Billy.

JIM O'CONNOR. This stallion was by Albert by Hickory Bill and out of a mare by Big Jim by Sykes' Rondo. He was bred by Jim O'Connor of Victoria, Texas.

JIM POLK. This bay stallion was foaled in 1881 and was by Shiloh and out of Hercules. He was owned by S. Stroud. This Shiloh was probably a son of the better-known Clayton's Shiloh. His half-brother Mikado, a gelding, was also a well-known short-horse.

JIM REED. Jim Reed was a gray stallion foaled in 1886. He was sired by Rebel Morgan by John Morgan (TB). His dam was Grey Alice by Steel Dust. He was bred and owned by J. M. "Jim" Brown of Giddings, Texas, and several other race-horse men.

JIM RIX. Jim Rix was a sorrel stallion foaled in 1927 by Election (TB) and out of Rix by The Senator. He was bred and owned by C. A. Allison of Weston, Wyoming.

JIM TRAMMELL. This stallion was a chestnut foaled in 1894 by Barney Owens by Cold Deck and out of a mare from Kentucky bred by A. P. Bush. Jim Trammell was bred by Thomas Trammell of Sweetwater, Texas, and later owned by J. Frank Norfleet of Hale Center, Texas.

JIM TRAMMELL, see TRAMMELL.

JIM WELLS. Jim Wells was foaled in the early 1900's. He was bred by Ott Adams and was sired by Little Joe and out of Katie M by Big Jim by Sykes' Rondo. He was first purchased by John Dial of Goliad, Texas, and then owned by Graves Peeler of Christine, Texas; John E. Parke of Kyle, Texas; J. L. Custer of Spofford, Texas; and the Franklin brothers of Tilden, Texas. Parke used to use him as a rope horse. He was also a race horse and outran Karnes' City Jim in San Diego, Texas, running 200 yards in 10¼ seconds.

JODIE (JOE D and JODIE CLICK). Jodie was by Little Joe by Traveler and out of Lucretia M by The Hero (TB). His second dam was Bird by Jack Traveler by Steel Dust. She was bred by Sam Watkins of Petersburg, Illinois, and purchased by George Clegg of Alice, Texas, who was the breeder of Jodie. Jodie was sold to J. B. Murrah and Pat Rose of Del Rio, Texas.

JOE BAILEY, OLD. Old Joe Bailey of Weatherford was the first and most important Joe Bailey. He was sired by Eureka and out of Susie McQuirter. Eureka was by Shelby by Tom Driver by Steel Dust. Tom Driver's dam was Mammoth by Shiloh. Susie McQuirter was by Little Ben by Barney by Steel Dust. He was bred by Dick Baker of Weatherford, Texas. He was later sold to Bud Parker, then to Jack Tindel, and finally to E. A. Whiteside of Sipe Springs, Texas. He was foaled in 1907 and died in 1934.

JOE BERRY HORSE, see COLD DECK, BERRY'S.

JOE BUTLER. This stallion was by Joe Reed by Joe Blair (TB) and out of Fanny Ashwell. He was bred by John W. House of Cameron, Texas.

119

JOE COLLINS. Joe Collins was foaled in 1883(?) and died in 1910(?). He was sired by Old Billy by Shiloh and out of Paisana by Brown Dick by Berkshire. He was bred by William B. Fleming of Belmont, Texas, and owned by Alex Gardner of San Angelo and Clay McGonigal of Midland, Texas. According to Charles Gardner, Joe Collins was a dark brown horse and a better sire than his brother, Pancho. Alex Gardner gave Fleming $1500 for Joe Collins, Pancho, and Dora in 1886.

JOE D, see JODIE.

JOE GARDNER, see CAPTAIN JOE.

JOE, HARP'S LITTLE. He was by Springer's Little Joe by Old Joe by Harmon Baker. His dam was a Springer mare. He was bred by the CS Ranch of Cimarron, New Mexico.

JOE, HEARD'S LITTLE. He was by China Suarez by Little Joe. Dam by Little Joe.

JOE HOOKER. Joe Hooker was by Monday (TB) by Colton and out of Mayflower (TB) by *Eclipse. He was foaled in 1872. Both he and his dam were foaled in California. In 1887 he was advertised at stud by the Rancho del Rio of Sacramento, which was owned by Theodore Winter. Winter also bred the well-known Salvator, who covered the mile in 1:35½. Joe Hooker's blood was very popular with short-horse breeders.

JOE HOWELL. This brown stallion was foaled in 1894 and was sired by Joe Harris by Sam Harper and out of Dora by Bill Garner by Steel Dust. He was bred by John Wilkins Jr. of San Antonio, Texas. He was registered in the appendix of the *American Stud Book* (Vol. VII, 1210).

JOE JOKER. This Thoroughbred bay stallion was foaled in 1907. He was by Peter McCue by Dan Tucker and out of

Darkey's Dream (TB). He was bred and owned by Walter Watkins of Oakford, Illinois.

JOE LEWIS. This Joe Lewis was foaled in 1878 and sired by Bobby Cromwell by Old Cold Deck and out of Grasshopper by Old Cold Deck. He was bred by Joe Lewis of Hunnewell, Kansas.

JOE, LITTLE. Little Joe, the best-known of the many Little Joe's, was a brown stallion, foaled in 1904, who died in 1929 on the O. W. Cardwell Ranch at Junction, Texas. He was by Traveler and out of Jenny by Sykes' Rondo. His second dam was May Mangum by Anthony by Old Billy. He was bred by Dow and Will Shely of Alfred, Texas, and purchased as a colt by George Clegg of Alice, Texas. For many years, he was owned by Ott S. Adams of Alfred, Texas.

JOE, McPETER'S LITTLE. He was by Red Joe of Arizona. His dam was a Clayton mare.

JOE MURRAY. Joe Murray, foaled in 1891, was by Anthony by Old Billy and out of Little Blaze by Old Billy. He was bred by William Fleming of Belmont, Texas, and later was owned by Lucius Buttrill of Marathon, Texas.

JOE, OLD. This Old Joe was by Harmon Baker by Peter McCue and his dam an Anson mare by Jim Ned. He was bred by Billy Anson of Christoval, Texas, and owned by the CS Ranch at Cimarron, New Mexico.

JOE, OLD. This Old Joe was a brown stallion foaled in 1870(?) by Whalebone by Old Billy and out of Paisana by Brown Dick by Berkshire. His second dam was Belton Queen by Guinea Boar. He was bred by William B. Fleming of Belmont, Texas, and later was owned by Crawford Sykes of Nixon, Texas.

JOE, OLD. Old Joe was by Cotton Eyed Joe by Little Joe and out of a John Dial mare. W. A. Napper of Alamo, Texas, says he bought Old Joe in 1934 from L. D. Johnson. He was fast as a two-year-old. He ran three races against a Copperbottom Quarter mare called Minnie from North Texas and beat her by a nose twice.

JOE PETER (JAZZBO). Joe Peter was by Joe Hancock by John Wilkins by Peter McCue. His dam is unknown, as is his breeder. He was owned by George Buchanan of Garland, Texas, who sold him, to be raced under the name Jazzbo, to an Indian in Oklahoma.

JOE RATLIFF. Joe Ratliff was a sorrel stallion foaled in 1912(?). He was by Watkins' Cotton Eyed Joe by Peter McCue and out of Babe Ruth by Sykes' Rondo. He was bred by William Nack of Cuero, Texas.

JOE, R. O.'S. The only breeding known of this horse was that he was by a Texas Quarter Horse and out of a Texas Quarter mare. He was owned by the Greene Cattle Company of Cananea, Sonora, Mexico. He was one of five Quarter Horse stallions purchased by the company early in 1916. William Anson helped the ranch select the stallions. The others were King, Little Kid, Mark, and Sykes.

JOE SHELY. This stallion was a sorrel foaled in 1905 and sired by Traveler. His dam was a Shely Quarter mare. He was bred and owned by Will Shely of Alfred, Texas.

JOE, SPRINGER'S LITTLE. This bay stallion was foaled in 1916 and died in 1941. He was by Old Joe by Harmon Baker by Peter McCue and out of Old English by Uhlan (TB). He was bred and owned by Ed T. Springer of the CS Ranch at Cimarron, New Mexico.

JOHN A. John A was foaled in 1889. He was a bay by Gabriel (TB) and out of Kitty by a Whip stallion. His second dam was Lady Williams by Fall's Gray Eagle by Gray Eagle, and his third dam was by Bick by Printer. He was probably bred on the Pacific Coast and named after John Adams of Woodland, California.

JOHN BACCHUS. John Bacchus was a bay stallion foaled about 1835. He was by Cone's Bacchus by the Bacchus by Sir Archy. His dam was Old Nell by Old Printer. His breeder is unknown, but he was owned by a Mr. Armstrong of Schoolcraft, Michigan. He was a full brother of Telegraph (Hamilton's). He stood 15 hands, 2 inches and was very muscular and a fast runner. He could go a half mile.

JOHN BROWN. John Brown was by John Wilkins by Peter McCue and out of Cora by Blue by Cornstalk. He was bred and owned by Gaston B. Mathis of Stinnett, Texas.

JOHN CALDWELL. This black stallion was by Texas Chief by Lock's Rondo and out of a good Quarter mare. He was bred by Joe D. Jeffries of Clarendon, Texas, and raced by Jim Gibson of the same city.

JOHN COOK. A bay stallion by Steel Dust, dam unknown. He was bred in Texas and owned by Jim Cook of Stephens County, Texas. He was sometimes called just John. He was said to be "too heavy to be a winner, but a great sire of short speed." One of his best-known colts was Thurman.

JOHN CROWDER. This chestnut stallion was foaled in 1878(?). He was by Old Billy by Shiloh and out of Paisana by Brown Dick by Berkshire. His second dam was Belton Queen by Guinea Boar. He was bred by William Fleming of Belmont, Texas, and owned consecutively by the Johnson brothers of Hondo, Texas; Will Shely of Alfred, Texas; Alex Gardner of San Angelo, Texas; and John Marksbury of Camp Verde, Arizona.

JOHN GARDNER. John Gardner was a sorrel stallion by Traveler and out of a Gardner Quarter mare. He was bred by John E. Gardner of San Angelo, Texas, and then owned by Jack Gates of Devine, Texas, and Ott S. Adams of Alfred, Texas. Ott Adams said he was a sorrel horse with white hairs, but not enough to be called a roan. He was a good race horse, although not as fast as his half brother, Captain Joe. Adams traded Captain Joe to Gates for John Gardner.

JOHN L. This race stallion was, according to *Goodwin's Turf Guide*, by Cold Deck by Old Billy and his dam unreported. He was raced during 1891, 1892, and 1893 by F. M. Fanning. He was a chestnut, foaled in 1888.

JOHN, LITTLE. This stallion was by Traveler and out of a Gardner mare. He was bred by John E. Gardner of San Angelo and owned by Pete Gardner of Big Foot, Texas.

JOHN, LITTLE. This stallion was foaled in 1926 and was by John Wilkins by Peter McCue and his dam an Oklahoma mare named Thunderbolt. He was bred and owned by Gaston B. Mathis of Stinnett, Texas.

JOHN MacKAY. This bay stallion was foaled in 1900. He was by Dan Tucker by Barney Owens and out of Alice Wood who was sired by his half brother, Peter McCue. John Mac-Kay was bred by Fred T. Wood of Abilene, Texas, and raced (and probably owned) by C. B. Willingham in Denver, Colorado.

JOHN MOORE, LITTLE, see JACK, LITTLE.

JOHNNIE BROWN. This bay stallion was foaled in 1919. He was sired by Star McGee (TB) and out of Bessie Keough by Peter McCue. He was bred by Joseph Brown of Petersburg, Illinois.

JOHNNIE REED. This brown stallion was foaled in 1928. He was by Dennis Reed (TB) and out of Indian Maid by Moss King. He was bred by the Waddell brothers of Odessa, Texas.

JOHNNY. Johnny was a sorrel stallion sired by Cotton Eyed Joe by Peter McCue and out of a mare sired by Karnes City

Jim. He was bred by Pedro Tijerino and purchased by a Mr. Galanto of Cuero, Texas. He was small and heavily built, but fast for all distances under 440 yards. His best-known son was Ace of Diamonds.

JOHNNY CORBETT. Johnny Corbett was by Little Steve by Pony Pete. Little Steve was out of Cherokee Maid. Dan Casement said Pony Pete was a Printer Quarter Horse, and that he had been bred by "Old Man Smalley" of Sylvan Grove, Kansas. Johnny Corbett was out of a Walker Quarter mare. He was bred by Charley Walker of Kiowa, Colorado. Sometimes Johnny Corbett is referred to as Corbett. This "Old Man Smalley" must be Mike Smiley of Sylvan Grove. See Little Steve.

JOHNNY, HOLMAN'S. This Johnny was by Dogie Beasley by Sykes' Rondo by McCoy Billy and out of a Holman mare. He was bred by J. S. "Jap" Holman of Sonora, Texas, and owned by George Whitehead of Del Rio, Texas.

JOHNNY KANE STUD, see SONNY BOY.

JOHNNY MOORE. This chestnut stallion, foaled in 1867, was by George Moore, a Quarter race horse stallion of unknown breeding and out of Sally Franklin by Illinois Medoc (TB). He was bred and owned by Mr. A. Musick of California. Helen Michaelis wrote that he contributed to the history of racing Quarter Horses in California.

JOHNNY WALKER. This brown stallion was by Uncle Jimmy Gray by Bonnie Joe (TB) and out of an unrecorded dam. He was owned by Brooks Sparks of San Antonio, and later by Whitehead and Wardlaw of Del Rio, Texas.

JOHNNY WALKER. This Johnny Walker was a brown stallion by Wyoming (TB) and out of a Little Steve mare. He was owned by A. F. Smillie of Granby, Colorado.

JOHNNY WALKER HORSE. This stallion was by Johnny Walker by Uncle Jimmy Gray by Bonnie Joe (TB) and out of a Whitehead-Wardlaw mare. He was bred by Whitehead and Wardlaw of Del Rio, Texas.

JOHN, OLD. Old John was a bay stallion foaled in 1935. He was by Jim Trammell by Barney Owens by Cold Deck and his dam is unknown. He was owned by John and Clarence Scharbauer of Midland, Texas.

JOHN REED. This chestnut Quarter running horse was foaled in 1884. He was by Little Pete by Pony Pete and out of Sorrel Nell. His breeder is unknown, but he was owned and raced by S. V. Gordan and G. F. Hammer in Arkansas, Colorado, and Iowa.

JOHN WILKES (JOHN WILKINS). John Wilkes was a chestnut stallion sometimes referred to as John Wilkins. He was foaled in 1912 and sired by Peter McCue by Dan Tucker and out of Big Alice by Pid Hart by Shelby. He was bred by Milo Burlingame of Cheyenne, Oklahoma. Later he was owned by Matt Renfro of Fort Sumner, New Mexico, and Barry Pursley of Spur County, Texas. Burlingame named him John Wilkins but, when Renfro bought him, he changed his name to John Wilkes.

JOHN WILKINS. This bay stallion was foaled in 1906 and died in 1930. He was by Peter McCue by Dan Tucker and out of Katie Wawekus (TB). He was bred by B. C. Watkins of Oakford, Illinois, and registered in the *American Stud Book*. E. J. and J. W. Moore of Mobeetie, Texas, brought John Wilkins, Billy Sunday, and Nannie Gum to Texas from Petersburg, Illinois. The J. A. Ranch owned John Wilkins at one time on their ranch near Palo Duro, Texas. Later, Walter E. Hancock of Perryton, Texas, owned him and then sold him to Gaston B. Mathis of Stinnett, Texas.

JOHN WILKINS, see JOHN WILKES.

JOHN W. NORTON. This sorrel stallion was foaled in 1876. He was by *Bonnie Scotland and out of Mary Gowan. He died October 10, 1891, in Pueblo, Colorado. He was bred by General W. B. Harding of Nashville, Tennessee.

JOKER. A chestnut stallion foaled in 1886 and sired by Joe Hooker and out of Daisy Miller. He was owned and raced in California by J. King.

JOLLY. This stallion was by John Wilkins by Peter McCue and out of a Hancock mare. He was bred and owned by Walter E. Hancock of Perryton, Texas. He was a top race horse.

JONAS. Jonas was by Joe Reed by Joe Blair (TB) and out of Fanny Ashwell by Ashwell (TB). He was bred and owned by John W. House of Cameron, Texas.

JOSELIA. This stallion was a bay by Hickory Bill by Peter McCue and out of a Clegg Quarter mare. He was bred by George Clegg of Alice, Texas, and owned by Therrill Rose of Del Rio, Texas.

JOY. This sorrel stallion was foaled in 1912 and died in 1931. He was sired by Jeff by Jeff C by Printer by Old Cold Deck (or a son of his) and out of Lou Trammell by Peter McCue. He was bred by Clyde McClain of Leedey, Oklahoma, and owned by C. O. Guase, Cheyenne, Oklahoma; Thomas Trammell of Sweetwater, Texas; and Ed Carney of Putnam City, Oklahoma. He was raced for a time by W. J. "Bill" Patton of Leedey, Oklahoma. That is why it is sometimes referred to as Patton's Joy. Trammell traded a horse called Coon Dog to Guase for Joy in 1923, but kept him only a year. Carney owned him from 1924 to 1931. Joy was a sorrel horse with a star and stood 15-1 hands.

JUDGE, LITTLE. Little is known about this stallion except that he was by Rocky Mountain Tom by Pid Hart and out of a short-running mare.

JUDGE WELCH. Judge Welch was foaled in 1898. He was by Traveler and out of Fannie Pace by Gulliver by Missouri

Rondo. He was bred by C. C. Seale of Baird, Texas, and owned by Eugene H. Leache of The Plains, Virginia.

JUDGE WILKINS. This chestnut stallion was foaled in 1914. He was by John Wilkins by Peter McCue and out of Nannie Gum by Nimrod (TB). His second dam was Pansy H by The Hero (TB). He was bred by J. W. "Bill" Moore of Mobeetie, Texas.

JULY. This sorrel stallion was foaled in 1925. He was by Mentor (TB) and out of June Sunday by Tom Sunday (TB). His second dam was a daughter of The Senator by Leadville (TB). He was bred and owned by the 7-11 Ranch of Hot Springs, South Dakota.

JUMBO. This stallion was a sorrel foaled in 1879. He was by California (TB) and out of Big Gun by Old George. He was bred and owned by Theodore Winter of Sacramento, California.

JUNE BEE. June Bee was foaled in 1924 and was brown. He was by Elmendorf (TB) and out of Nellie by Arch Oldham by Gallantry (TB). He was bred and owned by Mrs. W. S. Hall of Boerne, Texas.

JUNE BUG. This June Bug was a chestnut with a blaze and stockings. He stood 14-3 and weighed 1100 pounds. He was foaled in 1913 and died in 1925. He was by Tommy Twigg (TB) and out of Bonnie Bird II by Lock's Rondo by Whalebone. He was bred by Bob Burns of Hope, New Mexico, and owned by Andy Locklear of San Saba, Texas; Bob Spiller of Menard, Texas; and Ed Spiller of Voca, Texas. In 1945 Andy Locklear said he did more to improve the average quality of the horse in the San Saba-Brady-Menard area than any other stallion.

JUNE BUG. This stallion was foaled in 1920 and was by Captain Daughtery by Jack De Mund (TB). His dam was a

Renfro Quarter mare. He was bred and owned by the Renfro brothers of Menard, Texas.

JUPITER. This C.A.Q.R.H. stallion was a chestnut probably foaled in 1766. He was by *Janus, as was his dam. Both the *ASB* and Edgar list him.

JUST RIGHT. Just Right was a chestnut stallion foaled in 1930. He was by Just David (TB) and out of Rain No More by Rainy Day by Lone Star. He was bred by Martin Haby of Riomedina, Texas.

K

KAISER (KAYSER). Not much is known about this stallion. He was by Old Dedier (D. J.) by Henry Star (TB)(?). He was bred, owned, and raced in Louisiana.

KARNES CITY JIM (KENEDY JIM). This stallion was by Hondo by John Crowder and out of a Sykes mare by Rondo. He was foaled in 1901(?). He was bred by Jim Brown of Karnes City, Texas. This is not the well-known race-horse man Jim Brown, although both were sheriffs. He was matched with Carrie Nations, but the race never came off. "They turned them for a day or two, but never got them started."

KAYO. Kayo was by Spark Plug by Jack McCue and out of New Moore by Brettenham (TB). His second dam was Flugget by Jim Trammell by Barney Owens. He was bred by W. R. Norfleet of Kress, Texas.

KEELING HORSE. This stallion was foaled around 1920. He was by Brother Compton by Dr. Mack and out of a Keeling mare by Foster's Traveler by Traveler. He was bred and owned by Robert Keeling of San Angelo, Texas.

KEENEY HORSE. This stallion was by Yellow Wolf by Old Joe Bailey by Eureka and out of a Waggoner mare. He was bred by W. T. Waggoner of Fort Worth, Texas, and owned by Hed Guice of Stephenville, Texas.

KEENO. Keeno was by Joy by Jeff by Jeff C by Printer and out of a McClain mare. He was bred and owned by Clyde McClain of Leedey, Oklahoma.

KEGGY. Keggy was a chestnut stallion by Brown Jug by Texas Chief by Traveler and out of a mare by Dogie Beasley by Sykes' Rondo. He was bred by J. S. "Jap" Holman of Sonora, Texas, and owned by Mack Cauthorn of Sonora, Texas, and Husie Galoway of Del Rio, Texas.

KELLY (CLAY, KELLY BOY). Kelly was a gray stallion by Star Shoot by Hermus by Tom Campbell and out of a Kelly mare. He was bred by Jim and Earl Kelly of Las Vegas, New Mexico. He was later owned by John Williams of Stead, New Mexico, and Carl Sheppard, also of New Mexico. He was widely raced.

KENDRICKS. Kendricks was a bay stallion foaled in 1899. He was by The Hero (TB) and out of Hattie W by Hi Henry by Big Henry (TB). His second dam was Katie Wawekus by Wawekus (TB). He was bred by B. C. Watkins of Newmanville, Illinois.

KENEDY JIM, see KARNES CITY JIM.

KENNEDY. This black stallion was foaled in 1892 and was sired by Fonso (TB). His dam was May Kennedy by Faustus and his second dam by Printer by Gray Eagle. He was bred by B. J. Treacy of Lexington, Kentucky, and raced by J. C. Rogers.

KENO, see KEENO.

KENTUCKY WHIP, COOK'S and BLACKBURN'S. Kentucky Whip was a bay stallion of whom a contemporary wrote "it is questionable whether the world ever held his equal in smoothness, symmetry, and finish of form. He was the favorite horse in Kentucky for fifteen or twenty years, and went to nearly all of our best mares." He was sired by the imported stallion Whip (TB) and out of Speckleback by Celer (TB). He was foaled in 1805, bred by John Patrick of Charlotte County, Virginia. He was later taken to Kentucky and spent the rest of his life near Lexington. In Kentucky, he was owned by William B. Cook, Abraham Buford, J. Kinkaid, and E. M. Blackburn. His get, such as Short Whip and Tiger, were widely scattered into the new Western states and were responsible for many famous Quarter running horses. Kentucky Whip died in 1828.

KETCHUM. This Ketchum was by Joe Collins by Old Billy and out of a McGonigal dun mare. He was bred by George McGonigal of Midland, Texas.

KETCHUM. Ketchum was foaled in 1921(?). He was a bay stallion by Captain by Harmon Baker by Peter McCue. His dam was a Berry Ketchum Quarter mare. He was bred by Blackstone and Slaughter of Sheffield, Texas, and owned later by R. D. Johnson of San Angelo, Texas.

KID, LITTLE. This sorrel stallion was by Peter McCue by Dan Tucker and an unknown dam. He was bred by Mr. Gibson of San Antonio, Texas, and owned by the Greene Cattle Company of Cananea, Sonora, Mexico. He was one of five stallions the RO Ranch bought in 1916. Mr. Gibson was a hunchbacked man who lived five or six miles south of San Antonio. The RO stallion, King, was also purchased from Mr. Gibson.

KID McCUE, see OKLAHOMA SHY.

KID WELLER. This sorrel stallion was foaled in 1902. He was by Rancocas (TB) and out of Heeley by Blue Dick by Wade Hampton. His second dam was Mittie Stephens by

Shiloh Jr. by Shiloh. He was bred and owned by J. F. Newman of Sweetwater, Texas. He was raced.

KILBOURNE. This bay stallion was foaled in 1908. He was by Peter McCue by Dan Tucker and out of Patti Bellet (TB). He was bred and owned by Edwin Blakeley of Kelbourne(?), Illinois.

KINCH. Kinch was a chestnut stallion foaled in 1927. He was by Everett (TB) and out of Cappitola by Brother Compton. He was bred and owned by J. E. Renfro of Menard, Texas.

KING. By Steel Dust by Harry Bluff. No other facts known about this King.

KING (POSSUM). King or Possum, his Arizona name, was a roan stallion foaled in 1905 who died in 1925. He was by Traveler and out of Jenny by Sykes' Rondo and his second dam was May Mangum by Anthony by Old Billy. He was bred by Dow and Will Shely of Alfred, Texas, and owned first by Dick Herring of Devine, Texas, and then bought and taken to Arizona by J. J. Kennedy of Bonita, Arizona. He was a full brother of Little Joe.

KING, BARKER'S (KINGFISHER). This chestnut stallion was by Inkabrodis by Big King by One-Eyed Kingfisher and out of a Barker mare by Lock's Rondo. He was bred and owned for a while by Rufi E. Barker of Manchaca, Texas. Later he was owned by Bob Barker who sold him to Bill Moss of Llano County, Texas, who stood him for 16 years. Hazel Bowman said 80 per cent of his colts sold for polo.

KING, DAUGHERTY'S. This stallion was by Moss King by Big King and was owned by Ed Daugherty.

KING, DuBOSE'S. Sire and dam of this King are unknown. He was bred and owned by Friendly DuBose of Rancho Seco, Nueces County, Texas.

KING F. King F was by King (Possum) by Traveler. He was owned by Spence Jowell of Midland, Texas.

KINGFISHER, see KING, BARKER'S.

KINGFISHER, MOSS'. This stallion was by Moss King by Big King by One-Eyed Kingfisher by Old Kingfisher. He was bred and owned by Luke Moss of Llano, Texas. Tate Moss of Llano also had a similarly bred stallion he called Kingfisher.

KINGFISHER, OLD. Kingfisher apparently was a popular name. The first we are interested in was foaled in 1870 and died in 1890(?). He was by Rebel by Steel Dust. He was brought to Texas about 1885 by an old bachelor. Mr. Leeman Barker bred a daughter of Steel Dust to Kingfisher and got a stallion that was the foundation of the Barker Kingfisher horses. He called him Kingfisher after his sire. Many descendants of this son, bred by Barker, were afterwards called either King or Kingfisher. After the Barker horse lost an eye, he was generally referred to as One-Eyed Kingfisher.

KING, HARKEY'S. This sorrel stallion was foaled in 1930. He was sired by Dodger by Harmon Baker by Peter McCue and out of Kitty by Mineral. His second dam was a Berry Ketchum mare. He was bred and owned by Leigh Harkey of Sheffield, Texas.

KING, HOHMANN'S. The sire of this stallion was a bay horse of Kingfisher breeding. He was owned by Mr. Hohmann of Llano County, Texas.

KING JOHN. King John was a bay stallion foaled in 1926 by Walking John by Nimrod (TB). His dam was a heavy, polo-type mare. He was bred and owned by Arch Wilkinson of Menard, Texas.

KING, LITTLE. Little King was foaled about 1910. He was by Possum by Traveler and out of Nellie by Old Joe. He was bred by Jim Morris of Devine, Texas, and owned by John Nixon of Yancey, Texas.

KING OF HEARTS. The sire of this horse was an Ace of Hearts stud owned by Sam Pugh of Dinero, Texas.

KING, PARKER'S. This King was by Moss King by Big King by One-Eyed Kingfisher and out of an unknown dam. The breeder was unknown. He might be the same horse as Daugherty's King, but it is more likely he was a half brother. He was owned for a time by Walter Parker of Marble Falls, Texas.

KING, R. O.'S. This King was a sorrel considered to be of Peter McCue breeding. He was bred by Mr. Gibson of San Angelo and owned by the Greene Cattle Company of Cananea, Sonora, Mexico. See under Little Kid.

KING, SHORT'S LITTLE. This King was by One-Eyed Kingfisher. His dam and breeder are unknown, but he was owned by J. W. Short of Bandera, Texas.

KING, SIMM'S. This stallion was by Strawberry by Possum by Traveler and out of an unreported mare. He was foaled in Arizona and owned by a Mr. Simm of that state.

KING TAMMANY, OLD. This F.A.Q.R.H. was foaled about 1796 and was by Eaton's Little Janus by Meade's Old Celer and out of a Mark Anthony mare. He was bred by William Jackson of Franklin County, North Carolina. Maj. Cordie Ferrell rode the stallion in several races and told Edgar he was strong and swift and won immense sums of money. Old King Tammany was a pale sorrel with a streak in his face and two white hind feet. He was 14 hands high. He is also listed in the ASB.

KING TAMMANY, YOUNG. Young King Tammany was a F.A.Q.R.H. bred by William Jackson of Franklin County, North Carolina. He was sired by Old King Tammany and his dam was by Eaton's Garrick. He is listed in the *ASB*. He was foaled about 1790.

KING TUT. King Tut was sired by Shiek by Peter McCue and his dam was by Old Fred. He was bred and owned in Colorado.

KIRO. This bay horse was foaled in 1887 and was sired by the Thoroughbred Joe Hooker. He was bred by Andrew Wackman of Elk Grove, California, and later bought by the Trowbridges of Wellington, Kansas.

KNOX HORSE, see YELLOW JACKET, NACK'S.

L

LANESBORO. This bay stallion, foaled in 1908, was by Jim Dunn (TB) and out of Peachum by Peter McCue by Dan Tucker. He was bred and owned by T. J. Cunningham of Lanesboro, Iowa.

LA PLATA. La Plata was a sorrel stallion foaled in 1923. He was by Booger Red by Rancocas (TB) and out of Silver by Dave Waldo. He was bred and owned by D. Bryant Turner of Colorado Springs, Colorado.

LAYTON CHUT. This stallion was by Ben Hur by Rainy Day by Lone Star. He was owned by Dick Layton of Stafford, Arizona.

LEE BAY. Lee Bay was by Little Trouble by Trouble by Dan Tucker and his dam was by an unknown stallion. He was bred and owned by Oliver M. Lee of Alamogordo, New Mexico.

LEE SORREL. Lee Sorrel was by Cope by Trouble by Dan Tucker and out of a Lee mare. He was bred and owned by Oliver M. Lee of Alamogordo, New Mexico.

LEINSTER. Leinster was a brown stallion foaled in 1928. He was by Helmet (TB) and his dam was Rainbow by The Senator by Leadville (TB). He was bred and owned by Henry Leonard of Colorado Springs, Colorado.

LEMAN. Leman was a chestnut stallion foaled in 1909. He was by Dr. Curtis (TB) and his dam was Annie T by Traveler. He was bred and owned by D. W. "Webb" Christian of Big Spring, Texas. His second dam was Annie May, who was the dam of the Barney Lucas.

LENOX. Lenox was a bay stallion foaled in 1912 and by Bobbie Lowe by Eureka by Shelby and his dam was Christine C by Palm Reader (TB). His second dam was Annie T by Traveler and his third dam was Annie May. He was bred and owned by D. W. "Webb" Christian of Big Spring, Texas.

LEONELL. This stallion was by Ace of Hearts II by Ace of Hearts and his dam was a Saenz mare. He was bred by Anastacio "Tacho" Saenz of Premont, Texas.

LIBRARY. This gray stallion was foaled in 1909 and was sired by Tom Campbell by Old Bob Peters and out of Hazel by Pid Hart by Shelby. He was bred and owned by Dan C. Armstrong of Doxey, Oklahoma.

LIGHTFOOT B. This bay stallion was foaled in 1924. He was by Meteorite (TB) and out of a mare by Johnny Corbett by Little Steve. He was bred and owned by F. Dean Bidwell of North Powder, Oregon.

LIGHTNING, see RED LIGHTNING.

LIMBER JIM. Limber Jim was a sorrel stallion foaled in 1880. He was by Sleepy Dick and out of Switch. His breeder is unknown, but he was owned by Ogden and Neel of Illinois while he was racing.

LINDY. Lindy was by John Wilkins by Peter McCue and out of a Hancock mare. He was bred by Walter E. Hancock of

Perryton, Texas, and raced by Kenneth "Skip" Montgomery of Reydon, Oklahoma. He was foaled about 1924.

LONE MAN. This chestnut stallion was foaled in 1889 and was by Lock's Rondo by Whalebone and out of Fleetfoot by a Morris Ranch Thoroughbred. He was bred by Santana Cruz of Driftwood, Hays County, Texas, and owned by Sam Heard of Hays County.

LONE SIX. This sorrel stallion was foaled in 1883(?) and was by Black Wind and out of a mare by Harry Bluff. His second dam was of Short's Whip stock. He was bred in Illinois and raced by White and Barnes of the same state.

LONE STAR. This chestnut stallion was foaled in 1911. He was by Gold Enamel (TB) and out of a Quarter mare and was bred by Eugene Schott of Riomedina, Texas.

LONE STAR. Lone Star was foaled in 1927(?). He was by Uncle Jimmy Gray by Bonnie Joe (TB) and out of Mamie Hogett by Captain Joe. He was bred by Dell Wingate of Devine, Texas.

LONGFELLOW. This dun stallion was foaled in 1928. He was by Dennis Reed (TB) and out of a Kingfisher mare by Moss King by One-Eyed Kingfisher. He was bred and owned by the Waddell brothers of Odessa, Texas.

LONG JIM STUD, see NIG.

LONG JOHN. This chestnut stallion was foaled in 1880. He was by Black Nick by Stewart's Telegraph and out of a short-mare named Sprinter. He was owned and raced by C. Ward of Nebraska.

LONNIE GRAY. This sorrel stallion was foaled in 1913. He was by The Sharper (TB) and out of Mary T by Traveler. He was bred by W. E. Moody of Toyah, Texas.

LOVER. Lover was by RO Horse Number 2 (TB) and out of an RO mare named Kid by Peter McCue. He was bred by the Greene Cattle Company of Cananea, Mexico, and later owned by G. B. Mason of Hereford, Arizona. He was foaled in the 1920's.

LUCKY, see APACHE KID.

LUCKY MOSE, GARDNER'S. Lucky Mose was by Old Mose by Traveler.

LUCKY, OLD. This chestnut stallion was foaled in 1914 and died in 1937. He was sired by McGonigal Horse by McGonigal's Dexter. He was bred by Clay McGonigal of Midland, Texas, and owned by Berry Gardner of Douglas, Arizona. He changed hands many times and ended up in California.

LUCKY, OLD. Old Lucky was foaled in the 1920's and died in 1938. He was a small chestnut stallion bred by Clay McGonigal, or his father, George, of the Midland, Texas, area. He was owned by Will Gardner of Douglas, Arizona. The breeding of all of the McGonigal horses is unknown, but they gained fame as Quarter Horses in Midland County where the family ran the Apple brand.

LUCKY, PANKEY'S. This Lucky was born in the early 1930's and was by Apache Kid by Guinea Pig and out of Fuzzy by Three Finger Jack by Traveler. He was bred by J. M. "Tim" Brister of Lordsburg, New Mexico, and owned by Joe Pankey of Hot Springs, New Mexico.

LUMMIX, see OREGON LUMMIX.

LUPITE, see CLEMENTE GARCIA.

MAC. Mac was by Little Rondo by Lock's Rondo and out of an East Quarter mare. He was bred and owned by Arthur L. East of Sarita, Texas.

MAC (McMURTRY), see WILL STEAD.

MACK. Mack was by the Thoroughbred Delmor and out of Baby King by Possum. He was bred by Joe McKinney of Willcox, Arizona, and later owned by John Kane of Douglas, Arizona.

MACK, see MIKE, OLD.

MACK. This Mack was by Little Joe by Traveler and out of Dow Shely's Belton mare. He was bred and owned by the Shely's of Alfred, Texas.

MACK, R. O.'S. This sorrel stallion was a Quarter Horse out of Texas. He was one of five Quarter Horses bought by the RO's in 1916. He was purchased from a German who lived on the Guadalupe River about 50 miles east of San Antonio.

MAC, LITTLE. Little is known about this stallion except that he was by Rodney by Old D. J. (Dedier) and bred and raced in Louisiana.

MADSTONE. This brown stallion was foaled in 1886 and was by Vanderbilt by the TB Norfleet. His dam was Nina Turner. He was bred and owned by E. L. Liger of California.

MAGICIAN. This black stallion was by Rainy Day by Lone Star and out of Lady S by Jess Parsons who was by Traveler. He was bred by Will Wingate of Devine, Texas, and owned by Jim Crutchfield of San Antonio, Texas.

MAHOGANY. Mahogany was a bay, foaled in 1891, sired by the TB Bulwark and out of May Kennedy. His second dam was by a Printer stallion. He was bred by B. J. Treacy of Lexington, Kentucky.

MAJOR DOMO. This sorrel stallion was foaled in 1895 and was sired by Jim Ned by Pancho and out of a Quarter mare. He was bred by Billy Anson of Christoval, Texas, and owned by Mont Noelke of Mertzon, Texas.

MAJOR GRAY. This brown stallion was by Uncle Jimmy Gray by Bonnie Joe (TB) and out of Mamie Sykes by Sykes' Rondo. His second dam was May Mangum. He was bred and owned by W. A. Wright of Kingsbury, Texas.

MAJOR SPECK. This chestnut stallion was foaled in 1926. He was by Uncle Jimmy Gray by Bonnie Joe (TB) and his dam was Pink Cheek (TB). He was bred by Henry Pfefferling of San Antonio, Texas, who sold him to John K. Kenedy of Sarita, Texas. He was also owned or stood by Eligio Garcia and Ed Rachel. Garcia lived at Edinburg and Rachel at Falfurrias, Texas.

MALTSBERGER DUN. He was by Mano Chueco by the Strait Horse and was bred by Aubra Harr of Millett, Texas. He is also sometimes referred to as Despain Dun.

MAN-A-LIFE. This bay stallion was foaled in 1922. He was by Uncle Jimmy Gray by Bonnie Joe (TB) and out of a Schott mare. He was bred and owned by Eugene J. Schott of Riomedina, Texas.

MAN, LITTLE. Little Man was by Dr. Blue Eyes by A. D. Reed by Peter McCue and out of a mare by Chief by Peter McCue. He was bred by Reed Armstrong of Foss, Oklahoma, and owned and raced by Armstrong's son-in-law, Ben Force of Foss.

MAN, LITTLE. This Little Man was by Oklahoma Star by Dennis Reed (TB) and out of an unregistered race mare. He was bred in Oklahoma and owned by Everett Bowman of Temple, Arizona.

MANO CHUECO. This dun stallion was by the Strait Horse by Yellow Jacket. He was bred and owned near Cotulla, Texas.

MARCO SAN. This brown stallion was foaled in 1924. He was by Uncle Jimmy Gray by Bonnie Joe (TB) and out of

Anna Statia by Peter McCue. He was bred and owned by John Wilkins of San Antonio, Texas.

MARION WILSON. This chestnut stallion was foaled in 1914. He was by Barnsdale (TB) and out of Nellie Mier by Peter McCue. He was bred by George Newton of Del Rio, Texas.

MARSHALL NEY. Marshall Ney was a bay stallion foaled in 1896. He was by Tehachapi (TB), and out of Della Beach. He was bred and owned by J. W. Lillard of Richards, Missouri.

MARTIN HORSE. Martin Horse was by Paul El by Hickory Bill and out of a Little Joe mare. He was bred by a Mr. Martin, address unknown, and later owned by O. W. Cardwell of Junction, Texas.

MASTER GOULD. This bay stallion was foaled in 1916 and died in 1934. He was sired by First Chip (TB), and his dam was Gracie Gould. He was bred by Sam Waring of Eden, Texas, and then bought by J. E. White of Brady, Texas. White sold him to the Remount Service, and he was handled by several Texans, including J. S. Holman of Sonora, Texas.

MAXWELL. This stallion was by Paul Murray by Joe Murray by Anthony and out of a Quarter mare.

MAY BOY. May Boy was by Confidence (Old) by Walnut Bark and out of an Adams mare. He was bred by John Adams of Woodland, California.

McDERMETT. This stallion was sired by Harmon Baker by Peter McCue, and his dam was an Anson Quarter mare. He was bred by Billy Anson of Christoval, Texas, and owned by Charles C. McDermett of Burkett, Coleman County, Texas.

McGONIGAL. Three stallions were named for George McGonigal of Midland, Texas:

141

1. McGONIGAL HORSE, bred by G. McGonigal of Midland, Texas, and owned by his son, Clay, of Midland; he was later sold and taken to Amarillo.
2. McGONIGAL ROAN. A race stallion (perhaps gelded) that once outran 80 Gray. Bred and owned by G. McGonigal.
3. McGONIGAL BAY. This stallion was by Elm (TB), and out of a Mayes Quarter mare. He was bred and owned by Allen Mayes of Big Lake, Texas.

MEADY. Meady was by a Silver Dick Quarter Horse stallion. He was bred and owned in New Mexico.

MEDINA SPORT. Medina Sport was by Uncle Jimmy Gray by Bonnie Joe (TB) and out of Scooter's Sister by Lone Star by Gold Enamel (TB). He was bred by Eugene Schott of Riomedina, Texas. He was also owned by Bob Sutton of Cotulla, John Kenedy of Sarita, and George Clegg of Alice, all in Texas.

MEFFORD. This chestnut stallion was foaled in 1897. He was by Shannon (TB) and out of Miss Mitford by the Thoroughbred Joe Hooker. Second dam was Pearl by Brick. He was bred by the Adamses of Woodland, California.

MENARD, LITTLE. This sorrel stallion was foaled in 1915 and was sired by Barnsdale (TB) and out of Nellie Mier by Peter McCue. He was bred and owned by George Newton of Del Rio, Texas.

MENZO SHURTZ. This brown stallion was foaled in 1906. He was by Peter McCue by Dan Tucker and out of the Thoroughbred Patti Billet. He was bred and owned by Edwin Blakeley of Kilbourne, Illinois.

MERLE LEE. This bay stallion was foaled in 1913. He was by Barney Lucas by Traveler(?) and out of Maggie Gale (TB). He was bred and owned by D. W. "Webb" Christian of Big Spring, Texas.

MERRY GOLD. Merry Gold was by Little Joe by Traveler and his dam was a Big Jim mare by Sykes' Rondo. He was bred by Mr. Schmidt of Comfort, Texas.

MIACHO. This sorrel stallion was foaled in 1930 and was by Yellow Wolf by Old Joe Bailey by Eureka and his dam was a dun Waggoner mare. He was bred by A. T. Hayes of Greer, New Mexico, and later owned by Ray Barnes of Milrose, New Mexico.

MICKEY. This brown stallion was by Guinea Pig by Possum, and his dam is unknown. He was owned by Whitey Montgomery and Port Parker of Rimrock, Arizona.

MIDNIGHT. By Senator by Leadville (TB). He was a Colorado horse.

MIDNIGHT. This Midnight was by Uncle Jimmy Gray by Bonnie Joe (TB), and his dam was by Sykes' Rondo. He was bred by Clyde Thompson of Moore, Texas.

MIDNIGHT. Midnight was a gray stallion, foaled in 1916, who died in 1936. He was by Badger by Peter McCue and out of Nellie Trammell by Ace by Peter McCue. He was bred by Jess Cooper of Roosevelt, Oklahoma, and owned by: Hal Cooper, Roosevelt, Oklahoma; W. T. Waggoner of Fort Worth, Texas; J. A. Ranch, Palo Duro, Texas; and Aubra Bowers of Allison, Texas.

MIDNIGHT II. This Midnight was a bay foaled in 1933 by Old Midnight by Badger by Peter McCue and out of a JA mare. Bred and owned by the J. A. Ranch of Palo Duro, Texas.

MIDNIGHT, YOUNG. This bay stallion was sired by Midnight by Badger by Peter McCue and out of Trixie by Midnight by Badger by Peter McCue. His second dam was a mare by Norfleet by Brettenham (TB). He was bred by the

J. A. Ranch of Palo Duro, Texas, and owned by Aubra Bowers of Allison, Texas.

MIKE. This stallion was by Frank Dutton's Dun by Yellow Jacket and out of a Springer mare. He was bred by Ed Springer of the CS Cattle Company of Cimarron, New Mexico, and later owned by the Bell Ranch.

MIKE. This stallion was born about 1912. He was by Silvertail by Jim Ned by Pancho. His dam was Polly Murphy. He was a Colorado horse.

MIKE BEETCH. This dun stallion was foaled in 1921 and lived until 1934. He was by Beetch's Yellow Jacket by Yellow Jacket by Little Rondo and his dam was sired by Yellow Wolf by Old Joe Bailey. He was bred by Mike Beetch of Lawton, Oklahoma, and owned by Tom Burnett of Fort Worth, Texas. Jim Minnick had a colt by this horse that he called Mike Beetch also; this one was stolen in 1939, so there are no known colts after 1940.

MIKE, LITTLE, see MISSOURI MIKE.

MIKE, OLD, see MISSOURI MIKE.

MIKE, OLD (MACK). Old Mike was by Chickasha Bob, who was by Pid Hart or Rocky Mountain Tom and out of a Starke Quarter mare. He was bred by Barney Starke of Tulia, Texas, and owned by Filiberto Gallegos of Gallegos, New Mexico. He was sometimes called Mack.

MIKE SULLIVAN. Mike Sullivan was foaled in 1867, and he was sired by Sweet Owen by Gray Eagle and out of Camden. He lived in both Ohio and Kentucky.

MILLER BOY. This stallion was by Hobart and his dam was Wylie by Texas Chief. He was bred by Will Wylie of Palo Duro, Texas, and later owned by Milt Jasper of Silverton, Texas.

MILLINETTE. This sorrel stallion was foaled in 1887 and was by Joe Hooker (TB) and out of Chestnut Bell by Norfolk. He was bred by Theodore Winter of Woodland, California, and owned by George Hearst of San Simeon, California. Winters also had farms in Sacramento and in Nevada.

MINCO JIMMIE. This brown stallion was foaled in 1909. He was by Bonnie Joe (TB) and out of Bettie Campbell by Old Bob Peters. He was bred and owned by Charles B. Campbell of Minco, Oklahoma. He was a full brother of Uncle Jimmy Gray.

MINERAL, OLD. Sire and dam of this Quarter stallion are unknown today. He was owned and perhaps bred by the famous short-horse man, Berry Ketchum of Sheffield, Texas.

MISSOURI MIKE. Missouri Mike was a chestnut stallion foaled in 1876 and living until about 1900. He was by Printer by Cold Deck, and his dam was by Alsup's Brimmer. He was bred near Carthage, Missouri, near the place where Barney Owens was foaled. He was owned by Bill Stockton of Lockwood, Missouri, and run by Jack Weir of Weir City, Kansas. He also was referred to as Little Mike and as Old Mike.

MISSOURI RONDO (RONDO). This sorrel stallion was foaled in 1880 and was by Missouri Mike by Printer by Cold Deck. He was bred near Springfield, Missouri, and owned by Alex Chote of Lockwood, Missouri, and John Stockton of Trinidad, Colorado. He was often called just Rondo.

MISSOURI RONDO. This stallion was foaled around 1884 and was by Missouri Mike and out of an Alsup mare of Brimmer breeding.

MR. REX. This stallion was a bay foaled in 1926, and he was by Rex Beach by Conjuror (TB) and out of Edee Ree by Peter McCue. His second dam was Nona P. He was bred and owned by John Dial of Goliad, Texas. Edee Ree was a full sister of Harmon Baker. John Wilkins brought Nona P, her yearling Buck Thomas, and Peter McCue to San Antonio, Texas, all at the same time in 1907.

MITCH. This sorrel stallion was by Zurick by Old Mike and out of a Billy Smoot mare. He was bred by T. E. and Albert Mitchell of Albert, New Mexico, and later owned by Tom Caviness of Seligman, Arizona.

MODEL, THE, see TOM HARDING.

MOGGY. Moggy was a gray stallion bred by Peter Stewart of Greensville County, Virginia. He was 15 hands-1 inch high and sired by *Janus and out of a *Janus mare. He was sold to J. H. Dancey. His probable dates were 1767 to 1779. He is found in both the *ASB* and in Edgar.

MONDAY. A bay stallion foaled in 1864. He was by Colton and out of Mollie Jackson. He died in California in 1884, aged 20 years.

MONEYBACK. Moneyback was a bay stallion foaled in 1926 by Recluse (TB) and out of Christine C by Palm Reader (TB). His second dam was Anne T by Traveler and his third dam, Annie May. He was bred and owned by W. C. Smith of Ocheleta, Oklahoma.

MONKEY. Monkey was by Mr. Doc (TB) and out of Champs Girl. He was owned by Harry J. Saxon of Willcox, Arizona.

MONMOUTH. The sire and dam of this stallion, whose fame rests mostly on a race he had with Steel Dust, is unknown. He was bred in Kentucky. He could run and he was brought to Texas by Harrison Stiff of McKinney, Texas.

MONT BAKER. The sire and dam of this stallion are unknown, as is the breeder. He was influential in the production of short-horses in the Northwest. He was in Oregon, and then taken to Washington by a Mr. Gillespy.

146

MONTE CARLO. This palomino stallion was foaled in 1935. He was by Plaudit and out of a Phillips mare. He was bred by Waite Phillips of Cimarron, New Mexico.

MONTE CROSS. Monte Cross was by Baby King by Possum by Traveler and out of Loretta, a Kennedy Quarter mare. He was bred by J. J. Kennedy of Bonita, Arizona.

MONT MEGELLON. This stallion was foaled about 1922. He was by Gold Coin by The Senator by Leadville (TB). He was bred and owned by Axel E. Peterson of Elbert, Colorado.

MONTY. Monty was by Red Bird by Buck Thomas and out of Dainty Dancer by Young Fred by Old Nick. He was bred by Earl Moye of Arvada, Wyoming.

MONTY. This Monty was by San Antonio Sorrel by Hickory Bill and his dam was by Major Domo by Jim Ned. He was bred by Mont B. Noelke of Mertzon, Texas, and later owned by Howard Cargile of San Antonio, Texas. He was sometimes called Rocky.

MOON. Moon was a sorrel stallion foaled in 1923. He was by Concho Colonel by Jim Ned and out of Christabel by Old Joe by Harmon Baker. He was bred by Dan Casement of Manhattan, Kansas, and owned by Mr. Neumeyer of Monte Vista, Colorado, and Henry J. Wiescamp of Alamosa, Colorado.

MOON MULLENS. This stallion was a sorrel foaled in 1926. He was by Everett (TB) and out of Kiddo by Johnnie Wilkes by Peter McCue. He was bred by Matt Renfro of Sonora, Texas.

MOORE. Moore was a bay stallion foaled in 1918. He was by Dominus Arvi (TB), and out of Juanita Armstrong by Peter McCue. He was registered as a Thoroughbred. He was bred by John J. Armstrong in California. He was a half brother to Big Boy and to Crippled Dick.

MORELAND. Moreland was by Steel Dust and bred in Texas. About all that is known about this stallion is that he sired Trammell and Newman's Black George.

MORISSEY. Morissey was a sorrel foaled in 1889 by Fonso (TB) and out of May Kennedy by Faustus (TB). His second dam was by Printer by Gray Eagle. He was bred by B. J. Treacy of Lexington, Kentucky.

MOSCO. This chestnut stallion was by Master Gould by First Chip (TB) and out of a Quarter mare. He was bred by "Jap" Holman of Sonora, Texas, and owned by Dee Harrison of Del Rio, Texas.

MOSE. Mose was by Ashton (TB) and out of a Roberds' Quarter mare. He was bred by Coke Roberds of Hayden, Colorado.

MOSE. Mose was a brown stallion foaled in 1914 by Old Mose by Traveler and out of Squaw by Possum by Traveler. He was owned by Claude Gardner of Willcox, Arizona. He was sometimes called Little Mose, Lucky Mose, and My Mose.

MOSE BRIMMER. This stallion was foaled about 1858. He was by Alsup's Brimmer by a Brimmer stallion and out of an Alsup mare. He was bred and owned by the Alsup brothers in Tennessee and taken by them to Bald Knob, Douglas County, Missouri. This is the Old Mose Brimmer that sired Emily Walker.

MOSE, OLD. This Old Mose was foaled in 1904. He was sired by Traveler.

MOSES. Moses was a brown stallion foaled in 1929 by Edmon (TB) and his dam was by Billy Mason. He was bred by Mark Hersig of Cheyenne, Wyoming.

MOSS KING. Moss King was a sorrel stallion by Big King by One-Eyed Kingfisher and out of a Barker mare. He was bred by Bob Barker of Manchaca, Travis County, Texas. He was also known as Moss' Kingfisher, Bill Moss' Kingfisher, and the Moss Horse. He was owned for a time by Bill Moss of Marble Falls, Texas.

MOUNTS. A prominent stallion in the 1860's. He was by Steel Dust by Harry Bluff and was owned around Bosque and Eastland counties in Texas. He was the sire of Bay Puss, Old Lit, Methodist Bull, and Judy. He is sometimes referred to as Mount's Steel Dust.

MUCKLE JOHN. Muckle John was a sorrel stallion foaled in 1818. He was by Sir Archy (TB) and out of Bellona by Belle Air. He is listed in Wallace's *Stud Book*.

MUCKLE JOHN. Muckle John was a sorrel foaled in 1827. He was owned by Colonel Richardson of South Carolina in 1831. He was sired by Muckle John and his dam was by High Flyer. He is listed in Bruce's *American Stud Book*.

MUD LARK. Mud Lark was foaled in 1928 and was by Setback (TB) and out of Fay Larkin by Barney Lucas by Traveler. He was bred by H. P. Saunders of Roswell, New Mexico. Fay Larkin was bred by "Webb" Christian of Big Spring, Texas.

MUGGINS. Muggins was a bay stallion by Traveler and out of a Gardner mare. He was bred by John E. Gardner of San Angelo, Texas, and owned by Stanley Turner of Water Valley, Texas.

MURDOCK. Murdock was by Blue Eyes by Possum by Traveler and out of a Murdock mare. He was bred by Dave Murdock of Camp Verde, Arizona, and owned by Doc Pardee of Phoenix, Arizona.

MUSHMOUTH. Mushmouth was a sorrel stallion foaled in 1926. He was by Everett (TB) and out of Blackbird by Johnnie Wilkes by Peter McCue. He was bred by J. E. Renfro of Sonora, Texas.

MUSKOGEE STAR. This stallion was by Oklahoma Star and out of a John Dawson mare. He was owned and bred by John Dawson of Talala, Oklahoma.

MUSKRAT. This dun stallion was foaled in 1928 and was by Dennis Reed (TB) and out of Juicy Fruit. He was bred by the Waddell brothers of Odessa, Texas.

MUSTARD. This sorrel stallion was foaled in 1929. He was by Fayette C (TB) and out of a range mare. He was owned by Spence Jowell of Midland, Texas.

MUY PRONTO. This stallion was a sorrel foaled in 1926 by Esquire (TB) and out of Touch Me Not by Traveler. He was bred by Monty Corder of Sanderson, Texas.

N

NABOB. Nabob was a bay stallion foaled in 1930. He was by *Brave Bob (TB) and out of Agate by Joe T. He was bred and owned by Harry Clark of Boise City, Oklahoma.

NAVAJO. Navajo was by Jack Dempsey by Big Boy and out of Cotton Tail by a Remount stallion. He was owned by Albert Harrington of Correo, New Mexico.

NAVARRO. Navarro was a chestnut horse foaled in 1870. He was by Peacock by Flying Dutchman and out of Adelaide by Pudhomme (TB). He was bred by Marion Martin of Corsicana, Texas.

NEAFUS HORSE, see CHICKASHA BOB, YOUNG.

NECKTIE. This stallion was by Fuzzy by Three Finger Jack by Traveler and out of a Quarter mare. He was bred and owned in Arizona.

NED HARPER. Ned Harper was big and powerful, a dappled dun who weighed 1,375 pounds. He was sired by Tom Campbell by Old Bob Peters by Pony Pete, and his dam was School Girl. His breeder was C. B. Campbell.

NED OAKS. This stallion was by Peter McCue by Dan Tucker. He was bred in Oklahoma and owned by Harry Clark of Boise City, Oklahoma.

NED WILSON. Ned Wilson was a bay stallion foaled in 1924. He was by Red Seal by Sealskin by Harmon Baker and out of Jet Gel by Jetsam (TB). He was bred by Monty Corder of Sanderson, Texas.

NEDWOOD. Nedwood was by Possum by Traveler and bred in Arizona. He was owned by J. B. Cook of Willcox, Arizona.

NEEL GRAY. This gray stallion was foaled in 1925. He was by the imported Thoroughbred Bluecoat and out of a Steel Dust mare brought from New Mexico for racing purposes. He was owned by Henry Leonard of Colorado Springs, Colorado.

NELSON. Nelson was a bay stallion foaled in 1911. He was by Thicket (TB) and out of Lady McCue by Peter McCue. He was bred by J. M. Leavitt of San Jose, Illinois.

NICK, HUBBARD'S. This chestnut stallion was by Yellow Stone by Dundee (TB) and out of a Quarter mare sired by Loveland. Owned by R. Harry Hubbard of Oak Creek, Colorado.

NICK, LITTLE. Little Nick was by Nick by Shiek by Peter McCue and out of a mare by Jiggs by Fred Litze. He was bred by the CS Ranch of Cimarron, New Mexico, and owned by Henry J. Wiescamp of Alamosa, Colorado. Occasionally he is referred to as Nick Jr.

NICK, OLD. Old Nick was by Old Fred by Black Ball by Missouri Rondo and out of Silvertail by Jim Ned. He was bred by Si Dawson of Hayden, Colorado. His owners were Laughlin Brothers of Yampa, Colorado, and Henry Martin and Marshall Peavy, both of Steamboat Springs, Colorado.

NICK S. Nick S was a palomino stallion foaled in 1926 and he was sired by Shiek by Peter McCue and out of Sylvia by Bob H by Old Fred by Black Ball. He was bred by Marshall Peavy of Steamboat Springs, Colorado, and later owned by Warren Shoemaker of Watrous, New Mexico.

NIG (LONG JIM STUD). The pedigree and foaling date are unknown for this Nig. He was bred and owned in Washington. He was a great race horse from 220 to 440 yards. He was also known as the Long Jim Stud, so Long Jim may have been his sire.

NIGGER. There were three Niggers:
1. NIGGER by Buck Walton, owned by Nasworthy of San Angelo, Texas.
2. NIGGER by Dodger by Harmon Baker owned by Charles Scott of Sheffield, Texas.
3. NIGGER by Young Fred by Old Nick, bred by Earl Moye of Arvada, Wyoming.

NIGGER BABY. Nigger Baby was a black stallion foaled in 1934. He was by Dennis Reed (TB) and out of Napanee II by Moss King. He was bred by the Waddell brothers of Odessa, Texas.

NIGGER BOY. Nigger Boy was by Hamp by Recluse (TB). He was owned and bred in Oklahoma.

NO GOOD. No Good was by Barney Owens by Cold Deck and out of a Trammell mare. He was bred by Thomas Trammell of Sweetwater, Texas. He was later owned by Jim Kennedy and Mark DuBois, both of Bonita, Arizona, and by R. A. Pride of Willcox, Arizona. No Good was not by Red Cloud as sometimes reported.

NONPAREIL. This stallion was a beautiful sorrel foaled in 1823. He was by Edmundston's C.A.Q.R.H. Little Janus and out of a mare by Ball's Florizel. He was bred by Fayette Allan of Halifax County, Virginia. He was 15 hands high and, Edgar added, "as pretty as need be." He is found in the *ASB*.

NOOBLIS. This brown stallion was foaled in 1930. He was sired by *Batchlor's Bliss (TB) and out of Noo by Barney Lucas by Traveler. He was bred by H. P. Saunders of Roswell, New Mexico.

NO REMARKS. No Remarks was a sorrel colt foaled in 1887. He was by Aliunde (TB) and out of Miss Hackney by Engraver (TB). His second dam was a Quarter mare. He was bred and owned by H. A. Trowbridge of Wellington, Kansas.

NORFLEET. Norfleet was a sorrel stallion foaled in 1924 by *Brettenham (TB) and out of Five Dollars by Jim Trammell by Barney Owens. He was bred by J. Frank Norfleet of Hale Center, Texas, and owned by W. I. Driggers of Santa Rosa, New Mexico, Bill Thompson of Santa Rosa, New Mexico, and by J. H. Minnick of Crowell, Texas.

NORFLEET, see FRANK NORFLEET.

NORTHINGTON HORSE. This stallion was by Little Joe by Traveler and out of a brown Clegg mare that was also by Little Joe. The second dam was Caroline by Hickory Bill by Peter McCue. He was bred by George Clegg of Alice, Texas, and owned by Mentor Northington of Egypt, Texas.

NUBBIN. This Nubbin was a brown stallion foaled in 1909 by Conjuror (TB) and out of Dorothy Duncan by Thrine (TB). He was bred and owned by O. G. Parke of Kyle, Texas.

NUBBIN. Nubbin was foaled in 1927. He was by Old Joe Bailey by Eureka. He was from the Breckenridge, Texas, area.

O

OAKFORD. Oakford, a bay stallion foaled in 1907, was by Peter McCue by Dan Tucker and out of Patti Tennyson (TB). He was bred and owned by B. C. Watkins of Oakford, Illinois.

OBE JENNINGS. This bay stallion, who lived in the last half of the nineteenth century, was by Patete's Ariel by Simpson's Ariel and out of Betsy Baker by Wilden's La Blanch. He was bred and owned in Oregon.

O'CONNELL. O'Connell was a chestnut stallion foaled in 1890. He was sired by Harry O'Fallon (TB) and out of May Kennedy by Faustus (TB). His second dam was Printer by Gray Eagle. He was bred and owned by B. J. Treacy of Lexington, Kentucky.

ODD FELLOW. This stallion was a chestnut and he was foaled in 1873. He was sired by Bay Printer by Sweet Owen and out of Wise Mare (Bellona) by Franchi. He was bred by John M. Mathewson of Lowell, Michigan.

ODDFELLOW II. This stallion was a bay foaled in 1930 and by the Thoroughbred Captain Costigan. His dam was Nellie Reed by Dennis Reed (TB). His second dam was Pocahontas by Moss King. He was bred by the Waddell brothers of Odessa, Texas.

O JIMMY. O Jimmy was a sorrel foaled in 1923 by Uncle Jimmy Gray by Bonnie Joe (TB), and he was out of a Schott mare by Yellow Jacket by Little Rondo. He was bred by Eugene J. Schott of Riomedina, Texas.

OKEMA. Okema was registered as a (TB). He was by Reform and out of Maggie. He was owned by H. A. Trowbridge of Wellington, Kansas, and was foaled about 1880.

OKLAHOMA SHY. This stallion was sired by A. D. Reed by Peter McCue and his dam was Old Allie by Peter McCue. He was bred by Frank A. Malek of Rosenburg, Texas, and later owned by Curtis Sears of Logan, New Mexico. He was sometimes referred to as Kid McCue and as Billy the Kid.

OLE BULL. Ole Bull's breeding and breeder are unknown. In the appendix of the *ASB* (Vol. VII, 1277), he is simply called a Quarter Horse.

OLG WAG. Olg Wag was a dun stallion foaled in about 1922. He was by Yellow Jacket by Little Rondo and out of a Waggoner mare. He was bred by W. T. Waggoner of Fort Worth and owned by G. R. and J. E. White of Brady, Texas.

ONE DIME. One Dime was a bay stallion foaled in 1888. He was by Afton (TB) and out of Bertha by Morris (TB). His second dam was Fanchette by Bay Printer. He was bred by John M. Mathewson of Lowell, Michigan. His best-known get was John Griffin II foaled in 1902.

ONE-EYE. This C.A.Q.R.H. was a blood bay sired by *Janus and his dam was also by imported Janus. He was probably bred by Will Williams Sr. of Martin County, North Carolina, sometime prior to 1780. Edgar says he was a celebrated Quarter Racer and got capital racing stock for short distances. He accidentally lost an eye as a colt. He is listed in both the *ASB* and in Edgar.

ONE-EYED BILLY. This brown stallion was foaled in 1919. He was by Harmon Baker by Peter McCue and his dam was by Sam Jones by Black Nick. His second dam was by Jim Ned by Pancho. He was bred by Billy Anson of Christoval, Texas, and owned by Dick Burrus of Mountain Home, Texas, and John R. Scott of Mertzon, Texas. He was sometimes known as the Burris Horse or Burris' Billy Anson.

ONE-EYED KINGFISHER. One-Eyed Kingfisher was a black stallion foaled in 1885 and died in 1905. He was by

Old Kingfisher by Rebel and his dam was a Barker mare by Steel Dust. He was bred by Leeman Barker of Boerne, Texas, and owned by Jeff and John Brazier of Willow City, Gillespie County, Texas.

ONE-EYED KINGFISHER. This Kingfisher was by Old Kingfisher by Rebel by Steel Dust. His dam was Mollie by Steel Dust, a mare bred by C. R. Haley of Sweetwater. He was bred by Leeman Barker of Boerne, Texas, and was raced by Jeff and John Brazier. His approximate dates are 1885–1905. See Old Kingfisher.

Charles Duffy of Austin, Texas, told Helen Michaelis that One-Eyed Kingfisher was owned by Ruff Barker of Williamson County, Texas, and that Barker's wife poisoned the stallion so they would not run him any more. Some said he was never beaten and that they bet everything and anything they owned on every one of his races.

ONWARD. Onward was by The Senator by Leadville (TB). He was owned by Joe Maycock of Gillette, Wyoming.

OPERATOR. Operator was a bay stallion foaled in 1917. He was sired by First Chip (TB) and out of Gracie Gould. He was bred and owned by Sam Waring of Eden, Texas.

ORDEON. Ordeon was by Texas Chief by Traveler and his dam was a MacMurray Quarter mare by Doc Oldham. He was bred by B. MacMurray of Hebbronville, Texas, and owned by Anastacio Saenz of Rios, Texas.

OREGON CHARLIE. Oregon Charlie was probably sired by Old Dan, who was from Missouri and carried Printer and Whip blood. Oregon Charlie's exact dates are also unknown, but he lived between 1850 and 1880. His blood, of unquestioned Quarter Horse origin, led the Pacific Coast (especially Oregon and California) in producing the fastest short-horses during the last quarter of the nineteenth century. He was bred in Oregon and was sometimes referred to as Old Charlie and as Jenkin's Charlie. He was owned in his later years by John W. Adams of Woodland, California, a prominent short-horse breeder and racer between 1870 and 1890.

OREGON DAN, see DAN, OLD.

OREGON ECLIPSE. This chestnut stallion was foaled in 1887 and was by Joe Hooker and out of Lula Riggs by Humboldt. His second dam was by Crooked River Dan. He was bred and raised by A. James Foster of Paisley, Oregon.

OREGON LUMMIX. This stallion, one of the foundation Quarter Horses of the Pacific Coast area, was by Simtuck by Oregon Dick. His dam is unknown, as is his breeder and owner.

ORPHAN BOY. This stallion was foaled in California in 1903. He was by Wernberg (TB) and his dam was Plowmare. He was owned by Cuff Burrell of Hanford, California. He was probably bred by Lee Blasingame of Fresno, California.

ORPHAN'S PRIDE. Orphan's Pride was foaled in 1921. He was by Orphan Boy by Wernberg (TB) and out of Moana by Wernberg (TB); his second dam was Marie by Old Confidence by Walnut Bark. He was bred by Byron W. Jennings of Visalia, California, and owned by Roy Fulgham of Squaw Valley.

P

PABLO. Pablo was a sorrel stallion foaled in 1932. He was by Pablo (TB) and out of Maud by Little Billy. He was bred by A. H. Bodie of Pontotoc, Texas.

PACHECO. This stallion was by Silver King by Possum by Traveler and out of Diamond Bell by Marcus II. He was bred and owned by Louie Pacheco of Santa Maria, California.

PACIFIC. Pacific was by Plaudit by King Plaudit (TB) and out of Stella by Booger Red by Rancocas (TB). His second dam was Nancy by The Senator. He was bred by Ernest Myers of Hoehne, Colorado, and owned by Henry Wiescamp of Alamosa, Colorado.

PADDY. Paddy was foaled in the 1890's. He was by Berry's Cold Deck by Old Cold Deck and out of a Maxwell Quarter mare. He was owned by Lock Alsup of Bald Knob, Missouri. He was bred by N. B. Maxwell of Wendell, Tennessee.

PADDY WHACK (LITTLE TWIGG). This F.A.Q.R.H. stallion was foaled in 1778. He was by either *Jolly Roger, as Edgar says, or, as Fairfax Harrison rather logically contends, by *Janus. He was owned by John Goode Sr. of Mecklenburg County, Virginia, and later by Henry Deloney of the same county. His races with Twigg attracted wide interest in the newly independent United States. He is listed both in the *ASB* and by Edgar.

PADRIAC, see PAT.

PALMISTRY. Palmistry was a brown stallion foaled in 1907 by Palm Reader (TB) and out of Jaquette by Traveler. He was bred by "Webb" Christian of Big Spring, Texas.

PAL-O-MINE. This chestnut stallion was foaled in 1923, and he was by Rainy Day by Lone Star by Gold Enamel (TB) and out of a mare by Little Tom by Old Ben. He was bred and owned by Eugene Schott of Riomedina, Texas.

PAL-O-MINE. This sorrel stallion was foaled in 1927 and sired by Billy Sunday by Horace H and out of Dora du Mar by Little Joe. He was bred by Ott Adams of Alfred, Texas. He was a full brother to Rialto.

PANAMA. Panama was a sorrel foaled in 1891. He was by Glen Elm (TB) and out of Queen by Lynx (TB). He was bred by H. Kirkendall of Helena, Montana.

PANCHO. This Pancho was by Peter McCue by Dan Tucker. His breeder and owner are unknown.

PANCHO. This Pancho was by Peace Buddy (TB) and out of Miss Sleepy by Star Shoot. His dam was a Zurick mare. He was bred by John W. Zurick of Stead, New Mexico, and owned by Bill Thompson of Santa Rosa, New Mexico.

PANCHO. Pancho was a brown stallion who was foaled in 1886 and died in 1892. He was by Old Billy by Shiloh and out of Paisana by Brown Dick by Berkshire. He was bred by William Fleming of Belmont, Texas, and owned by Alex Gardner of San Angelo, Texas.

PANCHO, LITTLE. Little Pancho was by Pancho Villa by Little Joe by Traveler and out of a Saenz mare. He was owned by "Tacho" Saenz of Alice, Texas.

PANCHO VILLA. Pancho Villa was by Little Joe by Traveler and out of Jeanette by Billy by Big Jim. His second dam was by Sykes' Rondo. He was bred by Ott Adams of Alfred, Texas, and owned by Fred C. Binkley of Cotulla, Texas. He is sometimes referred to as the Binkley Horse.

PAN TOY. Pan Toy was a palomino stallion foaled in 1934 by High Fruit (TB) and out of a McIntyre Quarter mare. He was bred by Fowler McIntyre of Sterling City, Texas, and owned by Roy C. Davis, also of Sterling City, and by Richard Eurith of Livingston, Montana.

PARKER DUN. This stallion was by W. A. by Major Domo by Jim Ned and out of a Vail mare of TB breeding. He was owned by W. D. Parker of Sonoita, Arizona.

PAT. This Pat was a bay foaled in 1874(?). He was by Steel Dust by Harry Bluff and out of a Missouri mare. He was bred by Bill Rayburn of Hood County, Texas, and owned by Jim Brown of Giddings, Texas.

PAT (PADRIAC). Pat was a sorrel foaled in 1934. He was by Mustard Seed (TB) and out of Joanne by Old Joe by Harmon Baker. His second dam was a Springer mare. He was bred by the CS Ranch at Cimarron, New Mexico, and owned by Glaser Halleck of Nevada. He is also known as Padriac.

PAT TUCKER. This bay stallion was foaled in1891. He was by Dan Tucker by Barney Owens and out of Bird by Jack Traveler by Steel Dust. His second dam was Kitty Clyde. He was bred by Sam Watkins of Petersburg, Illinois. He was a good race horse and was gelded in 1896.

PAUL MURRAY. This stallion was foaled in 1906 and was by Joe Murray by Anthony by Old Billy. His dam was a Fleming Quarter mare. He was bred by Paul Murray of Pandora, Texas, and later owned by Fred Matthies of Seguin, Texas.

PAWHUSKA. This stallion was bay, and he was foaled in 1893. He was by Okema (TB) and out of Lady Lawrence by Wisconsin Harry. He was bred by S. E. Lawrence of Maple City, Kansas.

PAWHUSKA, YOUNG. Young Pawhuska was by Pawhuska by Okema (TB) and out of a running mare named Kamack. He was bred by Lawrence Smith of Smithtown, New York, and owned by Dan D. Casement of Manhattan, Kansas.

PEACOCK. Peacock was foaled in 1860. He was by Flying Dutchman by Gray Eagle and out of a Martin mare. He was bred and owned by Marion Martin of Corsicana, Texas.

PEACOCK, BRINKLEY'S. This pale sorrel stallion was foaled in 1760 and died at the age of 26. He was by *Janus and out of a mare imported from Spain. He was bred by Joseph John Alston of Halifax County, North Carolina, and later sold to a Mr. Brinkley of the same county. Edgar says, "He was one of the swiftest quarter of a mile racers in America of his day, and won upwards of $40,000." He is listed in both the *ASB* and in Edgar. Edgar says he was a F.A.Q.R.H.

PEARLY BELLS. This black stallion was foaled in 1930. He was sired by Election (TB) and out of Pearly C by The Senator by Leadville (TB). He was bred and owned by C. A. Allison of Weston, Wyoming, and was a full brother of Ben D and Pickarilla II.

PECOS. Pecos was a sorrel stallion by Little Texas Chief by Texas Chief by Traveler.

PECOS JR. Pecos Jr. was by Pecos by Little Texas Chief, and he was owned by Claude Cowan of Mabelle, Texas.

PECOS PETE. Pecos Pete was a bay stallion foaled in 1928. He was by Prepare Away (TB) and out of June by Captain Daugherty. He was bred and owned by Matt Renfro of Fort Sumner, New Mexico.

PEDRO RICO. Pedro Rico was a sorrel foaled in 1923. He was by Red Seal by Sealskin by Harmon Baker and out of Willie Grow by Traveler's Bay. He was bred by Monty Corder of Sanderson, Texas.

PEEKABOO, YOUNG. Young Peekaboo was by Bob H by Old Fred by Black Ball and out of Snip by Si Ding by Ding Bob. He was bred and owned by Leonard Horn of Wolcott, Colorado.

PEE WEE. This bay stallion was foaled in 1926. He was by Everett (TB) and out of Afton by Harmon Baker. He was bred by Matt Renfro of Sonora, Texas.

PENNY, LITTLE. Little Penny was a chestnut foaled in 1913. He was by Barnsdale (TB) and out of Bille of Kilborn by Peter McCue. He was bred by George Newton of Del Rio, Texas.

PETE KING. This stallion was a bay, and he was foaled in 1929. He was by Captain Costigan (TB) and out of Myrtle. He was bred by the Waddell brothers of Odessa, Texas.

PETE, LITTLE. Little Pete was foaled in 1878. He was by Pony Pete by Printer by Cold Deck and out of a mare by Old Man. He was bred by John Day of Asawata, Kansas. See Little Steve.

PETER BROWN. This stallion was a bay foaled in 1920. He was sired by Star McGee (TB) and out of Bessie Keough by Peter McCue. He was bred and owned by Joseph Brown of Petersburg, Illinois.

PETER McCUE. Peter McCue was a bay stallion who was foaled in 1895 and died in 1923. He was by Dan Tucker by Barney Owens by Cold Deck and out of Nora M by Voltigeur (TB). His second dam was the race mare Kitty Clyde. He was bred by Sam Watkins of Petersburg, Illinois. He was owned by John Wilkins of San Antonio, Texas; Milo Burlingame of Cheyenne, Oklahoma; Si Dawson of Hayden, Colorado; and Coke Roberds of Hayden, Colorado. When young, he was raced successfully and as a stud proved to be one of the greatest of sires for the Quarter Horse.

PETER McCUE, others. Other than the original, there were at least four fairly well-known sons of Peter McCue who were also called Peter McCue: (1) Boyer's in Colorado, (2) Thompson's in New Mexico, (3) Trammell's in Texas, and (4) Coke Roberds' in Colorado. There was another one sired by Peter's son Chief owned by George Parr in Texas, and still another called Peter McCue II, who had little if any blood of Peter McCue. Peter McCue II was by *King Zeek (TB) and out of a granddaughter of Little Joe. He was bred by W. S. Farish of Berclair, Texas.

PETER PAN. This stallion was a sorrel foaled in 1924. He was by Ben Hur by Rainy Day by Lone Star and out of

Bishop's mare by Little Ace by Ace of Hearts. He was bred by Jap Bishop of Marfa, Texas.

PETERS CUE. Peters Cue was a roan foaled in 1904. He was by Peter McCue by Dan Tucker and out of Patti Tennyson (TB). He was bred by Sam Watkins of Petersburg, Illinois.

PETERSON HORSE, see GLORY.

PETER TIJERINA. This Peter was by Cotton Eyed Joe by Peter McCue and out of a Graves Peeler short-mare. He was raced by his breeder, Graves Peeler, and later owned by the Franklin brothers of Tilden, Texas.

PHIL KING. Phil King was a brown stallion foaled in 1902. He was by the imported Thoroughbred Gallantry, and his dam was Lemonade by Anthony by Old Billy. He was bred by Wade McLemore of Belmont, Texas.

PHOENIX. Edgar says that Phoenix was a Famous American Quarter Running Horse, but gives no foaling date. He was undoubtedly foaled a little before 1783. He was bred by Col. Lewis Burwell of Mecklenburg County, Virginia. He was sired by *Shadow and out of a *Jolly Roger mare. He is also listed in the *ASB*.

PICKANINNY. Pickaninny was a bay stallion foaled in 1923. He was by Red Seal by Sealskin by Harmon Baker and out of Bonnie by Billy Tom. He was bred by Monty Corder of Sanderson, Texas.

PICKARILLA II. This stallion was a sorrel foaled in 1927. He was by Election (TB) and out of Pearly C II. His second dam was Pearly C by The Senator. He was bred and owned by C. A. Allison of Weston, Wyoming.

PICK POCKET. This stallion was by Captain Sykes by Sykes' Rondo by McCoy Billy and out of Shoo Fly. He was owned by West Riggs of Goliad County, Texas.

PID HART. Pid Hart was a chestnut stallion foaled in 1887(?). He was sired by Shelby by Tom Driver by Steel Dust, and he was out of Jenny Capps by Dash by Little Jeff Davis by Shiloh. His second dam was Bay Puss by Mounts by Steel Dust. He was bred by E. Shelby Stanfield of Thorp Spring, Texas, and owned by John C. Platt of Sipe Springs, Texas, and by C. B. Campbell of Minco, Oklahoma. He was one of the most noted race horses of his day. Rocky Mountain Tom, foaled in 1890, was Pid Hart's first foal. W. H. Cormack, who raced him in 1892, said he had the "biggest jaws I ever saw."

PI FULLER HORSE, see LITTLE FORT WORTH.

PINE KNOT. Pine Knot was a brown stallion foaled in 1871. He was by Whalebone by Old Billy by Shiloh and out of Paisana by Brown Dick by Berkshire. His second dam was Belton Queen by Guinea Boar. He was bred by Billy Fleming of Belmont, Texas. Later, he was taken into Mexico.

PINK REED. Pink Reed was by Anthony by Old Billy by Shiloh and out of Sweet Lip by Old Billy. His second dam was Paisana by Brown Dick by Berkshire. He was bred by Billy Fleming of Belmont, Texas. He was taken into Mississippi by Jack Hardy.

PLAY BOY. Play Boy was by Old Red Bird by Buck Thomas. He was owned by Harry Keeline of Gillette, Wyoming.

PLEAS WALTERS. This brown stallion was by John Crowder by Old Billy by Shiloh and his dam's name was Dutch. He was bred by Pleasant Walters of Oakville, Texas, and was owned by Dow and Will Shely of Alfred, Texas. He was a full brother of Ben and Hondo. Dutch was bred by Joe Mangum of Nixon, Texas, but her pedigree is unknown.

POLE CAT. Pole Cat was by Chickasha Bob. His dam, breeder, and owner are unknown.

POLE CAT. This Pole Cat was by Harmon Baker by Peter McCue, and his dam is unknown, as is his breeder. He was owned by William P. Bevans of Menard, Texas.

POLKA. This bay stallion was bred and owned by W. O. Breazeale of Louisiana, and lived in the early 1800's. He was by Kentucky Whip and out of a Brimmer mare. He is listed in the *American Stud Book*.

POLO KING. This stallion was bay, and he was foaled in 1929. He was by Election (TB) and out of Rix by The Senator. He was bred and owned by C. A. Allison of Weston, Wyoming.

PONCHO. Poncho was a dun stallion foaled in 1935. He was by Charm Peavine and out of Bonnie by Captain Montgomery. He was bred by Dan Evans of Stephensville, Texas.

PONY. Pony was by Wild Cat by Jim Ned by Pancho and out of an Old Fred mare. His second dam was by Primero. He was bred by Coke T. Roberds of Hayden, Colorado.

PONY PETE. Pony Pete was foaled in the late 1800's—a colorful race horse and sire who dominated his period. He was by Barney Owens by Cold Deck by Old Billy and his dam was of Printer breeding, probably Ricket's Printer by Snip Printer by Old Printer. Pony Pete was probably bred by Mike Smiley of Sylvan Grove, Kansas. See Little Steve.

POOLE HORSE. This dun stallion was by Little Rondo by Lock's Rondo by Whalebone, and the dam's pedigree is unknown, as is the breeder. He was owned by T. Hogue Poole of Cotulla, Texas. There was also another Poole horse referred to as Poole Jimmy Gray. This Poole horse was sired by Uncle Jimmy Gray by Bonnie Joe (TB), and his dam too is unknown.

POOR BOY, see SLIM JIM.

POP CORN. Pop Corn was by John Wilkes by Peter McCue by Dan Tucker and out of Cora by Blue. He was bred by Gaston B. Matthis of Stinnett, Texas, and owned in Oklahoma.

POP CORN. This Pop Corn was by No Good by Barney Owens by Old Cold Deck and out of a Gardner mare. He was bred and owned by Charles A. Gardner of Elgin, Arizona.

POP EYES. Pop Eyes was by Big Apple by Joe Collins by Old Billy and out of Donna by Barney by Danger. His second dam was Katy Bell by Buck Shot by Joe Collins.

POSSUM, see KING.

POSSUM. This Possum was a stallion sired by Young White Lightning by White Lightning, and his dam was a Stokes mare. He was bred by Tom Stokes, address unknown, and owned by Coke Blake of Pryor, Oklahoma.

POWDER RIVER. This bay stallion was foaled in 1930. He was by Captain Costigan (TB) and out of Dollie by Dennis Reed (TB). His second dam was Squaw by Moss Queen. He was bred and owned by the Waddell brothers of Odessa, Texas.

POWERS HORSE, see HARRISON.

PRIEST BOB. Priest Bob was foaled in 1886. He was by Anthony by Old Billy and out of Silver Heels. He was bred by Tom King of Belmont, Texas.

PRIMATE. This chestnut stallion was by Prince Royal (TB) and out of May Kennedy by Faustus (TB) and his second dam was by Gray Eagle's Printer by Gray Eagle.

PRIMERO. Primero was sired by Leadville (TB) and out of a race mare. He was bred by Sen. Borilla of Trinidad, Colorado, and owned and used by Coke Roberds when he farmed in western Oklahoma in the nineteenth century. He was killed in a train wreck in 1908 when Roberds was moving to Hayden, Colorado.

PRINCE. Prince was foaled in 1912. He was by Billy Bartlett by Traveler and out of Menyon by Rancocas (TB). His second dam was Heeley by Blue Dick. He was bred by the Morris Ranch of San Antonio, Texas, and owned by J. R. Mims of Water Valley, Texas.

PRINCE, see COKE T.

PRINCE. There were several other Princes:
1. PRINCE by Gold Enamel (TB), and bred by Schott of Riomedina, Texas.
2. PRINCE by Jim by Gotch by Hondo and bred by Pace of Kenedy, Texas.
3. PRINCE by Joe Bailey, and bred by Mercer of Gonzales, Texas.
4. PRINCE, Old; a red roan of unknown breeding owned in Gillette, Wyoming.

PRINCE ALBERT. This chestnut stallion was foaled in 1923. He was by Red Seal by Sealskin by Harmon Baker and out of Cherry by Billy Tom. He was bred by Monty Corder of Sanderson, Texas.

PRINCE CHARMING. Prince Charming was a sorrel stallion foaled in 1934. He was by Lion D'or (TB) and out of Judy by Old Joe Bailey by Eureka. He was bred by Jack Joyce of Graham, Texas, and owned by W. R. Downy of Mineral Wells, Texas.

PRINCE OLDHAM (PRINCE ODEM). This stallion, foaled in 1916, was by Rex Beach by Conjuror (TB). His dam was by Arch Oldham by Gallantry (TB) and his second dam was a Sykes' mare. He was bred by Crawford Sykes of Nixon,

Texas, and owned by Jim Brown of Giddings, Texas. He was sometimes referred to as Prince Odem.

PRINTER. According to the *American Stud Book* (Vol. II, 566), Printer was by *Janus, but actually he was by a son of *Janus, and foaled on or about the year 1800. He died in 1828. He was foaled in Virginia, taken to Pennsylvania, and later died in Fairfax County, Ohio.

PRINTER. Printer was by Old Cold Deck by Billy. He got his name from his dam who was by Printer Jr. (1829) by Old Printer. This Printer was foaled in or about 1867 and was the sire of Missouri Mike (1871) and Missouri Rondo (1884).

PRINTER. This Printer was foaled about 1870 or 1871. He was by Old Cold Deck by Old Billy and out of a mare by Printer Jr. by Ricket's Printer by Snip Printer by Old Printer. He was in Missouri for a while and later stood in Texas. He was probably bred either in Missouri or Illinois.

PRINTER TOM. This Printer was foaled in 1888. He was by Pony Pete by Barney Owens by Cold Deck and out of Cherokee Maid by Cold Deck by Old Billy. He was bred and owned by Mike Smiley of Sylvan Grove, Kansas, and later owned and raced by W. L. Thompson in Missouri and Colorado.

PROCTOR. Proctor was foaled in 1890 or a little before. He was by Dunman's Billy Fleming by Old Billy by Shiloh. He was bred by R. L. Dunman of Coleman, Texas.

PURE GOLD. This stallion, foaled in 1924, was by Jim Wells by Little Joe by Traveler and out of a mare of Sykes breeding. He was bred by J. L. Custer of Spofford, Texas.

R

RABBIT. Rabbit was by Harmon Baker by Peter McCue. He was owned and bred in Texas.

RABBIT, see GREY RABBIT.

RAFTER L. This stallion was by Chickasha Bob by Pid Hart and stood in Erath County, Texas.

RAINDROP. Raindrop was a sorrel foaled in 1923. He was by Rainy Day by Lone Star by Gold Enamel (TB) and his dam was a Schott mare by Paul Murray by Joe Murray by Anthony. He was bred and owned by Eugene Schott of Riomedina, Texas.

RAINMAKER. This brown stallion was foaled in 1929. He was by Helmet (TB) and out of Rainbow by The Senator by Leadville (TB). He was bred and owned by Henry Leonard of Colorado Springs, Colorado.

RAINY CLOUD. Rainy Cloud was by Rainy Day by Lone Star by Gold Enamel (TB). He was bred by Eugene Schott of Riomedina, Texas, and owned by H. J. Meyer of Hondo, Texas, and in 1927 by Tom Henderson of Eldorado, Texas.

RAINY DAY. This sorrel stallion was foaled in 1914 and died in 1928. He was by Lone Star by Gold Enamel (TB) and his dam was by Old Tom by Old Ben. He was bred by Eugene J. Schott of Riomedina, Texas. He was registered with the Jockey Club under the name Johnny Boy. His sire is given as Gold Enamel and his dam as Edee Ree by Peter McCue (*ASB*, Vol. XII, 153). He was a good race horse, but Joe Blair beat him.

RAINY DAY, HUGHES'. This Rainy Day was by Waggoner's Rainy Day by Ben Hur and was bred by W. T. Waggoner of Fort Worth, Texas. He was foaled in about 1933. He was sometimes referred to as Hughes' Rainy Day because Duwain E. Hughes of San Angelo owned him for a number of years.

RAINY DAY, LITTLE. This stallion was foaled in 1934. He was by Eagle Jr. by Eagle (TB) and his dam was by Rainy Day by Midnight.

RAINY DAY, MORRIS', see SID.

RAMBLER. Rambler was a bay born in or about 1920. He was by Tubal Cain by Berry's Cold Deck and out of Quail by Tanglefoot by Young Cold Deck. His second dam was Gray Kate by Young White Lightning. He was bred by Coke Blake of Pryor, Oklahoma, and owned by Jim Minnick of Crowell, Texas.

RAMBLING JACK. This stallion was foaled in 1931. He was brown and had been sired by Major Speck by Uncle Jimmy Gray. His dam was Mary Lou by Pride of India. He was bred and owned by John Cowey of Dewville, Gonzales County, Texas.

RAMBLING SAM. Rambling Sam was a brown stallion foaled in 1923. He was by Red Seal by Sealskin by Harmon Baker and out of Sophie by Billy Tom. He was bred by Monty Corder of Sanderson, Texas.

RAMON SAPPHO. This palomino stallion was by Sappho by Brown King by Arch Oldham and out of a Jack Zurick mare. He was owned and bred by W. B. Mitchell of Marfa, Texas.

RAMSEY. Ramsey was a bay stallion foaled in 1906. He was by Peter McCue by Dan Tucker and out of Flora V by Voltigeur. He was bred by Sam Watkins of Petersburg, Illinois.

RANCHER BANK. This gray stallion was foaled in 1929 and was by Hootch (TB) and out of a Quarter mare of Steel Dust breeding. He was bred by W. M. Anderson and Son of Cody, Nebraska.

RANGER. Ranger was an A.Q.R.H. He was sired by *Janus and his dam was by *Janus. He may have been bred by George Wilson in North Carolina. He is listed by both Edgar and in the *ASB*. He was foaled before 1765.

RANGER II. Ranger II was a bay stallion foaled in 1925. He was by Eagle Chief (TB) and out of Foxy by Chief by Peter McCue. He was bred by M. B. Huggins of Clinton, Oklahoma, and owned by O. H. Bouldin of Hartley, Texas.

RAT. Rat was a sorrel stallion foaled about 1890. He was by Rattler by Sam Bass by Steel Dust. He was bred in Texas and owned by Davis and Ivy of Seymour, Texas. He was a light sorrel with a blaze and some white on his feet. He stood 14-3 and weighed around 1,150 pounds. He was raced extensively and died around 1897(?).

RATTLER. This Rattler was foaled about 1886 and was by Sam Bass by Steel Dust and his dam was Desha Martin by Lock's Rondo. He was probably bred by Tom Martin of Kyle, Texas, and later he was owned by Bob Adams of Alfred, Texas.

RATTLER, NEWMAN'S. This Rattler was a sorrel foaled in 1890. He was by Hickory Jim by Dasher and his dam unknown. He was bred by Mann and Fields in Tarrant County, Texas, and owned by J. F. Newman of Sweetwater, Texas. Some feel he was the sire of Walling's Rattler.

RATTLER, WALLING'S. This bay stallion was foaled in 1908 and lived until 1916. He was by Barney by Grover and out of a mare by Buck Walton (TB). He was bred by W. P. Walling of Robert Lee, Texas. Some individuals have said he was by an older Rattler.

RAYD ORR. This chestnut stallion, foaled in 1930, was used primarily for the production of Polo ponies. He was by Ray D'or (TB) and out of Dolly Gould by Woodie Montgomery. He was bred by L. L. Evans of Brownwood, Texas, and owned by W. S. Evans of Brownwood.

READY MONEY. Ready Money was a sorrel, sired by Tom Glover by Sykes' Rondo and his dam was by Coleman. He was bred in Texas and owned by Herbert Schmidt of Comfort, Texas.

REBEL. This Rebel was foaled in the 1850's. He was sired by Steel Dust by Harry Bluff and his dam is unknown. He was bred by Mid Perry of Lancaster, Texas, and owned by Jim Brown of Giddings, Texas.

REBEL, NIXON'S. Rebel was foaled about 1925. He was by Joe Bailey by King by Traveler. He was bred by Dr. J. W. Nixon of Hondo, Texas.

RED. Red was a sorrel stallion by A. D. Reed by Peter McCue and out of a John Harrel mare. He was bred by John Harrel of Canute, Oklahoma.

RED. This sorrel stallion was by Little Fort by Black Bob by Bob Caraway, and his dam a Walter McGonigal Quarter mare. He was bred by P. L. Fuller of Snyder, Texas, and owned by Ernest Huffman of Muleshoe, Roy McMurty of Silverton, T. W. Bell of Turkey, and Red Sims of Snyder, all in Texas.

RED. This sorrel stallion was by Possum (King) by Traveler. He was owned by Clyde Smith of Big Foot, Texas. He sired the mare Old Red, the dam of Colonel Clyde and Little Shadow.

RED (COLORADO SORREL). This stallion was by Magnus Patch and out of Red Wing. His second dam was a Si Dawson Quarter mare. He was bred and owned in Colorado.

RED BACCHUS. Red Bacchus was a red bay horse, 14 hands-1 inch high, foaled in 1787. He was by F.A.Q.R.H. Old Bacchus and out of a mare by F.A.Q.R.H. Old Babram. He was bred by John Dickinson of Granville County, North Carolina. Edgar says he is a C.A.Q.R.H.

RED BALL, see RED TEXAS.

RED BALL. This stallion was a bay, and was foaled in 1927. He was by Oklahoma Star by Dennis Reed (TB). He was bred in Oklahoma and owned by M. J. Murray of Bartlesville, Oklahoma, and by Barton D. Carter of Pawhuska, Oklahoma.

RED, BIG. Big Red was by Red Bird by Buck Thomas and out of a mare by Jim Wells by Little Joe. He was bred by Earl Moye of Arvada, Wyoming, and sold to George Keeline of Gillette, Wyoming.

RED BIRD. Red Bird was by Jim Trammell by Barney Owens by Cold Deck and out of a Jim Newman mare. He was bred and owned by J. Frank Norfleet of Hale Center, Texas.

RED BIRD. This Red Bird was by Little Rondo by Lock's Rondo. He was foaled about 1890. He was out of a Shely mare. He was bred by Dow and Will Shely of Alfred, Texas.

RED BIRD. This Red Bird was foaled in 1933(?) and was sired by Scotsman (TB) and out of Old Allie by Peter McCue by Dan Tucker. He was bred by William Francis of Elk City, Oklahoma, and owned by Al Woolridge of Vinson, Oklahoma.

RED BOY. This stallion was a bay foaled in 1926. He was sired by Rancocas (TB) and out of Nessa Arch. He was bred by D. Bryant Turner of Colorado Springs, Colorado.

RED BUCK. This bay stallion was foaled in 1885. He was sired by Red Boy (TB) and out of Norma by Norwich (TB). His second dam was by Oregon Charlie. He was bred by R. H. Baker of Helena, Montana.

RED BUCK. This chestnut stallion was foaled about 1900. He was by Gold Coin, a Texas Quarter Horse, and his dam was Stray Mare's daughter. He was bred and owned by Little Brothers of Osage County, Oklahoma.

RED BUCK. This Red Buck was a chestnut foaled in 1929. He was by Everett (TB) and his dam was Sidney by Captain

Daugherty. His second dam was Alice by Renfro's Cold Deck. He was bred by Matt Renfro of Melvin, Texas, and owned by J. S. "Jap" Holman of Sonora, Texas. Renfro's address varies between several Texas and New Mexico towns.

RED BUCK, ALSUP'S. This stallion was by Grinder by Todd by Old Snort and his dam was by Big Joe by Chrisman's Swayback. His second dam was by Broke Leg by Alsup's Steel Dust. He was bred and owned by Ben Alsup in Tennessee and then taken by Alsup to Bald Knob, Douglas County, Missouri.

RED BUCK, HICK'S. This Red Buck was by Andy Gray by Uncle Jimmy Gray by Bonnie Joe (TB). He was bred by Raymond Hicks of Bandera, Texas.

RED CEDAR. Red Cedar was a sorrel foaled in 1928. He was sired by Buck McCue by Peter McCue and out of Dixie by Rhodes (TB). He was bred and owned by A. F. Willett of Des Moines, New Mexico.

RED CHIEF. This stallion was by Little Rex by Rex Beach by Conjuror (TB) and out of a bald-faced mare by Hickory Bill by Peter McCue. He was bred by George Clegg of Alice, Texas, and owned by Herbert Schmidt of Comfort, Texas.

RED CLOUD. This Red Cloud was a sorrel foaled in 1919. He was by King (Possum) by Traveler and out of Dottie by No Good by Barney Owens. His second dam was Birdie Hopkins by John Crowder by Old Billy. He was bred by Jim Kennedy of Bonita, Arizona, and later owned by Mark Dubois of Bonita; Ernest Shilling of Willcox; A. V. Mercer of Mammoth; and R. A. Pride of Willcox, all in Arizona.

RED CLOUD. Red Cloud was foaled in 1933 and was sired by Balleymooney by Concho Colonel by Jim Ned and out of Christabel by Old Joe by Harmon Baker. His second dam was a Springer mare sired by Uhlan. He was bred by Dan D.

Casement and Jack Casement of the Triangle Bar Ranch west of Whitewater, Colorado. Later he was owned by W. D. Wear of Willcox, Arizona; G. W. Wiggett of Ventura, California; and Tom Mattart of Salinas, California.

RED DECK. This stallion was foaled in 1905. He was a sorrel and had been sired by Diamond Deck by Old Cold Deck by Billy and his dam was a Missouri Mike mare by Printer by Old Cold Deck. He was bred in Missouri and owned later by Tom Stephenson of Gonzales, Texas, and Conrad Dickinson of the same town.

RED DENNIS. This bay stallion was foaled in 1928. He was by Dennis Reed (TB) and out of Red Wing by Moss King by Big King by One-Eyed Kingfisher. He was bred and owned by the Waddell brothers of Odessa, Texas.

RED DEVIL. This Red Devil was by Idle Jack by Tubal Cain by Berry's Cold Deck and out of Belle Starr by Big Danger by Berry's Cold Deck. He was bred by Coke Blake of Pryor, Oklahoma.

RED DEVIL. This bay stallion was foaled in 1922. He was by Booger Red by Rancocas (TB) and out of Graceful, who was a polo mare. He was bred by D. Bryant Turner of Colorado Springs, Colorado.

RED DEVIL. This sorrel stallion was foaled in 1935. He was by Galopin Son (TB) and out of Boots by Alkatraz. He was bred by J. D. Cowsert of Junction, Texas.

RED DOG. Red Dog was by Uncle Jimmy Gray by Bonnie Joe (TB) and his dam was by Billy Bartlett. He stood around Sterling City and Water Valley, Texas.

RED EAGLE. Red Eagle was a chestnut stallion foaled in 1928. He was by Lion D'or (TB) and out of Texas Lassie. The breeder is unknown, but he was owned by Ralph Smith of Range, Oklahoma.

RED FISH. This chestnut stallion was foaled in 1913. He was by Peter McCue by Dan Tucker and out of Swing Corners (TB). He was bred and owned by Dan Armstrong of Doxey, Oklahoma.

RED GOLD. Red Gold was a sorrel foaled in 1926. He was sired by Esquire (TB) and out of Bonnie by Billie Tom. He was bred by Monty Corder of Sanderson, Texas.

RED GOLD. This Red Gold was a chestnut foaled in 1930. He was by Red Lantados by Lantados (TB). He was bred in Sierra Blanca, Texas, and owned by Ross Perner of Seligman, Arizona.

RED, HARRINGTON'S. This stallion was foaled in 1917. He was by Jack Harrington by Grover Cleveland and out of Miss Texas by Rocky Mountain Tom by Pid Hart by Shelby. He was bred by Albert Harrington of Correo, New Mexico.

RED KITE. This bay stallion was foaled in 1928. He was sired by Walking John by Nimrod (TB) and out of Kate. He was bred and owned by Frank Walston of Menard, Texas.

RED KNIGHT. This bay stallion was by Cotton Eyed Joe by Little Joe by Traveler. He was bred, probably, by Bill Nack of Cuero. He was owned later by Ray and Reuben Holbein of Hebbronville, Texas.

RED LANTADOS. Red Lantados was a sorrel foaled in 1925(?). He was bred by a Baldwin in California and owned by Ross Perner of Sierra Blanca, Texas, and W. B. Mitchell of Marfa, Texas.

RED LIGHTNING. This bay stallion was by Joy by Jeff by Jeff C and out of Miss Patton by Joy by Jeff. His second dam was by Tom Campbell by Old Bob Peters. He was bred by Bill Patton of Leedey, Oklahoma.

RED LINK. Red Link was foaled in 1919 by Golden Link (TB) and out of a short-race mare. He was owned by Albert Nelson of Burwell, Nebraska.

RED LION and others. Red Lion was foaled in 1922. He was by Booger Red by Rancocas (TB) and out of a Turner polo mare. He was bred by D. Bryant Turner of Colorado Springs, Colorado. Turner also bred several other stallions sired by Booger Red whose names started with Red, for example, Red Rascal, Red Mouse, Red Star, Red Light, Red Zoo, Red Zoolock, Redich, Rediva, and Redno.

RED, LITTLE. This sorrel stallion was by Fishtail, a Quarter Horse, and out of an Anson mare. The second dam was by Jim Ned. He was bred by Marcus Snyder of Seminole, Texas.

RED, LITTLE. This stallion was by Joy by Jeff by Printer and out of Nellie Trammell by Ace by Peter McCue. He was foaled around 1920.

RED MACK, see DR. MACK, YOUNG.

RED MAGIC. This stallion was a bay foaled in 1929. He was by Free Hand (TB) and out of Dixie by The Senator. He was bred by Samuel Russell Jr. of Middletown, Connecticut.

RED MAN. Red Man was by Idle Jack by Tubal Cain by Berry's Cold Deck and out of Belle Starr by Big Danger by Berry's Cold Deck. He was bred by Coke Blake of Pryor, Oklahoma.

RED RAY. Red Ray was a bay foaled in 1903. He was by Lord Dalameny (TB) and out of Red Nellie by Boston Boy. His second dam was Heeley by Blue Dick by Wade Hampton. He was bred by Jim Newman of Sweetwater, Texas.

RED REED. Red Reed was a chestnut stallion. He was by A. D. Reed by Peter McCue and out of a John Harrel mare. He was bred by John Harrel of Canute, Oklahoma.

RED ROVER. This Red Rover was a bay stallion sired by John Gardner by Traveler and out of a Gates Quarter mare. He was bred by Jack Gates of Devine, Texas.

RED ROVER. Red Rover was a sorrel foaled around 1907. He was by Harmon Baker by Peter McCue, and his dam was by Duck Hunter by Peter McCue. He was bred by George Berry Ketchum of Sheffield, Texas, and owned by Gus Duncan of Duncan, Arizona.

RED ROVER, FLEMING'S. This Red Rover was a sorrel stallion foaled in 1875 who lived until 1899. He was by Old Billy by Shiloh and out of Paisana by Brown Dick by Berkshire. His second dam was Belton Queen by Guinea Boar. He was bred by William B. Fleming of Belmont, Texas, and owned by Jim Brown of Giddings, Texas, and Berry Ketchum of Sheffield, Texas. He was also called Rover.

RED SEAL. Red Seal was a bay stallion foaled in 1920. He was by Sealskin by Harmon Baker by Peter McCue and out of Eve by First Chip (TB). His second dam was Gracie Gould. He was bred by Sam Waring of Eden, Texas, and owned by Monty Corder of Sanderson, Texas.

RED SEAL II. Red Seal II was a bay stallion foaled in 1927. He was by Red Seal by Sealskin by Harmon Baker and out of Sun Down by Billie Tom. He was bred and owned by Monty Corder of Sanderson, Texas.

RED TEXAS (SMILEY). Red Texas was a chestnut foaled in 1902. He was by Little Steve by Pony Pete by Barney Owens and out of a mare by Croton Oil. His second dam was Cherokee Maid by Old Cold Deck. He was bred by Mike Smiley of Sylvan Grove, Kansas, and owned by Hanley Brothers of Scott City, Kansas. He was also known as Smiley and Red Ball.

RED VIGIL. This stallion, brown, was foaled in 1923. He

was by Booger Red by Rancocas (TB) and out of Pansy by Dave Waldo (TB). His second dam was Silvie T, a famous running Quarter mare said to be of Steel Dust breeding. Red Vigil was bred by Bryant Turner of Colorado Springs, Colorado.

RED WING. This stallion was by Jack McCue by Peter McCue and out of an Andes Quarter mare. He was bred by M. E. Andes of Portales, New Mexico.

RED WING. This Red Wing was by Red Bug by Everett (TB) and out of a Holman race mare. He was bred by J. S. Holman of Sonora, Texas, and owned by Espy–Vander Stucken Ranch of Sonora.

RED WING SIR. This stallion was foaled in 1934. He was by Chicaro (TB) and out of Medina Doll by A. M. White by Everett (TB). He was bred by Eugene Schott of Riomedina, Texas.

REGENT. This bay stallion was foaled in 1867 and was by *Bonnie Scotland and out of a Quarter mare. He died in Deer Lodge, Montana, on August 1, 1892.

REINCOCAS. This bay stallion was by Mose by Old Mose by Traveler and out of Frogeyes. He was bred by Roy Kimble of Clayton, New Mexico, and owned by George Thomas of Guy, New Mexico; John Williams of Stead, New Mexico; and Andrew Hamilton of Clayton, New Mexico.

RENDON. This brown stallion was foaled in 1894. He was by B. G. Bruce (TB) and out of Black Girl by Cold Deck. He was bred by W. Lissley of Oklahoma City and later owned by T. A. Cook of Oklahoma City.

RENO REBEL. Reno Rebel was a chestnut stallion foaled in 1905. He was sired by Rancocas (TB) and out of Mildred Juhl by Peter McCue. He was bred by Jim Newman of Sweetwater, Texas.

REPUTATION JR. This stallion was a bay foaled in 1897. He was by Reputation (TB) and out of Polly J by Spinning (TB). His second dam was Dell by Cold Deck by Billy. He was bred and owned by James Owens of Berlin, Illinois.

REVENUE. This Revenue was a sorrel foaled in 1912. He was sired by Bulger by Traveler and out of an unknown dam. He was bred in Arizona and owned by H. Cooper of Globe, Arizona.

REVENUE, OLD. This bay stallion was foaled in 1887 and was sired by Shelby by Tom Driver. He was bred in Texas and owned by John Lasater of Seymour, Texas, and S. B. Burnett of Fort Worth, Texas.

REX. Rex was by Billy Sunday by Roman Gold by Old Nick. He was bred by Leonard Horn of Wolcott, Colorado.

REX. This brown stallion was foaled in 1929. He was by Columbus by Ben Bolt by Aquinaldo and out of Mabel by Ben Bolt. He was bred by Corinne Huettig of Kyle, Texas, and owned by M. G. Michaelis of Kyle, Texas.

REXALL. Rexall was by Rex Beach by Conjuror (TB) and out of a Cooney mare. He was owned by Frank Rooke of Woodsboro, Texas.

REX BEACH. This brown stallion was foaled in 1912. He was sired by Conjuror (TB) and out of a mare by Tio Beach by Bobby Beach. He was bred by O. G. Parke of Kyle, Texas, and later by George Tips of Kenedy, Texas. Some said his dam was by Lock's Rondo.

REX JR. This brown stallion was foaled in 1926. He was by Rex Beach by Conjuror (TB) and out of Imy Carway by Handy Shot. He was bred by Henry Talley of Nixon, Texas.

REX, LITTLE. Little Rex was foaled about 1923. He was by Rex Beach by Conjuror (TB) and out of Mamie Jay by Little

Joe by Traveler. He was bred by John Dial of Goliad, Texas, and later owned by George Clegg of Alice and the King Ranch of Kingsville. He also was called Rex Beach Jr., occasionally, and Rex Beach II.

REY K. Rey K was a brown stallion foaled in 1925. He was by Tad H (TB) and out of Beauty by Billy Mason. His breeder is unknown, but he was owned by Gordon Stewart of Castle Rock, Colorado.

RHEUBE. This chestnut stallion was foaled in 1848. He was by Boston by Timoleon by Sir Archy and out of Mary Porter by Muckle John. His second dam was by Old Printer. He was bred by Webb Ross of Scott County, Kentucky, and owned by J. H. Dailey of Canada. He was a half brother of Flying Dutchman.

RICHARD. Richard was by Little Ben by Joe Bailey by Eureka. He was bred by J. M. Rickles of Bridgeport, Texas, and owned by Alvin Rickles of Chico, New Mexico.

RIGSBY. This bay stallion was foaled in 1908. He was by Palm Reader (TB) and out of Mary T by Traveler. He was bred by "Webb" Christian of Big Spring, Texas.

RILEY. Riley was by Jack McCue by Peter McCue and out of Two Bits by Little Dan. He was owned by Charles Logan of Tucson, Arizona.

RING MASTER. This stallion was a bay foaled in 1925. He was sired by Red Seal by Sealskin by Harmon Baker, and out of Silk Stockings by Billie Tom. He was bred by Monty Corder of Sanderson, Texas.

RIO. Rio was a chestnut stallion foaled in 1927. He was by Everett (TB) and out of Black Bird by Johnny Wilkes by Peter McCue. He was bred by J. E. Renfro of Menard, Texas, and owned by Matt Renfro of Sonora, Texas.

RIVER STUD, THE, see ROYAL FORD JR.

ROAN DICK. Roan Dick was foaled in 1877 and died in 1904. He was sired by Black Nick by Stewart's Telegraph and out of a mare by Greenstreet's Boanerges, a grandson of Printer. He was bred by Robert T. Wade of Plymouth, Illinois, and later owned by Charley Neeley of Littleton, Illinois, and Grant A. Rea of Carthage, Illinois. Rea bought Roan Dick and Nettie Overton at a public sale. The famous Quarter running gelding Bob Wade was sired by Roan Dick and named after his breeder.

ROAN DICK, YOUNG. Young Roan Dick was foaled in 1902. He was by Roan Dick by Black Nick by Stewart's Telegraph and out of a Rea mare. He was bred by Grant A. Rea of Carthage and Adrian, Illinois.

ROBERT A. Robert A was a bay stallion foaled in 1928. He was by Setback (TB) and out of Noo by Barney Lucas by Traveler. His second dam was Aunt Nan-Noo by Abe Frank (TB). He was bred by H. P. Saunders Jr. of Roswell, New Mexico, and owned by Vernon George of Raton, New Mexico.

ROBERT T. This black stallion was by Lon Martin by Little Rondo by Lock's Rondo and out of a Waggoner mare named Big Liz. He was bred by J. R. Tinsley of Gonzales, Texas, and later owned by Andrew Cordaway of Karnes City, Texas.

ROBIN HOOD. Robin Hood was a sorrel stallion foaled in 1926. He was by Esquire (TB) and out of Queen by Traveler's Boy by Traveler. He was bred by Monty Corder of Sanderson, Texas.

ROB ROY. Rob Roy was a gray stallion sired by Chulo Mundo by Traveler and out of Blue Gown by Joe Collins by Billy. He was bred by W. F. Jenkins of Menard, Texas, and owned by Tom and Clive Jones of Eldorado, Texas.

ROCK AND RYE. Rock and Rye was a brown stallion foaled in 1913. He was by Bobby Lowe by Eureka by Shelby and out of Mozette (TB). He was bred by D. W. Christian of Big Spring, Texas.

ROCKY, see MONTY.

ROCKY MOUNTAIN TOM. This black stallion was foaled in 1890. He was by Pid Hart by Shelby by Tom Driver by Steel Dust and out of Lady Gladys by Bill Garner by Steel Dust. He was bred by Shelby Stanfield of Thorp Spring, Texas, and owned by Sam Payne of Quanah, Texas; George Tummins of Springtown, Texas; and by J. H. Helm of Newark, Texas.

ROLLING DECK. Rolling Deck was foaled in 1879. He was sired by Bobby Cromwell by Old Cold Deck and out of Grasshopper by Old Cold Deck. His second dam was a full sister to June Bug by Harry Bluff. He was bred by Joe Lewis of Hunnewell, Kansas.

ROMAN GOLD (TUG DALE'S GOLDY). This palomino stallion was foaled in 1924. He was by Old Nick by Old Fred and out of Babe by Wildcat by Jim Ned by Pancho. He was bred by Ben Savage and owned by C. M. Dale, both of Steamboat Springs, Colorado.

RONALD STAR. This brown stallion was foaled in 1935. He was by Oklahoma Star by Dennis Reed (TB) and out of a Mason mare by Smuggler by Tubal Cain. He was bred by Ronald S. Mason of Nowata, Oklahoma, and owned by S. A. McCormack of Delaware, Oklahoma.

RONDO, see MISSOURI RONDO.

RONDO, ALSUP'S. This stallion was foaled about 1854 and lived until the 1870's. He was sired by Alsup's Brimmer by a Brimmer stallion. He was bred by Ben Alsup in Tennessee and owned by him after he moved to Bald Knob, Missouri, in Douglas County.

RONDO, CLARK'S. This chestnut stallion was foaled in 1884. He was by Vanderbilt by Norfolk (TB) and out of Dutchy. He was bred and owned in California and was raced by Bill Clark between 1890 and 1895.

RONDO, FLEMING'S. This Rondo was owned by Billy Fleming of Belmont, Texas. John Bouldin said he was "of the Steel Dust strain," but that his pedigree was unknown. He was a small heavily muscled horse, "branded all over." He was allegedly foaled in Missouri.

RONDO, LANE'S LITTLE. This Little Rondo probably was foaled just before 1900. He was a sorrel and sired by Sykes' Rondo by McCoy Billy by Old Billy and out of a Sykes' mare. He was bred by Crawford Sykes of Nixon, Texas, and later his owners were George Clegg of Alice, Texas, Frank Wiley of Cuero, Texas, and Sam Lane of Hebbronville, Texas. Little Rondo was a light sorrel horse with a flax mane and tail; he stood fifteen hands and weighed about 1,100 pounds.

RONDO, LITTLE. Little Rondo was foaled around 1895 and died in 1915. He was by Lock's Rondo by Whalebone and out of Minnie Franks by Project. He was bred by a Mr. Peevy of Bastrop County, Texas, and owned by Jim Martin of Kyle, Ashley Bunton of Uvalde, and Will Shely of Alfred, Texas.

RONDO, LOCK'S. This chestnut stallion was foaled in 1880 and lived until 1897. He was by Whalebone by Old Billy by Shiloh and out of Mittie Stephens by Shiloh Jr. His second dam was Nelly Gray by Dan Secres. He was bred by Charles R. Haley of Sweetwater, Texas, and afterwards owned by J. M. Brown of Giddings, Texas, Thomas G. Martin of Kyle, Texas, W. W. Lock, Kyle, Texas, and Charley Francis of Erick, Oklahoma. This was the original and most famous Rondo.

RONDO, NORFLEET'S. Norfleet's Rondo was by Pole Cat
and out of a Norfleet mare. He was bred by J. Frank Norfleet of Hale Center, Texas, and owned by Jack Anders of
Anton, Texas, in 1924.

RONDO, RABURN'S. Same horse as Fleming's Rondo.

RONDO, STEFFEK'S. This Rondo was by Little Rondo by
Sykes' Rondo. His breeder is unknown, but he was owned by
Joe Steffek of Hallettsville, Texas.

RONDO, STONE'S. Stone's Rondo was by Lock's Rondo by
Whalebone and out of one of Lock's Quarter mares. He was
bred by W. W. Lock of Kyle, Texas, and owned by Mit Stone
of Dripping Springs, Texas.

RONDO, SYKES'. Sykes' Rondo was a dark sorrel foaled in
1887 who died in 1907. He was sired by McCoy Billy by Old
Billy by Shiloh and out of Grasshopper. He was bred and
owned by Joe M. Mangum and Crawford Sykes of Nixon,
Texas.

RONDO II. Rondo II was foaled in 1884. He was by Mike
McCool by Alsup's Rondo. He was owned in 1909 by Luther
Hancock of Shalton, Missouri.

RONDO, WADDELL'S. This Rondo was a bay stallion foaled
in 1927. He was by Dennis Reed (TB) and out of Indian Maid
by Moss King. He was bred by the Waddell brothers of
Odessa, Texas.

ROOSTER. This sorrel stallion was foaled in 1926. He was
sired by Daedalus (TB) and out of Topsy by Fox by Young
Dr. Mack. He was bred and owned by the Reynolds Cattle
Company of Fort Worth, Texas.

ROSE HORSE, see SYKES HORSE, ROSE'S.

R. O. SORREL. R. O. Sorrel was by Old Biscuit by Sykes by
Peter McCue and out of an R. O. mare. He was bred and

owned by the Greene Cattle Company of Cananea, Sonora, Mexico.

ROVER, see RED ROVER, FLEMING'S.

ROWDY. This palomino stallion was foaled soon after 1920. He was by Cheppy (TB) and out of a Bixby Quarter mare. He was owned by Goodyear Farms of Litchfield Park, Arizona.

ROYAL D. This stallion was by Little Tennessee by Abe Frank (TB) and his dam was by Barney Owens. He was bred and owned by John T. Sims Jr. of Snyder, Texas.

ROYAL FORD JR. (THE RIVER STUD). Royal Ford Jr. has been described as both dun and gray. He was foaled in or around 1930. He was by Royal Ford (TB) and his dam was a Waggoner mare by their Rainy Day by Ben Hur by Old Rainy Day. He was bred by W. T. Waggoner of Fort Worth.

ROY HUDSPETH. This stallion was by Dodger by Harmon Baker and bred and owned by Roy Hudspeth of San Angelo, Texas. In 1939, he was owned by Barney Brooks of San Angelo, Texas.

RUBY DAVIS. This brown stallion was by Dogie Beasley by Sykes' Rondo and out of a Holman mare. He was bred by J. S. Holman of Sonora, Texas, and owned by Ruby Davis of Rocksprings, Texas, and L. B. Wardlaw of Del Rio, Texas.

RUNNING MALLARD. This bay stallion was foaled in 1903. He was by Peter McCue by Dan Tucker and out of Millie D by Tennyson (TB). His second dam was Nora M by Voltigeur (TB). He was bred by Samuel Watkins of Petersburg, Illinois.

RUSH. Rush was a dun stallion foaled in 1925. He was by Hadrian (TB) and out of a mare of Steel Dust breeding called Bess. He was bred by Monty Corder of Sanderson, Texas, and owned by J. M. Reynolds of Rush Springs, Oklahoma.

RUSTY. Rusty was a sorrel stallion sired by Brown Dick by *Derring Doe (TB) and out of a bay mare by Wild Cat. His second dam was by Silver Tail by Jim Ned. He was bred by Coke T. Roberds of Hayden, Colorado, and owned by B. G. Anderson of Craig, Colorado.

S

SAENZ. Saenz was by Ace of Hearts II by Ace of Hearts and out of a Saenz mare. He was bred by Anastacio (Tacho) Saenz of Rios, Texas.

SAILOR BOY. Sailor Boy was by Field Marshall (TB) and out of Wampus Cat by Reclus (TB). His second dam was Queen of the West by Rex. He was bred and owned by Ronald Mason of Nowata, Oklahoma.

ST. DAMIAN. St. Damian was a brown stallion foaled in 1923. He was by Dark Friar (TB) and out of Rainbow by The Senator by Leadville (TB). He was bred and owned by Henry Leonard of Colorado Springs, Colorado.

ST. PAT. St. Pat was a palomino stallion foaled in 1932 and killed by a truck in 1942. His sire is unknown, but his dam was a R. O. mare. He was bred by Harry Hughes of Carrizo, California, and later owned by H. A. Pollard of Lakeview, Oregon.

SAINT TAMMANY. This stallion, listed by Edgar as a C.A.Q.R.H., was by Old King Tammany and out of a mare by Atkinson's Janus. He was bred by Alexander Shrewsberry of Franklin County, North Carolina. He was foaled in the late 1700's.

SALADIN. This palomino stallion was by Ding Bob by Brown Dick by *Derring Doe (TB) and out of Fleet by Bob H by Old Fred. He was bred by Marshall Peavy of Steamboat

Springs, Colorado, and later owned by L. B. Peavy of Clark, Colorado.

SALTOSH. This brown stallion was foaled in 1922. He was sired by Walking John by Nimrod (TB). His dam was May Newman by Portland (TB). He was bred by T. O. Atwell of Miles, Texas.

SALTY, OLD. Old Salty was by Henry Barrow by Berry Ketchum(?). He was bred and owned by Clarence Scharbauer of Midland, Texas.

SAM. This Sam was by Solis by The Old Sorrel by Hickory Bill and his dam was by Martin's Best. He was bred and owned by the King Ranch of Kingsville, Texas.

SAM. This Sam was by Joe Bailey of Gonzales by King (Possum) and his dam is unknown, as is his breeder. He was owned by J. P. Stokes of Breckenridge, Texas.

SAM. This Sam was a brown stallion foaled in 1901. He was sired by Priest Bob by Anthony by Old Billy and his dam was Fashion by Anthony. He was bred by Tom King of Belmont, Texas, and owned by John McKnight of Seguin, Texas.

SAM BASS. This sorrel stallion was by Rialto by Billy Sunday and out of a Taylor mare. He was bred by John Taylor of Kendleton, Texas, and later owned by M. G. Johnson of Edna, Texas.

SAM BASS. This Sam Bass was foaled in 1874 and was sired by Steel Dust by Harry Bluff. His dam was unknown as was his breeder. He was owned at one time by George McGonigal of Midland, Texas.

SAM C. Sam C was by Texas Chief by Traveler and out of a MacMurray mare by Doc Oldham by Gallantry (TB). His second dam was an Arab-Barb mare. He was bred by Bob MacMurray of Hebbronville, Texas, and bought later by Mr.

Gibbons of Three Rivers, Texas, who owned him when he beat Spike Webster. Sam C had a full brother named Ordeon. One account gave his sire as Ace of Hearts, but George Clegg said he was by Texas Chief.

SAM HARPER. Sam Harper was a bay horse, foaled in 1871, by Rebel. He died in southwest Texas in 1884, aged thirteen years. *American Stud Book* (Vol. V, 785).

SAM HARPER JR. This dark bay stallion was foaled in the late 1800's and was sired by Sam Harper (TB). His dam was Lucy Cherry, also referred to as the Cherry Filly. He was bred by Walter Priestley Dickson of Flatonia, Gonzales County, Texas, and later owned by G. B. Morris, J. DeLong, and W. Van Kuren, also of Texas. He was run by the last three individuals.

SAM JONES. This black stallion was foaled in 1886 and was sired by Black Nick by Stewart's Telegraph. His breeder is unknown, but he was owned by a C. Neel, or Nell, address unknown. He was later owned by Shields and Leonard of San Angelo, and ultimately by William Anson of Christoval, Texas.

SAM JONES. This sorrel stallion was foaled in 1890. He was by Waller (TB) and out of a Quarter mare named Annie Lee. His breeder is not known, but he was owned most of his life by Wade McLemor and Tom King of Belmont, Texas.

SAM MOUNT. This brown stallion was foaled in 1889 and was sired by Ironclad by Woodburn (TB) and out of Daisy Dean by Wheatley (TB). He was owned and raced in California by J. Leach.

SAMMY. Sammy was a brown stallion by Skeet by Yellow Wolf by Old Joe Bailey and out of Inky by a Castello Joe Bailey horse. He was bred and owned by C. E. Castello of Woodson, Texas.

SAMOSET. This sorrel stallion was foaled in 1930. He was sired by Captain Costigan (TB) and out of Red Wing by Moss King. He was bred and owned by the Waddell brothers of Odessa, Texas.

SAM SPARKS. This bay stallion was foaled in 1911, sired by Dr. Curtis (TB) and out of Christine C by Palm Reader (TB). He was bred by "Webb" Christian of Big Spring, Texas.

SAM WATKINS. This bay stallion was foaled in 1911 and was sired by John Wilkins by Peter McCue and out of Nannie Gum by Nimrod (TB). His second dam was Pansy H by The Hero (TB). He was bred and owned by J. W. Moore of Mobeetie, Texas.

SAM WATKINS. Sam Watkins was a bay colt foaled in 1913. He was by Hickory Bill by Peter McCue and out of Hattie W by Hi Henry. His second dam was Katie Wawekus, a Thoroughbred. He was bred by Sam Watkins of Petersburg, Illinois, and later owned by George Clegg of Alice, Texas. After he was wire cut, he was sometimes referred to as the Clegg Cut Foot Horse.

SAN ANTONIO. This sorrel stallion was foaled in 1909. He was by Peter McCue by Dan Tucker and out of Nona P by the Duke of Highlands, which makes him a full brother of Harmon Baker. He was bred and owned by John Wilkins of San Antonio, Texas.

SAN ANTONIO, CLEGG'S. This San Antonio was a sorrel, and he was sired by Hickory Bill by Peter McCue, and he was out of a full sister of Texas Chief, sired by Traveler. He was bred by George Clegg of Alice, Texas, and owned by Mont B. Noelke of San Angelo, Texas.

SANCHO. Sancho was sired by Harmon Baker by Peter Mc-Cue and out of an Anson mare. He was bred by William Anson of Christoval, Texas.

SAN FERNANDO SYKES. This stallion was by Sykes by Peter McCue by Dan Tucker and out of an R. O. mare. He was bred and owned by the Greene Cattle Company of Cananea, Sonora, Mexico.

SAN JUAN. San Juan was foaled in 1933 (?) and was sired by Pal O'Mine by Billy Sunday by Horace H. His dam was by Pugh's Ace of Hearts. He was bred by W. T. Wright of Alice, Texas, and later owned by Dan Sullivan of Falfurrias, Texas.

SANTA CLAUS. This roan stallion was by Rancocas (TB) and out of Watercress. His second dam was a Quarter mare. He was bred by George Thomas of Guy, New Mexico, and owned by Louie C. Baca of Rosebud, New Mexico.

SANTA CLAUS. Santa Claus was a sorrel stallion sired by Red Buck and out of Polly by Tom Campbell by Bob Peters. He was bred by E. Alden Meek of Durham, Oklahoma, and owned by Hardin Myers and Charley White Skunk of Hammon, Oklahoma.

SAPPHO. This palomino stallion was sired by Brown King by Arch Oldham and out of a palomino mare by St. Charles. He was owned by W. B. Mitchell of Marfa, Texas.

SAPPHO, WILSON'S. This Sappho was by Sappho by Brown King and out of a Mitchell mare. He was bred by W. B. Mitchell of Marfa, Texas, and owned by W. A. Wilson of Alpine, Texas.

SCARAMOUCHE. Scaramouche was foaled in 1925. He was sired by Sam King by Hondo by John Crowder. He was owned by Fred Mudge of Junction, Texas.

SCARECROW. This dark sorrel stallion was foaled in 1925. He was by A. D. Reed by Peter McCue by Dan Tucker and out of Oklahoma Queen (second). He was bred and owned by John A. Harrell of Canute, Oklahoma. He was a full brother of Duck Hunter, and his name was sometimes given as Scarcrow.

SCAR LEG. Scar Leg was by Pid Hart by Shelby by Tom Driver and his dam was Cut Foot. He was owned by Bird Ramey of Weatherford, Oklahoma.

SCHOOL BOY. School Boy was foaled in 1894. He was by Barney Owens by Cold Deck by Billy and out of a Trammell mare. He was bred by Thomas Trammell of Sweetwater, Texas. He was purchased by the XIT Ranch as a two-year-old.

SCOOTER. Scooter was by Mark by Red Cloud by Possum and out of Donna by Barney by Danger. His second dam was Katy Bill by Buckshot by Joe Collins. He was bred by Roy Sorrills of Nogales, Arizona, and owned by Tom Rush of Springerville, Arizona.

SCOOTER, see TOM.

SCOTT. This dun stallion was foaled in 1913 and died in 1930. He was by Yellow Jacket by Little Rondo by Lock's Rondo and out of a Parke Quarter mare. He was bred by O. G. Parke of Kyle, Texas, and owned by William Pyle of Midland, Texas.

SEALARK. Sealark was a bay stallion foaled in 1932. He was by White Seal (TB) and out of Fay Larkin by Barney Lucas by Traveler. He was bred and owned by H. P. Saunders, Jr. of Roswell, New Mexico.

SEALEM. Sealem was a brown stallion foaled in 1890. He was by the Thoroughbred Famous and out of Kitty Waddle by Jack Traveler by Traveler. His second dam was Kittie Clyde. He was bred by Samuel Watkins of Petersburg, Illinois. Kittie Waddle was also known as Kitty Watkins.

SEALSKIN. Sealskin was a brown stallion foaled in 1916. He was sired by Harmon Baker by Peter McCue and out of Bess

A (Bessie A). He was bred by Hawley C. Allen of San Angelo, Texas, and later owned by Sam Waring of Eden, Texas. Bess A was a large brown mare bred by Tom Avery of Ballinger, Texas.

SELAM II. Selam II was by Jim Wells by Little Joe by Traveler. He was bred by P. L. Fuller of Snyder, Texas.

SELECT. Select was a brown stallion foaled in 1927. He was by Esquire (TB) and out of Lightfoot by Traveler. He was bred by J. M. Corder of Sanderson, Texas.

SELIM. Selim, foaled about 1840, was by Barnes' Black Whip and his dam was by a son of Printer.

SELLEX. This bay stallion was foaled in 1896. He was by The Hero (TB) and out of Hattie W by Hi Henry. His second dam was Katie Wawekus by Wawekus (TB). He was bred by the Watkinses of Petersburg, Illinois.

SENATOR. This chestnut stallion was foaled in 1925. He was by Red Seal by Sealskin by Harmon Baker. His dam was Dimples by Billy Tom. He was bred by J. M. Corder of Sanderson, Texas.

SENATOR DON. This bay stallion was foaled in 1930. He was by Beauty Boy (TB) and out of May Senator by The Senator by Leadville (TB). He was owned by R. J. Kurruish of Littleton, Colorado.

SENATOR ELECT. This stallion was brown and foaled in 1926. He was by Election (TB) and out of Orpha by The Senator by Leadville (TB). His second dam was a Walker mare. He was owned by J. H. Deboard of Gillette, Wyoming.

SENATOR JR. Senator Jr. was by The Senator by Leadville (TB) and out of an Oregon Quarter mare. He was probably bred by R. J. Kurruish of Littleton, Colorado.

SENATOR, THE. The Senator was a sorrel stallion foaled in 1897. He was sired by the Thoroughbred Leadville and was out of Wooley by Little Steve. He was bred by Casimiro Borilla of Trinidad, Colorado. He was later owned by Frank and Horace Byers of Hot Sulphur Springs, Colorado; Charles T. Walker of Kiowa, Colorado; John Rennert of Elbert, Colorado; Ed Orin of Elbert, Colorado; Cash Spencer of Peyton, Colorado; and Ralph Brooks of Castle Rock, Colorado.

SENATOR WEST. This Senator was by Dr. West by Dr. Mechum (TB) and out of Orpha by The Senator. He was a full brother of Senator Elect. He was owned by Lloyd Cain of Arvada, Wyoming, and by William Eaton of Weston, Wyoming.

SHAD. Shad was a dark chestnut stallion foaled in 1761. He was sired by *Janus and his dam was by imported Silver-Eye. He was bred by James Haskins of Brunswick County, Virginia. He is listed in both Edgar and *ASB*.

SHALAKO. Shalako was by Crippled Dick by Dominus Arvi (TB) and out of Trixie by Delmor (TB). He was owned by James Wilford Ashcroft of Ramah, New Mexico.

SHANNON (TUESDAY). Shannon was a bay Thoroughbred stallion foaled in 1872. He was by Monday and out of Hennie Farrow. Shannon was sometimes called Tuesday, and Hennie was originally known as Bettey Money. She was a bay mare foaled in 1853 and bred by A. Turner of California. Shannon's sire was by Colton and his dam was by *Shamrock. Shannon was later owned by John Adams of Woodland, California.

SHANNON. This chestnut colt, foaled in 1878, was by Shannon and out of Bell by Oregon Charlie. His second dam was by Pilgrim. He was bred and owned by John Adams of Woodland, California. Shannon was by Monday and out of Hennie Farrow.

SHELBY. Shelby was foaled in 1878. He was by Tom Driver by Steel Dust by Harry Bluff and out of Mittie Stephens by Shiloh Jr. by Shiloh. His second dam was Nellie Gray by Dan Secres. He was bred by Charles R. Haley of Sweetwater, Texas, and owned by E. Shelby Stanfield of Thorp Spring, Texas.

SHELY HORSE, see JOE SHELY.

SHERIFF, THE. The Sheriff was a sorrel stallion foaled in 1890. He was by Barney Owens by Cold Deck and his dam was said to be a paint race mare. His breeder is unknown, but he was bred in Illinois and owned by Fred T. Wood of Abilene when he was in Texas. When racing, he was often entered as having been sired by Bailey Payton. He was considered one of the top race horses of his day. In St. Louis, in 1892, he was matched against Dan Tucker for ¼ mile and lost in 22 seconds flat, which was, Helen Michaelis adds, "the best time recorded for that state up to that time, and maybe since." At least he was beaten by a member of his family.

SHILOH, CLAYTON'S. This chestnut stallion was foaled in 1875. He was by a son of Lexington. He was bred by Dr. H. H. Clayton of Tennessee and owned by W. W. McClunn of Batesville, Virginia. His dam was by Brown Dick.

SHILOH FLEMING. Shiloh Fleming was a bay stallion by Anthony by Old Billy and out of Sweet Lip by Old Billy. He was bred by William B. Fleming of Belmont, Texas, and later owned by T. H. King of Belmont, Texas.

SHILOH, HALEY'S. Shiloh was a dark sorrel stallion foaled in 1883. He was by Lock's Rondo by Whalebone by Old Billy and out of a Haley Quarter mare. He was bred by Charles R. Haley of Sweetwater, Texas, and later owned by W. J. Miller of Mobeetie, Texas.

SHILOH JR. (PIERCE'S YOUNG SHILOH). Shiloh Jr., also called Young Shiloh, was foaled in 1863. He was by Shiloh

195

by Van Tromp by Thomas' Big Solomon and out of Old Puss by Freedom by *Emancipation. He was owned by Charles R. Haley of Sweetwater, Texas.

SHILOH, OLD. Old Shiloh was foaled in Tennessee in 1844 and brought to Texas by Jack Batchler in 1849. He died in 1874. He was sired by Van Tromp by Thomas' Big Solomon by Sir Solomon by Sir Archy. Jack Batchler lived in Lancaster, Texas. Shiloh and Steel Dust were foundation Quarter Horses in Texas. Helen Michaelis believed his dam to be by Union.

SHOOTING STAR. Shooting Star was a sorrel foaled in 1924. He was by Red Seal by Sealskin by Harmon Baker and out of Bonnie by Billie Tom. He was bred by J. M. Corder of Sanderson, Texas.

SHORT BOB. Short Bob was by Bill Garner by Steel Dust and out of a Morgan-bred mare. He was owned by Joe Morgan of Comanche, Texas, and raced by Ed Harris of Comanche, Texas.

SHORTY. Shorty was by Barlow by Lock's Rondo and out of Maud Baker. He was bred by Charles L. Francis of Floyd, New Mexico.

SHOW BOY. Show Boy was foaled in 1920. He was by Little Dick by Sleepy Dick and his dam was by Big Bill. He was bred by Dr. H. J. Meyer of Hondo, Texas, and later owned by Mack Cauthorn of Sonora, Texas.

SI. Si was a sorrel by Joe Lucas by Traveler and out of Little Suzie. He was bred by Walter Trammell of Sweetwater, Texas. He has been referred to as Cy.

SID (MORRIS' RAINY DAY). Sid, sometimes referred to as Morris' Rainy Day, was a sorrel stallion by Rainy Day by Lone Star by Billy Sunday and out of a Butler Quarter mare.

He was bred by Emmett Butler of Kenedy, Texas, and later owned by Ed Morris of Rocksprings, Texas, and then by R. C. Tatum of Junction, Texas.

SI DING. Si Ding was a palomino stallion sired by Ding Bob by Brown Dick by *Derring Doe (TB) and out of Flossie by Shiek by Peter McCue by Dan Tucker. He was bred and owned by Marshall Peavy of Steamboat Springs, Colorado.

SILVER CLOUD. Silver Cloud was a palomino stallion foaled in 1935. He was by Red Cloud by Red Buck by Buck Thomas and out of a Burnett mare. He was bred by Tom Burnett of Fort Worth, Texas, and owned by Edgar Watts of Pinon, New Mexico.

SILVER, COPE'S. This sorrel stallion was foaled in the 1920's and was a well-known short-race horse, winning several matches in Tijuana, Mexico. He was later owned by Herbert Cope and Clyde Bowen of Sterling City. His breeding is unknown.

SILVER DICK. This Silver Dick was a gray foaled in 1892. He was by Roan Dick by Black Nick by Stewart's Telegraph. His dam was named Fury. He was bred in Illinois and owned by Robert T. Wade of Plymouth, Illinois. Later the following owned and raced Silver Dick: J. H. Beckwith, Joliet, Illinois; W. Kimfray, Webster, Illinois; Mr. Koontz, also of Illinois; and Mr. Donaldson of Wayaconda, Missouri.

SILVER DICK. Silver Dick was a bay stallion foaled in 1897. He was sired by Billy Caviness, a Texas horse strong in Billy blood. His dam was Fannie White, a short-mare of Thoroughbred breeding. He was bred by Kirk Williams of Mancos, Colorado, who owned him for a number of years and raced him widely.

SILVER DOLLAR. This palomino stallion was foaled in 1934. He was by Tarzan by Yellow Wolf by Old Joe Bailey and out of Campbell's Yellow. He was bred by W. H. Campbell of Gainesville, Texas, and later owned by R. W. Holland of Perryton, Texas.

SILVER M. This stallion was by Sam King by Hondo by John Crowder and out of an Anson mare sired by Harmon Baker. He was bred by O. W. Cardwell of Junction, Texas, and owned by George D. Miers of Villa Acuna, Mexico.

SILVER, SPIRES'. This stallion was by the Yates Horse by Little Joe by Traveler and out of a Tankersly mare. He was owned by Leroy Spires of Roscoe, Texas.

SILVER STREAK. This palomino stallion was foaled in 1932. He was by Wag by Yellow Jacket by Little Rondo and out of Cauthorn's Billy by Dogie Beasley. He was bred by C. R. White of Brady, Texas, and later owned by Punk Snyder of Melvin, Texas, and O. H. Nichols of Bangs, Texas.

SILVER TAIL. Silver Tail was foaled in 1895. He was by Jim Ned by Pancho by Old Billy and out of an Anson mare. He was bred by Billy Anson of Christoval, Texas, and later owned by Si Dawson of Hayden, Colorado.

SIMPLE SAM. Simple Sam was a bay stallion foaled in 1905. He was sired by Prince Plenty (TB) and out of Red Nellie by Boston Boy (TB). His second dam was Heeley by Blue Dick by Wade Hamilton.

SIMPLETON. Simpleton was by Joe Collins by Old Billy and out of a McGonigal mare. He was bred by George McGonigal of Midland, Texas.

SIMTUCK. This stallion was sired by Oregon Dick and he was out of Mag, a Printer mare. He was bred by Keeney Brothers of Long Creek, Oregon.

SIROCK. This gray stallion was foaled in 1909. He was by Silver Dick by Roan Dick by Black Nick by Telegraph. His dam was Mary S. He was bred by Robert T. Wade of Plymouth, Illinois.

SIR ROWDY. Sir Rowdy was a black stallion foaled in 1929. He was by Woodrow Wilson by The Senator by Leadville (TB) and out of Shorty. He was bred by Leo Crouse of Elbert, Colorado.

SKEET. Skeet was a dun stallion foaled in 1929. He was sired by Yellow Wolf by Old Joe Bailey by Eureka and out of a Parrott mare by Buncombe, the old dun horse. He was bred by Tom Parrott of Throckmorton, Texas, and owned by R. A. Brown of Throckmorton and Frank W. Austin of Fort Worth, Texas.

SKEEZIX. This bay stallion was foaled in 1929. He was by John Wilkins by Peter McCue by Dan Tucker. His dam is unknown, as is his breeder. He was first owned by Bob McCoy of White Deer, Texas, and later by Fred Lowry of Lenapah, Oklahoma.

SKIPPER DELIGHT. This bay stallion was foaled in 1925. He was by Red Seal by Sealskin by Harmon Baker and out of Traveler Gal by Red Seal. He was bred by J. M. Corder of Sanderson, Texas.

SKYROCKET (PYLE'S WAGGONER HORSE). Skyrocket was a dun stallion sired by Yellow Jacket by Little Rondo by Lock's Rondo and out of a Waggoner mare. He was bred by W. T. Waggoner of Fort Worth, Texas, and owned by Roy Parks of Midland, Texas. He has also been called Pyle's Waggoner Horse after a one-time owner, William Pyle of Midland, Texas.

SLEEPY. Sleepy was a black stallion sired by Gotch by Hickory Bill by Peter McCue and his dam was also by Hickory Bill. He was bred by William Brewster of Edenburg, Texas, and later owned by Jess Perkins of San Antonio, Texas, and Vance Rhea of Pampa, Texas.

SLEEPY DAVE. Sleepy Dave was a bay stallion foaled in 1884. He was by Roan Dick by Black Nick by Stewart's Telegraph. His dam and breeder are unknown. He was raised in Illinois, but owned and raced in Oregon.

SLEEPY DICK. This stallion was by Jim Trammell by Barney Owens and his dam is unknown. He was owned by Robert Parsons of Weston, Colorado.

SLEEPY DICK. This Sleepy Dick was a sorrel foaled about 1894 who died in 1917. He was by Little Rondo by Sykes' Rondo by McCoy Billy and his dam a Webb Smith mare. He was bred by Webb Smith of DeWitt County, Texas. and later owned by Luke A. Greer of Hallettsville, Texas.

SLEEPY DICK. This Sleepy Dick was foaled in the early 1900's. He was by Old Fred by Black Ball by Missouri Mike and his dam's ancestry is not recorded. He was bred by Coke Roberds of Hayden, Colorado, and later was owned by Charlie Walker of Kiowa, Colorado.

SLEEPY DICK. This Sleepy Dick was foaled in the early 1920's. He was by Little Dick by Sleepy Dick by Little Rondo. His dam was Nellie by Panmure (TB). He was bred by Charles F. Meyer of Ellinger, Texas. He was a full brother to Sadie M, the dam of My Texas Dandy.

SLEEPY SAM. Sleepy Sam was by Billy Sunday by Horace H (TB) and his dam was Sarazan by Billy Sunday and his second dam Lurianca by Little Joe by Traveler. He was bred by Ott Adams of Alfred, Texas, and later owned by H. A. Drumgoole of Eagle Lake, Texas.

SLIM JIM (POOR BOY). Slim Jim was a sorrel stallion foaled in 1932. He was by Little Dick by Sleepy Dick by Little Rondo and out of a mare by Chicaro. He was bred by C. L. Steffek of Hallettsville, Texas. He was sometimes raced under the name Poor Boy.

SLIP ALONG RED. Slip Along Red was a bay stallion foaled in 1925. He was by Red Seal by Sealskin by Harmon Baker. His dam was Cherrie by Billy Tom.

SLIP SHOULDER. Slip Shoulder was a stallion foaled in 1890. He was sired by Missouri Mike by Printer by Cold Deck and the pedigree of his dam was not recorded. He was bred by Bill Stockton of Lockwood, Missouri. He was later owned in Oklahoma.

SMILEY, see RED TEXAS.

SMITHY. Smithy was a brown stallion foaled in 1910. He was by Dr. Curtis (TB) and out of Jaquette by Traveler. He was bred and owned by "Webb" Christian of Big Spring, Texas.

SMOKEY, BEETCH'S. Smokey was a dun stallion foaled in 1929. He was by Beetch's Yellow Jacket by Yellow Jacket by Little Rondo and out of Mayflower by Naildriver. He was bred by Mike Beetch of Lawton, Oklahoma.

SMOKEY, J. A.'S. This Smokey was foaled in the 1930's. He was by Beetch's Smokey by Beetch's Yellow Jacket by Yellow Jacket and out of a mare by Adair's Yellow Wolf. He was bred and owned by the J. A. Ranch of Palo Duro, Texas.

SMUGGLER. Smuggler was a sorrel stallion sired by Tubal Cain by Berry's Cold Deck and out of Lady Fox by Grey Wolf by Young Cold Deck. He was bred by S. Coke Blake of Pryor, Oklahoma. He headed Blake's stud in 1922. Coke Blake described him as a beautiful sorrel, 15 hands-½ inch high and weighing 1,400 pounds in good flesh.

SNAKE BIT HORSE. This stallion was by Little Joe by Traveler and out of a good Adams mare. He was bred by Ott Adams of Alfred, Texas, and owned by George Clegg of Alice, Texas.

SNIP. Snip was a bay stallion by Old Tom by John Crowder by Old Billy and out of a Shely mare. The breeder lived in Hondo, Texas, and the stallion was bought by Frank Stean of Del Rio, Texas, and later owned by George R. Herndon of North Uvalde, Texas.

SNIP. This Snip was by Rafter L by Chickasha Bob by Pid Hart(?) and out of a Keller mare by Spark Plug. He was bred by George Keller of Erath County, Texas, and later went to New Mexico.

SNOOPER. Snooper was a black stallion sired by Oklahoma Star by Dennis Reed (TB) and out of Biddy by Smuggler. He was bred by Everett Bowman of Hillside, Arizona.

SOLOMON, THOMAS' BIG. Thomas' Big Solomon was by Sir Solomon by Sir Archy and foaled about 1820. His breeder and the exact date of birth are unknown. He was owned by a Mr. Thomas, who was also probably his breeder. This stallion sired Van Tromp.

SONNY BOY. Sonny Boy was by Ben Hur by Rainy Day by Lone Star and out of Biddy by Smuggler. He was bred by Everett Bowman of Hillside, Arizona, and owned by Leon C. Saylors of Marysville, California.

SONNY BOY. Sonny Boy was a dun stallion sired by Headlight by Yellow Wolf by Old Joe Bailey and out of Goldie. He was bred by Ed Thompson of Stinnett, Texas.

SONNY BOY. This Sonny Boy was a sorrel foaled in 1929. He was sired by Joe Bailey by King by Traveler and out of a Billy Fleming mare. He was bred by Ab Bateman of Gonzales County, Texas. He was later owned by Will Hysaw of Luling, Texas, and by Sam Sessions of Brady, Texas.

SONNY BOY. Sonny Boy was by Mack by Delmor (TB) and out of a mare named Kitty by Tony by Guinea Pig by Possum. He was bred and owned by John E. Kane of Douglas, Arizona. He was occasionally referred to as the Johnny Kane Stud.

SON OF SYKES. This stallion was a chestnut. He was by Sykes by Peter McCue and out of an RO mare. He was bred and owned by the Greene Cattle Company of Cananea, Sonora, Mexico.

SONORA HARMON. Sonora Harmon was a bay stallion foaled in 1931 who died about 1943. He was by Sealskin by Harmon Baker by Peter McCue and out of a Corder mare. He was bred by John Williams of San Angelo, Texas, and owned by Marion Stokes of Sonora, Texas.

SORREL JOHN. Sorrel John was a full brother of Honest John. He was by Sleepy Jim (TB) and out of Sorrel Nell, a good race mare. His breeder is unknown, but he was raced in Missouri by Adsitt and Robbins.

SPADILLE, OLD. This C.A.Q.R.H. stallion, foaled in 1762, was by *Janus and out of Selima by the Godolphin Arabian. He was owned by Wyllie Jones of Halifax County, North Carolina, and is listed by both Edgar and *ASB*.

SPARK PLUG. This Spark Plug was by Booger Red by Rancocas (TB) and was raced in Colorado.

SPARK PLUG. This Spark Plug was a sorrel foaled sometime between 1921 and 1924. He died in 1937. He was by Jack McCue by Peter McCue by Dan Tucker and out of Silver by Chickasha Bob by Pid Hart(?). He was bred by Will Stead of Tulia, Texas, and later owned by W. R. Norfleet of Olton, Texas.

SPARK PLUG (SPARKY). This Spark Plug was by Midnight by Badger by Peter McCue and out of a Waggoner mare. He was bred by W. T. Waggoner of Fort Worth, Texas, and owned by N. L. Welton of Pampa, Texas. He was sometimes called Sparky.

SPARKY. Sparky was foaled in 1928, and was sired by A. D. Reed by Peter McCue by Dan Tucker. He may have been bred by W. T. Waggoner of Fort Worth, Texas. He was owned in 1930 by Edd Wright of Lefors, Texas. Later, he was acquired by Herbert G. Moss of Erick, Oklahoma, and by Elmer Gaston of Pampa, Texas.

SPARKY. This Sparky was a brown stallion foaled in 1934. He was by Spark Plug by Jack McCue by Peter McCue and out of a three-quarter Thoroughbred mare. He was bred by Ed Deahl of Panhandle, Texas, and owned by Vance Rhea of Pampa, Texas.

SPEEDY. Speedy was by Kelly by Star Shoot (TB) and out of Red Wings by Reincocas by Mose. He was bred and owned by John Williams of Stead, New Mexico.

SPEEDY BALL. This sorrel stallion was foaled in 1904. He was sired by Tom Campbell by Old Bob Peters by Pony Pete, and his dam was Stockings. He was bred and owned by Dan C. Armstrong of Doxey, Oklahoma. Armstrong got Stockings from C. B. Campbell.

SPIDER. Spider was a C.A.Q.R.H. stallion sired by *Janus and out of an imported mare. He was a full brother of Peacock. He was bred by Captain John Alston of Halifax County, North Carolina. He was foaled in 1764. He is listed in both Edgar and the *ASB*.

SPIEGEL. Spiegel was foaled in 1933 or 1934. He was by Mont Megellon by Gold Coin by The Senator. His dam was Silver Finn by The Senator by Leadville (TB). He was bred and owned by Axel E. Peterson of Elbert, Colorado. According to another source, this horse was sired by the Thoroughbred Mont Majella; who was owned at the time by J. R. Bradley of Colorado Springs, Colorado.

SPOKANE. Spokane was a bay stallion who was foaled about 1931 and died about 1938 or 1939. He was by Paul El by Hickory Bill by Peter McCue, and his dam was Maud by Arch Oldham. He was bred by Columbus Sykes of Stockdale, Texas. Later he was owned by the following breeders: Walter Askey, Gonzales, Texas; Bert Carnes, Floresville, Texas; Jim Clamp, Bracketville, Texas; Earl Sellers, Del Rio, Texas; and finally by Raymond Dickson, Zaragoza, Coahuila, Mexico.

SPRING WATER. Spring Water was a bay stallion foaled in 1883. He was by Hubbard (TB) and out of a mare by Oregon Lummix by Simtuck by Oregon Dick. He was owned and raced in California by F. Work.

STALKS. Stalks was a roan stallion foaled about 1911 or 1912. He was sired by John Wilkins by Peter McCue by Dan Tucker and out of Cora by Blue by Cornstalk. He was bred and owned by Gaston B. Mathis of Stinnett, Texas, who had John Wilkins during the 1910 and 1911 seasons.

STAND PAT. This sorrel stallion was foaled in 1930. He was sired by Captain Costigan (TB) and out of Eagle by Moss King by Big King by One-Eyed Kingfisher. He was bred by the Waddell Brothers of Odessa, Texas.

STAR LAD. This sorrel stallion was foaled in 1934. He was by High Star (TB) and out of Texas Lassie by Suffragist (TB). His second dam was Emma Hill by Peter McCue. He was bred by W. H. Askey of Sisterdale, Texas. Star Tex was a full brother.

STARLIGHT. Starlight was a brown stallion foaled in 1926. He was by Esquire (TB) and out of Cherry by Billie Tom. He was bred by J. M. "Monty" Corder of Sanderson, Texas.

STARLIGHT. This Starlight was by Young Fred by Old Nick by Old Fred and out of Ruby by Wildcat by Jim Ned. He was bred and owned by Earl Moye of Arvada, Wyoming.

STAR LIGHT. Star Light was by Concho Colonel by Jim Ned by Pancho and out of a little range mare named Raska. He was bred by Dan D. Casement of Manhattan, Kansas, and later sold to Samuel Russell Jr. of Middletown, Connecticut.

STAR SHOOT (STAR). Star Shoot, sometimes referred to as Star, was a black stallion foaled in 1914. He was by Hermus by Tom Campbell by Bob Peters and out of Little Deer by Idle Boy. He was bred by Earl Kelly of Las Vegas, New Mexico, and later owned by Jim Kelly of Nara Visa, New Mexico, and by John W. Zurick of Stead, New Mexico. He was also used by the Bacas on the Gallegos Ranch. He was sometimes referred to as the Zurick Horse, after his last owner.

STAR TEX. Star Tex was a sorrel stallion foaled in 1933. He was sired by High Star (TB) and out of Texas Lassie by Suffragist (TB). His second dam was Emma Hill by Peter McCue. He was bred by B. A. Gunn and H. L. Poston of Austin, Texas. Star Lad was a full brother.

STATESMAN. This stallion was by *Janus and his dam was by *Fearnought. Edgar terms him a capital Quarter Horse. He died sometime before 1780. He is listed in both Edgar and the *ASB*.

STEAM BEER. This bay stallion was foaled in 1887. He was by Uncle Billy by Joe Hooker and out of Pearl by Brick by Oregon Charlie. His second dam was Nellie by Walnut Bark by Blevin's Little Tom. He was bred, owned, and raced by John Adams of Woodland, California.

STEAMBOAT CHARLEY. Steamboat Charley was foaled in 1876. He was by Oregon Charlie, and his dam is unknown. He was widely raced in Oregon, California, and Washington in the 1880's by K. G. Baldwin.

STEEL DUST. Steel Dust was foaled in 1843 and died in the late 1860's. He stood 15 hands and weighed at maturity 1,200 pounds. He was foaled in Kentucky and brought to Texas, near Lancaster, by Middleton Perry and Jones Greene in 1844. He was sired by Harry Bluff who was by Short Whip by Kentucky Whip and out of Big Nance, who was of Timoleon stock. Timoleon was by Sir Archy. Steel Dust was the first of the legendary heroes of the modern Quarter Horse.

STEEL DUST, ALSUP'S. This Steel Dust was sired by the Coontz horse by Old Snort, and his dam is unknown. He was owned by the Alsup brothers, who took him from Tennessee to Douglas County, Missouri.

STEEL DUST, JENKINS'. This Steel Dust was a roan stallion foaled in 1882 and died in 1902. He was by Cold Deck by Billy, and his dam is unknown. Although bred in Texas, he was taken to Newkirk, Oklahoma, by Abe Pellum and George Jenkins.

STEP BACK. Step Back was a brown stallion foaled in 1929. He was sired by Step Back (TB) and out of Olna by Traveler. He was bred and owned by D. W. "Webb" Christian of Big Spring, Texas.

STEPPING ON IT. He was a bay stallion foaled in 1930 by Hadrian (TB) and out of Jet Gal by Jet Sam (TB). He was bred and owned by J. M. Corder of Sanderson, Texas.

STEVE, LITTLE. This famous stallion was foaled in 1879(?). He was by Pony Pete. Helen Michaelis believed that Pony Pete was by Barney Owens by Cold Deck. My research has led me to believe that Pony Pete was by Printer by Cold Deck. In either case the breeding is very similar. Little Steve was bred by Old Man "Mike" Smiley of Sylvan Grove, Kansas, and later owned by Jim Durkey and Charles T. Walker of Kiowa, Colorado. Little Steve's dam was Cherokee Maid by Old Cold Deck. He died about 1918. Jack Casement said he stood 14 hands, 2 inches and 15 hands at the hips. Bill Cassidy of Oklahoma disagrees with this pedigree, saying that Little Steve was by Frank James (TB). With all other details he agrees.

STOCKLEY HORSE. Stockley Horse was a brown stallion by Uncle Jimmy Gray by Bonnie Joe (TB). His dam is unknown, as is his breeder, although it was probably Henry Pfefferling of San Antonio, Texas. He was later owned by Frank C. Stockley of Cloete, Coahuila, Mexico. He was raced.

STRAIGHT EDGE. Straight Edge was by Pure Gold by Jim Wells by Little Joe and out of an Anson mare. He was bred and owned by J. L. Custer of Spofford, Texas.

STRAIGHT SHOT. Straight Shot was a bay stallion foaled in 1935. He was by Line Up (TB) and out of Bonnie Bird by Paul El by Hickory Bill. He was bred by Witherspoon and Sanders of Hereford, Texas, owned by N. G. Elliston of Hereford, and then went to New Mexico in the ownership of Ervin H. Elliston of Logan, New Mexico. Later he was acquired by Filiberto F. Gallegos of Gallegos, New Mexico.

STRAIT HORSE. Strait Horse was a dun stallion sired by Yellow Jacket by Little Rondo by Lock's Rondo and out of a Gardner Quarter mare. He was bred by O. G. Parke of Kyle, Texas, and owned by Yancey C. Strait of Big Wells, Texas.

STRAWBERRY. Strawberry was by King (Possum) by Traveler and out of Bulger by Traveler. His second dam was by Pancho by Billy. He was bred by J. J. Kennedy of Bonita, Arizona, and owned in 1934 by Claude Gardner of Willcox, Arizona.

STREAK. This stallion was by Snake Bit Horse by Little Joe by Traveler, and his dam was by Hickory Bill by Peter McCue. His second dam was by Traveler. He was bred by George Clegg of Alice, Texas, and owned by J. D. Hudgins of Hungerford, Texas, and then by Cecil K. Boyt of Devers, Texas.

SUDDEN CHANGE. This bay stallion was foaled in 1933. He was by Chicaro (TB) and out of Prides Ella by Pride of India (TB). His second dam was Emma Hill by Peter McCue. He was bred by John Dial of Goliad, Texas, and later owned by the King Ranch of Kingsville, Texas.

SULLIVAN HORSE, see SAN JUAN.

SUNDAY. Sunday was by Mike by the Frank Patton dun and out of a Mitchell mare. He was bred by Albert K. Mitchell of the Bell Ranch, New Mexico, and later owned by Herbert Moss of Erick, Oklahoma.

SUNLIGHT. Sunlight was a sorrel stallion foaled in 1926. He was by Walking John by Nimrod (TB) and out of Adeline. Sunlight was bred and owned by Ed Mears of Menard, Texas.

SUN MAN. Sun Man was a sorrel stallion foaled in 1935. He was by Leonard B (TB) and out of Lightfoot by June Bug by Captain Daugherty. He was bred and owned by A. J. Beck of Brownwood, Texas.

SUN SET. This stallion was by Arch Oldham by Gallantry (TB). His dam is unknown, as is his breeder. He was owned by S. P. Williams of McCamey, Texas, and Deming, New Mexico.

SUN SHOT. Sun Shot was a sorrel stallion foaled in 1929. He was by the imported Thoroughbred Comet and out of Carrie Nations by Handy Shot by Call Shot. He was bred and owned by the Hewell brothers of Nixon, Texas.

SURPRISE. This sorrel stallion was foaled in 1925. He was by Tad H (TB) and out of Teeter by Concho Colonel. He was bred by R. P. Lamont, Jr., of Larkspur, Colorado.

SUTHERLAND. Sutherland was a sorrel stallion sired by Hickory Bill by Peter McCue by Dan Tucker. His dam was a full sister of Texas Chief, sired by Traveler. He was bred by George Clegg of Alice, Texas, and owned later by a Mr. Strickland and then by the Sutherland brothers of Eagle Lake, Texas. George Clegg said that he bred the horse and gave the pedigree. Ott Adams agreed with the pedigree but said that the Shelys bred the stallion.

SUTTON HORSE, PAGE'S, see TIM PAGE.

SWAGGER. Little is known about the breeding of Swagger except that he came from Missouri and was said to be of Brimmer stock. He was owned by Crawford Sykes and Joe Mangum of Nixon, Texas.

SWANKY. Swanky was a sorrel stallion sired by Brown Smoot by Billy Smoot by Bob Wade(?). His dam was Gray Planter by Planter (TB). He was bred by H. L. Forker of Nara Visa, New Mexico.

SWAYBACK, CHRISMAN'S. Swayback was by Alsup's Brimmer by Brimmer by Harris' Eclipse (TB) and out of a Chrisman mare. He was bred by Chrisman in Tennessee and owned by the Alsup Brothers in Tennessee and in Missouri.

SWEET DICK. This sorrel stallion was foaled in 1921. He was by Rex Black by Conjuror (TB). He was bred by George Tips of Kenedy, Texas, and later by Ed Pfefferling of San Antonio, Texas.

SWEETHEART. Sweetheart was by Skeet by Yellow Wolf by Old Joe Bailey. He was owned by John L. Swartz of Fort Worth, Texas.

SWEET OWEN. This bay stallion was foaled in 1851. He was by Gray Eagle by Woodpecker (TB) and out of Mary Porter by Muckle John. His second dam was by Printer. He was bred by Webb Ross of Scott County, Kentucky, and later owned by J. R. Viley of Kentucky. Mary Porter was also called Blinkey. Sweet Owen was a full brother of Flying Dutchman, Printer, and Viley.

SWENSON. This palomino stallion was by Yellow Wolf by Yellow Wolf by Old Joe Bailey. He was bred on the Swenson Ranch at Stamford, Texas, and later owned by J. H. Nail of Albany, Texas.

SWIFTLY HOME. Swiftly Home was a brown stallion foaled in 1927. He was by Straight Home (TB) and out of Senatress by The Senator. He was owned by C. F. Cusack of Denver, Colorado.

SYKES, ALLEN'S. This bay stallion was foaled in 1902. He was by Sykes' Rondo by McCoy Billy by Old Billy and out of Blaze by Sykes' Rondo by McCoy Billy. His second dam was May Mangum by Anthony by Old Billy. He was bred by Crawford Sykes of Nixon, Texas, and later owned by Moore and Allen of Cline, Texas; by Frank C. Stockley of Montell, Texas; and W. E. Weathersbee of Del Rio, Texas. He has also been referred to as Stockley's Sykes.

SYKES HORSE, CUSTER'S. This stallion was by Allen's Sykes by Sykes' Rondo by McCoy Billy and out of a mare by John Crowder by Old Billy. He was bred by Grant Green of Uvalde, Texas, and later owned by J. L. Custer of Spofford, Texas; by Joe Smythe of Uvalde, Texas; by Frank C. Stockley of Montell, Texas; and by Hal L. Mangum of Muzquíz, Coahuila, Mexico. He has been referred to as Grant's Green Horse.

SYKES HORSE, GONZALES', see BILLY COWEY.

SYKES HORSE, ROSE'S. This sorrel stallion was by Allen's Sykes by Sykes' Rondo by McCoy Billy and out of a John Stockley mare. He was bred by Will Allen of Uvalde, Texas, and owned by Abb Rose of Del Rio, Texas.

211

SYKES, R. O.'S. R. O.'s Sykes was a sorrel stallion foaled in 1911 and died in 1937. He was by Peter McCue by Dan Tucker by Barney Owens and out of a Texas Quarter mare. He was bred in Texas while Peter McCue was standing in San Antonio in the ownership of John Wilkens. He was bought by the Greene Cattle Company of Cananea, Sonora, Mexico. Sykes was one of five stallions purchased by the R. O. Ranch in 1916.

T

TAFFY. This sorrel stallion was foaled in 1927. He was by Joe T (TB) and out of Pet by Ned Oaks by Peter McCue. He was bred and owned by Harry Clark of Boise City, Oklahoma.

TAFFY. Taffy was by Second Lieutenant by Concho Colonel by Jim Ned. He was bred and owned by Dan D. Casement of Manhattan, Kansas.

TAFFY. This palomino stallion was by Young Fred by Old Nick by Old Fred. His breeder is unknown, but he was owned by Fred Rule of Eagle, Colorado.

TAR RIVER. Tar River was a brown stallion foaled in 1853 and died in 1875. He was by Nicholas (TB?) and out of Ivy's Glory by Cymon. He was bred in Virginia and owned in Texas.

TARZAN. Tarzan was a palomino foaled in 1935. He was sired by Shiek by Peter McCue by Dan Tucker and out of a Matador mare. He was bred by the Matador Land and Cattle Company of Channing, Texas. He was later owned by John Keeran of Inez, Texas.

TARZAN. This Tarzan was a dun stallion by Yellow Wolf by Old Joe Bailey by Eureka. His dam was a Waggoner mare.

212

He was bred by W. T. Waggoner of Fort Worth, Texas, and later owned by J. D. Croft of Jacksboro, Texas.

T. C. WHEAT BAY. This bay stallion was foaled in 1928. He was sired by Uncle Jimmy Gray by Bonnie Joe (TB) and out of Rosa Lee. He was bred by Henry Pfefferling of San Antonio, Texas.

TEDDY. Teddy was a sorrel stallion foaled in 1930. He was by Billy Dick by Billy by Columbus, and his dam was Big Enough by Billy Boy by Dominus Arvi (TB). He was bred by Albert Harrington of Correo, New Mexico, and owned by J. W. Ashcroft of Ramah, New Mexico.

TEDDY. This Teddy was a bay foaled about 1931. He was sired by Brave Bob (TB) and out of Silver Heel by Red Squirrel. He was bred and owned by William Shelts of Spearman, Texas.

TEDDY. This Teddy was a bay stallion sired by Coke T by Brown Dick by imported Derring-Do (TB). His dam was by Peter McCue by Dan Tucker, and his second dam by Old Fred by Black Ball by Missouri Mike. He was bred and owned by Frank Stetson of Oak Creek, Colorado.

TEDDY. This Teddy was by Dodger by Harmon Baker by Peter McCue and out of a black Anson Quarter mare. He was bred and owned by Millard Smith of Van Horn, Texas.

TELEGRAPH. This Telegraph was foaled about 1830. He was by Cone's Bacchus by Bacchus by Sir Archy and out of Nell by Printer. He was owned by John Hamilton of Flint, Michigan, and was a full brother of John Bacchus.

TELEGRAPH (STEWART'S TELEGRAPH). Telegraph was foaled in 1857. He was by Harry Bluff by Short Whip by Kentucky Whip, and his dam was a mare by Wild Irishman. He was Steel Dust's half-brother.

TELEGRAPH, WINTER'S. Telegraph was sired by El Rio Rey (TB) in 1893, and he was out of Hettie Humphries by

Joe Hooker. He was bred by Theodore Winter of the Rancho del Sierra stud in Nevada. Winter also had farms in Sacramento and in western Yolo County, California. See under Joe Hooker.

TEMPEST. Tempest was a sorrel stallion foaled in 1929. He was sired by Libyan Sands (TB) and out of Little Sister by Jim Ned by Pancho by Old Billy. He was bred by Sam Harkey of Sheffield, Texas, and owned by the Spade Ranch of Colorado City, Texas.

TEN FILE. Ten File was by Filemaker (TB) and out of Western Beauty by Bobby Lowe by Eureka by Shelby. His second dam was Christine C by Palm Reader (TB). He was bred and owned by Louis Sands of Glendale, Arizona.

TERNS TRICK (TURNS TRICK). This bay stallion was foaled in 1907 and may have run under the name Turns Trick. He was by Peter McCue by Dan Tucker by Barney Owens and out of Tern (TB). He was bred by Samuel Watkins of Petersburg, Illinois, and later was taken to California.

TEX. Tex was foaled about 1927. He was by Cowboy by Yellow Jacket by Little Rondo and out of Mancos Pearl by Charles Sumner, supposedly a Thoroughbred. He was bred by the Brown brothers of Farmington, New Mexico, and owned by Pie Wilson of Albuquerque, New Mexico.

TEX. This Tex was a brown stallion foaled in 1934. He was by Texas by Jack McCue by Peter McCue and out of Diamond A. He was bred by Jim Black of El Paso, Texas, and owned by Phil M. Clark of Tucson, Arizona.

TEXAS. Texas was a brown stallion sired by Jack McCue by Peter McCue by Dan Tucker and out of a Booth Quarter mare. He was bred by J. S. Booth of Deming, New Mexico, and owned by J. W. Phillips of Deming and later by Sam Watkins of El Paso, Texas.

TEXAS CHIEF. This sorrel stallion was foaled in 1890. He was by Lock's Rondo by Whalebone by Billy and out of Daisy L by Project. He was bred by W. W. Lock of Kyle, Texas, and later owned by Joe D. Jeffries of Clarendon, Texas; by the J. A. Ranch of Palo Duro, Texas; by John H. Burson of Silverton, Texas; and by a Dr. Bell of Silverton, Texas.

TEXAS CHIEF. Texas Chief was a red sorrel with a prominent blaze. He was foaled about 1905 and was by Traveler and out of a Hallettsville mare who, according to George Clegg of Alice, Texas, had Rondo blood. Since Clegg bought the mare from the Shelys, he may be correct about Texas Chief's dam. In any case, Texas Chief was bred by Will and Dow Shely of Alfred, Texas, and was later owned by Ott Adams of Alfred, Texas, and then by the Waggoner Ranch of Fort Worth, Texas.

TEXAS CHIEF, LITTLE. Little Texas Chief was by Texas Chief by Traveler and out of a Clegg mare. He was foaled in 1919, bred by George Clegg of Alice, Texas, and owned by Mont B. Noelke of Mertzon, Texas, and Will Noelke of Sheffield, Texas.

TEXAS JACK. Texas Jack was a sorrel stallion foaled in 1930. He was by Jack McCue by Peter McCue by Dan Tucker and out of a Francis Quarter mare. He was bred by J. W. Francis of Floyd, New Mexico, and owned by Sam Martin of Fort Sumner, New Mexico; L. L. Martin of Stephenville, Texas; and Tom L. Burnett of Fort Worth, Texas. He died in 1943(?).

TEXAS REYNOLDS. This sorrel stallion was by Norfleet by the imported Thoroughbred Brettenham and out of Isla Sunshine by Frank Norfleet by Joe Rutledge. He was bred by J. Frank Norfleet of Hale Center, Texas, and later owned by Clyde Reynolds of Sterling City, Texas.

TEXAS ROAN. This stallion was by Chaquiz by Little Rondo by Lock's Rondo and out of a mare by Little Rondo. He was bred and owned by Abraham Perez of Bruni, Texas.

THOMPSON DUN, see GRULLA, OLD.

THREE FINGER JACK. This stallion was sired by Traveler and out of a Gardner Quarter mare. He was bred by Alex Gardner of San Angelo, Texas, and owned by Charles A. Gardner of Elgin, Arizona, and a Mr. Holstein of Deming, New Mexico.

THURMAN. Thurman was by John Cook by Steel Dust by Harry Bluff, and his dam was by Bill Garner by Steel Dust. He was bred by E. Shelby Stanfield of Thorp Spring, Texas. He was owned by R. H. Horton of Quanah, Texas.

TIGER. This mahogany bay stallion stood 15½ hands high and was foaled about 1822 or 1823. He was by Kentucky Whip by imported Whip (TB) and out of a Paragon mare by Hunt's Paragon. He was owned by D. W. Parrish, whose farm was in Clark County, Kentucky, about 12 miles south of Lexington. His blood was an important asset to the nineteenth-century Quarter Horse.

TIGER. This Tiger was a brown stallion foaled in 1835. He was sired by Printer by Holmes' Printer. He was owned by Charles Love of Indiana.

TIGER, LITTLE. Little Tiger was a full brother of Old Tiger. He was foaled in 1817, sired by Kentucky Whip by imported Whip and out of Jane Hunt by Hampton's Paragon. He was bred and owned by John Harris of Kentucky.

TIGER, MANGUM'S. This black stallion was foaled in 1861. He was by Tiger II by Old Tiger and out of an unknown mare. He was bred in Kentucky and later brought to Texas and finally owned by Joe M. Mangum of Nixon, Texas,

TIGER, OLD. Old Tiger was a bay stallion foaled in 1812 and died in 1832. He was by Kentucky Whip by imported Whip and out of Jane Hunt by Hampton's Paragon. He was owned in Kentucky by Elisha J. Winter and was probably bred by John Harris of Kentucky.

TIM. Tim was a brown stallion by Saladin by Ding Bob by Brown Dick and out of Goldie by Fred S (TB). His second dam was Stockings by Old Fred by Black Ball by Missouri Mike. He was bred by Marshall Peavy of Clark, Colorado, and later owned by B. T. Kinney of Steamboat Springs, Colorado.

TIMOLEON. Timoleon was by Sir Archy, and his dam was by imported Saltram, and his granddam the Wildair mare. As John H. Wallace says, "Beyond that the pedigree is hopeless."

TIM PAGE. Tim Page was a brown stallion by a Bob Sutton horse by a Billy Quarter Horse. His dam was a bay Sykes Quarter mare. He was bred by R. C. Sutton of Cotulla, Texas, and later sold to P. P. Page of Willcox, Arizona.

TINKERTOY. This black stallion was foaled in 1929. He was sired by Toyland (TB) and out of Big Knee by John Wilkes by Peter McCue. He was bred and owned by J. E. Renfro of Menard, Texas.

TOBEY, ROBERTS'. Tobey was by the Frank Patton dun by Yellow Jacket by Little Rondo and out of a Tobe Roberts' one-half Thoroughbred race mare. He was bred by Tobe Roberts, Texas address unknown, and later sold to Buck Coody of Knox City, Texas.

TOCHO GARCIA. Tocho Garcia was bred by Ott Adams of Alice, Texas, although his sire and dam are unknown at this time. He was purchased by Fructuoso (Tocho) Garcia of Piedras Negras, Coahuila, Mexico. He was bought to race and was very successful in Mexico. His only recorded get are the two famous race mares Marvomira and Peanut. Both were out of John Crowder mares.

TOM (SCOOTER). This gray stallion was foaled in 1925 and died in 1938. He was by Midnight by Badger by Peter McCue and out of Trixie by Press, an Arabian. He was bred by Keller Cooper of Elk City, Oklahoma, and owned by J. H. Minnick of Crowell, Texas, and Tom L. Burnett of Fort Worth, Texas. He was called Scooter originally.

TOM BENNETT. This stallion was sired by Joe Collins by Old Billy by Shiloh and his dam's breeding is unknown. He was owned by the CS Ranch of Cimarron, New Mexico. He is listed as the sire of Dora, the dam of Christina.

TOM, BLEVIN'S LITTLE. Blevin's Little Tom was foaled in 1840(?). He was sired by Veto or by Old Veto, Veto's sire. Old Veto was by Contention by Sir Archy. Old Veto stood at Madison, Kentucky. Little Tom, along with Oregon Charlie, did much to establish Oregon as a primary source of short-horses for the Pacific Coast area. Little Tom was driven overland with a wagon train, starting at St. Louis in 1847 and going to Oregon. Little Tom sired, among other well-known horses, the famous California sire Walnut Bark. The *ASB* says Little Tom was of Quarter stock, and adds that he was sired by Old Veto.

TOM CAMPBELL (GREY TOM). This gray stallion was foaled in 1895. He was by Bob Peters by Pony Pete by Barney Owens and his dam was also by Bob Peters. He was bred by C. B. Campbell of Minco, Oklahoma, and later owned by Charley Keith and then by the Armstrong brothers of Elk City, Oklahoma.

TOM CAT. This stallion was by Booger Red by Old Fred by Black Ball. His dam and breeder are unknown. He was owned by Leonard B. Pierson of Hayden, Colorado.

TOM D II. Tom D II was a bay stallion foaled in 1893. He was by the Duke of Highlands (TB) and out of Kitty Watkins (Kitty Waddle) by Jack Traveler by Steel Dust. He was bred and owned by B. C. Watkins of Newmanville, Illinois.

TOM DRIVER. Tom Driver was by Steel Dust by Harry Bluff by Short Whip and out of Mammoth by Shiloh by Van Tromp. He was bred and owned by Henry T. Batchler of Lancaster, Texas.

TOM GAY. This sorrel stallion was foaled in the 1890's. He was by Jack Hardy (TB) and out of Maley by Tar River. He was bred and owned by Henry T. Batchler of Lancaster, Texas.

TOM GAY. This stallion was bay, and he was foaled in 1927. He was by Red Seal by Sealskin by Harmon Baker and out of the Standardbred mare Patsey. He was bred and owned by J. M. Corder of Sanderson, Texas.

TOM GLOVER. Tom Glover was by Sykes' Rondo by McCoy Billy by Old Billy and out of a Mangum mare. He was bred by Joe M. Mangum of Nixon, Texas, and owned by Paul Ingenhuett of Comfort, Texas, and by Fritz Bierschwale of Harper, Texas.

TOM HARDING (THE MODEL). Tom Harding was a bay stallion foaled in 1889. He was by General Harding (TB) and out of Kitty Watkins (Kitty Waddle) by Jack Traveler by Steel Dust. He was bred by Samuel Watkins of Petersburg, Illinois, and later raced by Scoggan Brothers in Illinois.

TOM, LITTLE. Little Tom was by Abe Frank Jr. by Abe Frank (TB) and out of a Trammell mare. He was bred by Tom Trammell of Sweetwater, Texas, and owned by John Sims of Snyder, Texas.

TOMMIE GRAY. This bay stallion was foaled in 1928. He was by Uncle Jimmy Gray by Bonnie Joe (TB) and out of

Janet V by Elmendorf (TB). His second dam was Emma Hill by Peter McCue. He was bred by Ed and Henry Pfefferling of San Antonio, Texas.

TOM MIX. Tom Mix was by Uncle Jimmy Gray by Bonnie Joe (TB) and his dam was a Haby mare by Old Ben by Tom Grey. He was bred by Dick Haby of Hondo, Texas, and owned by Henry Rosenow of Uvalde, Texas, and by George R. Herndon of Leakey, Texas.

TOMMY. This stallion was by Young Joe Collins by Joe Collins by Old Billy. He was owned by the Diamond Cattle Company of Dexter, New Mexico, or by Hal Bogle of Dexter, New Mexico.

TOM, OLD. This Old Tom was by John Crowder by Old Billy. He was bred at Hondo, Texas, and owned by F. G. Senne of Hondo. He was also known as Tom and as One-Eyed Crowder Horse.

TOM, OLD. Old Tom was by Big Apple by Joe Collins and out of Little Sorrel by King Wood (TB). He was bred by George McGonigal of Midland, Texas, and owned by Joe Kane of Nogales, Arizona.

TOM POLK. Tom Polk was a sorrel foaled in 1926. He was sired by Everett (TB) and out of Fanny by John Wilkes by Peter McCue. He was bred and owned by J. Renfro of Sonora, Texas.

TOM ROY. Tom Roy was by Free Hand (TB) and out of Godiva by The Senator. He was owned by Samuel Russell Jr. of Middleton, Connecticut.

TOM THUMB. Tom Thumb was by Little Joe by Traveler and out of a Cotton Wright mare by Cherokee. He was bred and owned by Cotton Wright of Banquite, Texas.

TOM THUMB JR. Tom Thumb Jr. was by Tom Thumb by Little Joe by Traveler and out of a Clegg mare sired by

Hickory Bill by Peter McCue by Dan Tucker. His second dam was by Little Joe by Traveler. He was bred by George Clegg of Alice, Texas, purchased by the Paterson-Rieck Ranch of Roosevelt, Texas, and in 1931 was owned by Earl Huffman of Junction, Texas.

TOM TUG. Tom Tug was a bay stallion foaled in 1894. He was by Fonso (TB) and out of May Kennedy by Faustus (TB) and his second dam was Printer by Gray Eagle. He was bred and owned by Mrs. M. Treacy of Lexington, Kentucky. She was undoubtedly the wife of B. J. Treacy.

TONY COTTONTAIL. This Tony was by Tony by Guinea Pig by Possum and out of a Quarter mare. He was bred by W. D. Wear of Willcox, Arizona, and later owned by George (Gabby) Hayes of Studio City, California.

TONY, DEAHL'S (DEALS). This stallion was by Pal by Palomar, and was owned by Tom Deahl of Fritch, Texas.

TONY REILS. Tony Reils was by Big Jim by Sykes' Rondo by McCoy Billy. He was bred by Jim McFaddin of Victoria, Texas.

TONY ROGERS. This bay stallion was foaled in 1927. He was sired by Uncle Jimmy Gray by Bonnie Joe (TB) and out of Flossy Brown. He was bred and owned by Mose Franklin of San Antonio, Texas.

TONY, WARDLAW'S. This stallion was sired by Gus Wheat's Tony by Allen's Sykes by Sykes' Rondo and his dam was by Little Rondo by Sykes' Rondo. He was owned by L. B. Wardlaw of Del Rio, Texas.

TONY, WHEAT'S OLD. This Tony was by Allen's Sykes by Sykes' Rondo and his dam was by Traveler. His breeder is unknown, but he was owned by L. B. Harrington of Rocksprings, Texas; by Dave Sweeten and Lee Wallace of Barksdale, Texas; by Sam Rainey of Barksdale; and by Gus Wheat of Sonora, Texas.

TOP HAT. Top Hat was a sorrel stallion foaled in 1933. He was by Red Bug by Everett (TB) and out of a mare by Master Gould (TB). His second dam probably was by Dogie Beasley by Sykes' Rondo by McCoy Billy, but she may have been a granddaughter of Dogie Beasley. He was bred by J. S. Holman of Sonora, Texas, and owned by T. D. Beasley of San Antonio, Texas.

TOP HAT, SPILLER'S. This Top Hat was a sorrel foaled in 1933 by Red Bug by Everett (TB) and out of a Master Gould mare. His second dam was a Dogie Beasley mare. He was a three-quarter brother of the other Top Hat. He was bred by Jap Holman of Sonora, Texas, and owned later by Hugh Spiller of Menard, Texas.

TOP KICK. Top Kick was by Brown Dick by Mose by Old Mose by Traveler and out of Little Blaze by Possum by Traveler. He was an Arizona horse.

TORMENTOR. Tormentor was a sorrel stallion foaled in 1914. He was sired by Barnsdale (TB) and out of Maggie King by Peter McCue. He was bred and owned by George Newton of Del Rio, Texas.

TOT LEE. Tot Lee was a bay stallion foaled in 1905. He was sired by Peter McCue by Dan Tucker by Barney Owens and out of Nona P by The Duke of Highlands (TB). He was a full brother of the famous Texas horse, Harmon Baker. He was bred by Sam Watkins of Petersburg, Illinois, and owned by Hugh Watkins of Oakford, Illinois.

TOY BOY. Toy Boy was a bay foaled about 1918. He was sired by Deuce of Hearts by Ace of Hearts by the Dunderstadt horse and out of a Thoroughbred mare. He was bred by the King Ranch(?) of Kingsville, Texas, and was owned by the East Ranch, and then by Bob McMurray of Hebbronville, Texas.

TRAMMELL (OLD TRAMMELL, JIM TRAMMELL). Trammell was foaled in 1925(?). He was by Cappy by Dr.

222

Mack and out of a Reynolds' mare. He was bred by the Reynolds Cattle Company of Fort Worth, Texas, and owned by H. W. Davis of Clairemont, Texas.

TRAMP. Tramp was by Tubal Cain by Berry's Cold Deck and his dam traced back to Alsup's Red Buck. Tramp was bred by S. Coke Blake of Pryor, Oklahoma, and owned by E. Grove Cullum of Fort Reno, Oklahoma. Blake gave Colonel Cullum Tramp in 1941.

TRAVELER. There have been many conflicting stories about Traveler, the great South Texas sire of the early 1900's. He was foaled shortly before 1900 and sired his last colt in 1911. Much has been written about Traveler; one of the best articles is by Lewis Nordyke for the *Quarter Horse Journal* in December, 1954. As far as facts are concerned, little is known about him prior to the time he was found pulling a scraper for the railroad; there are conflicting stories about him afterwards. He was a great sire, as well as a great race horse. After racing for a time, he was used as a ranch stallion by Chris Seale of Baird, Texas. He then passed through several hands and finally became the main stallion on the Shely Ranch at Alfred, Texas.

TRAVELER, BLAKE'S. This stallion was foaled in 1914 and lived until about 1930. He was sired by Gold Button by Slip Shoulder by Missouri Mike and out of Flaxie B by Tubal Cain by Berry's Cold Deck. He was bred by Coke Blake of Pryor, Oklahoma, and owned by I. W. Blake of Morrow, Arkansas. Coke's brother, Watt, calf-roped this horse extensively.

TRAVELER, CUNNINGHAM'S. This stallion was by Traveler and out of a Cunningham mare. He was bred by Jack Cunningham of Comanche, Texas, and owned by "Webb" Christian of Big Spring, Texas.

TRAVELER, DOLAN'S. This Traveler was by Traveler and out of a Gardner mare. He was bred by John E. Gardner of

San Angelo, Texas, and owned by Tom Dolan and by Stanley Turner, both of Water Valley, Texas.

TRAVELER, LITTLE. Little Traveler was by Traveler and out of a Gardner Quarter mare. He was bred by Alex Gardner and later Charley Gardner took the horse to Arizona.

TRAVELER, others. There were several other Travelers about whom little is known. Booger Red's Traveler was by Dolan's Traveler and owned by Samuel Thomas Privett (Booger Red) of San Angelo. Then there was Foster's Traveler, who was by Traveler, owned by W. L. Foster of Sterling City. There was also Martin's Traveler, breeding unknown, owned by T. G. Martin of Kyle, Texas. This Traveler ended up in the Big Bend Country of Texas. Another Traveler was Irvine's. He was by Traveler and out of an unknown dam. He was owned by the Irvine Cattle Company of Tustin, California. Another son of Traveler, carrying his name, was Shely's, bred by Will and Dow Shely of Alfred, Texas. There was also a Traveler Jr., out of Traveler and an unknown mare. Junior was owned by Ira Carson of Ozone, Texas. J. M. Corder of Sanderson had a Traveler colt he called Traveler's Boy.

TROUBLE. Trouble was by Dan Tucker by Barney Owens by Cold Deck and out of an Oklahoma Quarter mare. He was bred by Thomas Trammell of Sweetwater, Texas, and owned by Oliver M. Lee of Alamogordo, New Mexico.

TROUBLE, LITTLE. This is the same horse as Trouble Jr. and Young Trouble. He was by Trouble by Dan Tucker and out of Nellie by Pat Garrett. He was bred and owned by Oliver M. Lee of Alamogordo, New Mexico.

TRUANT BOY. This stallion was foaled in 1928. He was sired by Lone Star by Billy Sunday by Horace H (TB) and out of a mare by Yellow Wolf by Old Joe Bailey. He was bred by John Dial of Goliad, Texas, and owned by W. B. Warren of Hockley, Texas, and Ray Moore of Richmond, Texas.

TRUCKER MILLER. This bay stallion was foaled in 1907. He was by Peter McCue by Dan Tucker by Barney Owens and out of Lady Lyon II (TB). He was bred by Maggie Watkins of Oakford, Illinois.

TUBAL CAIN. Tubal Cain was a sorrel stallion foaled in 1903 who died in 1918(?). He was by Berry's Cold Deck by Cold Deck by Steel Dust and out of Lucy Maxwell by Alsup's Red Buck by Grinder. His second dam was a line-bred Brimmer mare. He was bred by Coke Blake of Pryor, Oklahoma.

TUERTO. This bay stallion was sired by Hickory Bill by Peter McCue by Dan Tucker and out of a Fred Raymond mare by Little Joe by Traveler. His second dam was Lucretia M by The Hero (TB). He was bred by Fred Raymond of Raymondville, Texas, and later owned by Eligio Garcia of Rachal(?), Texas.

TUESDAY, see SHANNON.

TULAN CHIEF, see TULARE CHIEF.

TULARE CHIEF. This bay stallion was foaled in 1888. He was by Sleepy Dick by Roan Dick by Black Nick by Telegraph and his dam was Fallen Leaf. His breeder is unknown, but he was raced widely under the name Tulan Chief and Tulare Chief. He was raced in California by W. B. Fudge of Tulare, California.

TULLOS STUD, see DROWSY HENRY.

TURCO. Turco was by Grano de Oro by Little Joe by Traveler and out of Leona by Canales Horse by Leonell. His second dam was Vensidora by Joe Shely by Traveler. He was bred by Luis Reuteria of Edinburg, Texas.

TURK. Turk was a well-known Pacific Slope racing stallion. He was by Phil Sheridan by Mont Baker and spent some little time in the state of Washington.

TURN BACK. Turn Back was a bay stallion foaled in 1927 by Set Back (TB) and out of Daisy Lucas by Barney Lucas by Traveler. He was bred and owned by "Webb" Christian of Big Spring, Texas.

TWICKHAM. This bay C.A.Q.R.H. stallion was foaled in 1778 by *Janus and out of a *Janus mare. He was bred by Mr. Hardiman Abbington of Bertie County, North Carolina. He is listed in both Edgar and the *ASB*.

TWIGG, GOODE'S OLD. Goode's Old Twigg was a C.A.Q.R.H. stallion foaled in 1778. He was by *Janus and out of the C.A.Q.R.M. Puckett's Switch, who was herself by *Janus. Twigg was heavily made with a large blaze and two white feet. He was 14 hands-1 inch high, and was very compact with great muscular powers. He was bred by John Goode Sr. of Mecklenburg County, Virginia. He died in the ownership of a Mr. Hudson of Halifax County, North Carolina. Twigg is listed in both Edgar and the *ASB*.

TWIGG, LITTLE, see PADDY WHACK.

TWIN CITY. Twin City was a sorrel stallion foaled in 1924. He was sired by A. M. White by Everett (TB) and out of Lilly White by Horace H (TB). His second dam was Carrie Nation by Peter McCue. He was bred by Eugene J. Schott of Riomedina, Texas, and later owned by M. G. Michaelis Jr. of Kyle, Texas.

U

UNCLE BILLY. This sorrel stallion was foaled in 1885. He was by Joe Hooker (TB) and out of Bell by Oregon Charlie.

His second dam was Choctaw's Sister by Obe Jennings. He was bred and owned by John W. Adams of Woodland, California.

UNCLE JIMMY GRAY. Uncle Jimmy Gray was a brown stallion foaled in 1906 who lived until 1930. He was sired by Bonnie Joe (TB) and out of Bettie Campbell by Bob Peters by Pony Pete and his second dam was a Campbell Quarter mare by Pid Hart by Shelby by Tom Driver. He was bred by Charles B. Campbell of Minco, Oklahoma, and later owned by Till Johnson of Minco, Oklahoma. In 1921 he was owned by the United States Remount Service. While owned by the Remount, he stood in Cotulla, Texas, leased by T. Hogue Poole and later by W. F. Smith of Big Foot, Texas. Other breeders also used him. He died in the ownership of Henry Pfefferling of San Antonio, Texas.

UNCLE JIMMY GRAY, SIMINOFF'S. Siminoff's Uncle Jimmy Gray was by Bull Dog by Uncle Jimmy Gray by Bonnie Joe (TB) and out of Queen of Hearts by Ace of Hearts by the Dunderstadt Horse. He was bred by George Clegg of Alice, Texas, and owned by Yale Siminoff of Phoenix, Arizona. He is sometimes referred to as Arizona Jimmy Gray.

UNION. Union was foaled in the late 1830's. He was by Van Tromp by Thomas' Big Solomon by Sir Solomon. He was Shiloh's sire. Little more is known about him.

UTE CREEK REED, see A. D. REED II.

VALENTINO. Valentino was by Camaron by Texas Chief by Traveler and out of Jeanette by Harmon Baker by Peter McCue. His dam was an Anson Quarter mare. He was bred by C. Manuel Benevides of Laredo, Texas.

VANDERBILT. Vanderbilt was a bay stallion foaled in 1872. He was by Norfolk (TB) and out of Sally Franklin by Illinois Medoc (TB). His dam was a running Quarter mare. He was bred and owned by A. Musick of California.

VAN TROMP. Van Tromp was a bay stallion foaled in 1825. He was by Eaton's Van Tromp and his dam was by Sir Archy (*ASB*, Vol. II, 529). He was bred by W. N. Edwards and owned by E. M. Wagoner of Adair County, Kentucky. He is listed in Bruce's *American Stud Book*.

VAN TROMP. This Van Tromp was foaled in 1835. He was by Van Tromp by Thomas' Big Solomon by Sir Solomon and out of a Muckle John mare. He is listed in Bruce.

VAN TROMP, EATON'S. Eaton's Van Tromp was the original Van Tromp. He was foaled in 1809 and sired by Florizel by imported Diomed and out of Malbrook by imported Mexican. He was bred by Major John R. Eaton of Granville County, North Carolina. He is in Edgar's *Studbook*.

VETO, OLD. Old Veto was a sorrel stallion foaled in 1827. He was by Contention by Sir Archy and out of Colombia by Sir Archy. He was bred by the Hon. Mark Alexander of Mecklenburg County, Virginia. He is listed in Bruce's *Studbook*. See Blevin's Little Tom.

VILEY. Viley was a bay stallion foaled in 1854. He was sired by Gray Eagle by Woodpecker by Bertrand and out of Blinkey (Mary Porter) by Muckle John by Muckle John by Sir Archy. His second dam was by Old Printer. He was bred by Webb Ross of Scott County, Kentucky. He was a full brother to Flying Dutchman, Printer, and Sweet Owen.

VIOLIN. Violin was a sorrel stallion sired by Martin's Best (TB). His dam was a King Ranch mare. He was bred and owned by the King Ranch of Kingsville, Texas.

VIRGINIAN, THE. The Virginian was by Judge Welsh by Traveler and out of a Seale mare. He was bred by C. C. Seale of Baird, Texas.

VITO. Vito was a bay stallion foaled in 1933. He was by Gold Bug (TB) and out of Good Luck by Booger Red by Rancocas (TB). He was bred by Robert Land of Southold, Long Island, New York.

VIVIAN B. Vivian B was a sorrel foaled in 1910. He was by John Wilkins by Peter McCue by Dan Tucker and out of Big Ciss by Wawekus (TB). He was owned by Edwin Blakeley of Kilbourne, Illinois.

W

WAGGONER, HICKMAN'S. Hickman's Waggoner was a dun stallion by Yellow Wolf by Old Joe Bailey by Eureka and out of a Waggoner range mare. He was bred by W. T. Waggoner of Fort Worth, Texas, and owned by W. A. Hickman of Bronte, Texas. In 1935, he was purchased by William P. Bevans of Menard, Texas.

WAGGONER, JACKSON'S. Jackson's Waggoner was a dun stallion sired by Yellow Jacket by Little Rondo by Lock's Rondo and out of a Waggoner mare. He was bred by W. T. Waggoner of Fort Worth, Texas, and owned by Harold Jackson of Abilene, Texas.

WAGGONER, JONES'. Jones' Waggoner was by Yellow Jacket by Little Rondo by Lock's Rondo and out of a Waggoner mare. He was bred by W. T. Waggoner of Fort Worth, Texas, and owned by O. P. Jones of Midland, Texas.

WAGGONER, SCHARBAUER'S. Scharbauer's Waggoner was a dun sired by Yellow Wolf by Old Joe Bailey by Eureka and out of a Waggoner mare. He was bred by W. T. Waggoner of Fort Worth, Texas, and owned by Clarence Scharbauer of Midland, Texas.

WAGGONER, SMITH'S. Smith's Waggoner was sired by a son of Yellow Wolf by Old Joe Bailey and his dam was by Midnight by Badger by Peter McCue. He was bred by W. T. Waggoner of Fort Worth, Texas, and owned in 1931 by W. F. Smith of Big Foot, Texas.

WAKE UP JAKE. Wake Up Jake was a bay stallion foaled in 1907. He was sired by Peter McCue by Dan Tucker by Barney Owens and out of Katie Bar the Door by Duke of Highlands (TB). He was bred by Samuel Watkins of Petersburg, Illinois.

WALKING JOHN. Walking John was a bay stallion foaled in 1909. He was by Nimrod (TB) and out of Metropolis by Peter McCue by Dan Tucker. He was bred by W. C. Watkins of Oakford, Illinois, and owned by Richard J. Godfrey of Menard, Texas.

WALKING PRINCE. Walking Prince was a bay stallion foaled in 1928. He was by Hendricks (TB) and out of Princess Peep by Walking John by Nimrod (TB). His second dam was Madam Peep by Bo Peep, a Quarter Horse. He was bred and owned by Arch Wilkinson of Menard, Texas.

WALL PAPER. Wall Paper was a gray stallion foaled in 1891. He was sired by Buck Walton (TB) and out of Gypsy Queen. He was bred by John R. Nasworthy of San Angelo, Texas.

WALNUT BARK. This chestnut stallion was foaled in 1853 and spent most of his life in California. He was used extensively by John Adams of Woodland. He was by Blevin's Little Tom. His dam was Bessie Tar Tar by a son of Tarter by Arch.

WALTER HOWARD. This bay stallion was foaled in 1889. He was by the imported Thoroughbred Tubal Cain and out of a Quarter mare named Maud. He was bred by William M. Sumners of Lineville, Iowa.

WALTER OVERTON. Walter Overton was a bay stallion foaled in 1885. He was by Joe Hooker (TB) and out of Bay Kate by Norfolk (TB). His second dam was Big Gun (Kate George) by Old George. He was bred by T. J. Knight of Beatrice, California.

WALTER P. Walter P was a bay stallion foaled in 1901. He was by Peter McCue by Dan Tucker by Barney Owens and out of Velma by Fib (TB). He was bred by Samuel Watkins of Petersburg, Illinois.

WANDERING JEW. Wandering Jew was a bay stallion foaled in 1908. He was by Palm Reader (TB) and out of Annie T by Traveler. He was bred and owned by "Webb" Christian of Big Spring, Texas.

WANDERING JEW. This Wandering Jew was a bay foaled in 1927. He was sired by Set Back (TB) and out of Fay Larkin by Barney Lucas by Traveler. He was bred by H. P. Saunders Jr. of Roswell, New Mexico.

WANDERLUST. Wanderlust was a brown stallion foaled in 1926. He was sired by Allen's Choice (TB) and out of Bonnie by Billy Mason. He was owned by Elmer Mourning of Kiowa, Colorado.

WARRIOR, BUTLER'S. This sorrel stallion was by Captain Sykes by Sykes' Rondo by McCoy Billy. His dam is unknown, as is his breeder. He was owned by Sylvestra Shoat of Kenedy, Texas, and by the Butler brothers of Kenedy, Texas.

WEAVER. Weaver was a bay stallion foaled in 1883. He was by Big Henry (TB) and out of Nanie Owens by Barney Owens by Cold Deck. He was bred by Thomas Watkins of Petersburg, Illinois.

WEAZLE. Weazle was foaled in 1822. He was by Kentucky Whip by the imported Thoroughbred Whip and out of Old Crop, a Kentucky race mare. He was bred by Lewis Sanders Jr. of Kentucky.

WEBB'S CHOICE. Webb's Choice was a sorrel foaled in 1922. He was by Barney Lucas by Traveler and out of Overknight by Benighted (TB). He was bred by "Webb" Christian of Big Spring, Texas, and owned by Charles S. Springer of the CS Ranch at Cimarron, New Mexico.

WHALEBONE. This sorrel stallion was foaled in 1868. He was by Old Billy by Shiloh by Van Tromp and out of Paisana by Brown Dick by Berkshire. His second dam was Belton Queen by Guinea Boar. He was bred by William B. Fleming of Belmont, Texas, and owned by Crawford Sykes and Joe Mangum of Nixon, Texas. In 1879, he was owned by Charles R. Haley of Sweetwater, Texas.

WHALEBONE. This Whalebone was by Texas Chief by Traveler and out of Kitty by Blue Eyes by Sykes' Rondo. He was bred by Dow and Will Shely of Alfred, Texas.

W. H. ASHLAND. W. H. Ashland was a bay stallion foaled in 1900. He was by Ashland II (TB) and out of Level Lady by Leveller (TB). His second dam was Lady Lawrence (Polly) by Wisconsin Harry by Harry Miller. He was bred and owned by S. E. Lawrence of Maple City, Kansas.

WHIP, COOK'S or BLACKBURN'S, see KENTUCKY WHIP.

WHISKAWAY II. This sorrel stallion was by Whiskaway by A. D. Reed by Peter McCue and out of a Gallegos mare. He was bred by Filiberto F. Gallegos of Gallegos, New Mexico, and owned by N. T. Baca of Gallegos, New Mexico.

WHISKEY. Whiskey was a sorrel stallion foaled in the 1920's. He was by Elexa Lad by Cap by Tom Glover. He was out of a little bay mare by Hickman's Waggoner. He was bred and owned by Henry Marr of Menard, Texas.

WHITE HEEL. This bay stallion was foaled in 1899. He was sired by Rancocas (TB) and out of Nellie Havre by Havre (TB). He was bred by Charles R. Haley of Sweetwater, Texas.

WHITE LIGHTNING. This gray stallion was influential in establishing the modern Quarter Horse but little information has been uncovered about him, probably because he was stolen out of Missouri. (See *The Quarter Horse, A Story of Two Centuries*, 128.) He sired Grey Rebel, and White Lightning mares provided a foundation for the Blake horses.

WHITE LIGHTNING, YOUNG. Young Lightning was a gray stallion by White Lightning and out of an Alsup mare. He was bred by Jack Alsup of Bald Knob, Douglas County, Missouri, and later owned by S. Coke Blake of Pryor, Oklahoma. For more information, see Grey Rebel and White Lightning.

WILD CAT. Wild Cat was by Jim Ned by Pancho by Old Billy and out of an Anson Quarter mare. He was bred by William Anson of Christoval, Texas, and his owners were Si Dawson of Hayden, Colorado, and Dan Casement of Manhattan, Colorado. He was bought from Anson in 1911.

WILKENS. Wilkens was foaled in 1918. He was by John Wilkins (Wilkes) by Peter McCue by Dan Tucker and out of a J. A. mare. He was bred by the J. A. Ranch of Palo Duro, Texas, and owned by Ross Chisum of Dumas, Texas. The J. A.'s sold him in 1921.

WILL ALLEN HORSE, see SYKES HORSE, ROSE'S.

WILLIE (DEB WALKER). Willie was a gray stallion sired by Ace of Hearts by the Dunderstadt Horse by Sykes' Rondo. He was bred by Will Copeland of Pettus, Texas, and later owned by Deb Walker of Sweetwater, Texas.

WILLIE NORFLEET, LITTLE. Little Willie Norfleet was by Norfleet by Brettenham (TB) and out of a Norfleet mare. He was bred and owned by J. Frank Norfleet of Hale Center, Texas.

WILLRUN. Willrun was a sorrel foaled in 1932. He was by Runmore (TB) and out of Lady Blackburn by Barney Lucas by Traveler. He was bred by Dick Gray of Gorman, Texas.

WILL STEAD. Will Stead was by Billy McCue by Jack Mc-Cue by Peter McCue and out of Silver by Chickasha Bob by Rocky Mountain Tom. He was bred by W. R. Stead of Tulia, Texas, and owned by A. L. McCurtry of Silverton, Texas, and the J. A. Ranch of Palo Duro, Texas.

WILL WRIGHT. Will Wright was a sorrel sired by Little Joe by Traveler and out of a mare by Hickory Bill by Peter McCue. His second dam was by Traveler. He was bred by George Clegg of Alice, Texas, and owned by W. T. Wright of Alice, Texas; George W. Reynolds of Alfred, Texas; and by Alonzo Taylor of Hebbronville, Texas.

WINDIGO. Windigo was a brown stallion foaled in 1927. He was sired by H. T. Waters (TB) and out of Ucheno by Billy(?). He was bred and owned by J. W. Bond of Ramah, New Mexico.

WOLF, see APACHE KID.

WONDER, LITTLE. Little Wonder was foaled in 1915. He was by Rex Beach by Conjuror (TB) and out of a Lock Quarter mare. He was bred by O. G. Parke of Kyle, Texas, and owned by O. T. Sheeran of Cotulla, Texas.

WONDER WORLD (TIM PAGE'S BILLY). This stallion was by Tim Page by a Bob Sutton horse by a Billy Quarter Horse. He was bred by P. P. Page of Willcox, Arizona, and later owned by C. M. Nuttall of Cochise, Arizona; and L. Burns Blanton of Bowie, Arizona.

WOODPECKER. Woodpecker was a bay stallion foaled in 1927. He was sired by Dennis Reed (TB) and out of Red Wing by Moss King by Big King by One-Eyed Kingfisher. He was bred by the Waddell brothers of Odessa, Texas.

WOODROW WILSON. This stallion was a sorrel, and he was foaled in 1916 and died in 1937. He was sired by The Senator by Leadville (TB) and out of Minnie S by Raymond M. His second dam was Nellie B. He was bred by Cash Spencer of Peyton, Colorado, and owned by Julius Peterson of Elbert, Colorado.

WORKMAN HORSE. This stallion was foaled in 1926. He was by Rambler by Tubal Cain by Berry's Cold Deck and out of a polo mare. He was bred by J. H. Minnick of Crowell, Texas, and owned first by Bill Workman of Shidler, Oklahoma, and later by Byrne James of Pawhuska, Oklahoma.

WYOMING CLOWN. Wyoming Clown was a bay foaled in 1928. He was by Historicus (TB) and out of Nancy by Honest Jim. He was owned by Arthur D. Young of Moorcroft, Wyoming.

Y

YAKIMA. Yakima was by The Captain by Keeno by Joy and his dam a Cub Roberts' mare. He was bred by Cub Roberts of Leedey, Oklahoma.

YAMPAH. This brown stallion was foaled in 1929. He was by Desperate (TB) and out of Sweetheart by Johnny Corbett by Little Steve by Pony Pete. His second dam was Fly by Little Steve by Pony Pete by Printer. He was bred by R. W. McDonald of Glenwood Springs, Colorado.

YANKEE DOODLE. Yankee Doodle was a palomino stallion foaled in the late 1930's. He was sired by Clover Leaf by

Fleeting Time (TB), and he was out of a Waggoner mare by Buck Thomas by Peter McCue. He was bred by W. T. Waggoner of Fort Worth, Texas, and owned by B. B. Van Vacter of Carter, Oklahoma.

YELLOW BEAR. Yellow Bear was a dun stallion foaled in 1913. He was sired by Old Joe Bailey by Eureka by Shelby and out of Old Mary by Ben Burton by Blind Barney by Steel Dust. His second dam was Mandy by Old Dutchman by Lock's Rondo by Whalebone. He was bred by Dick Baker of Weatherford, Texas, and owned by W. T. Waggoner of Fort Worth, Texas. He was a full brother of Yellow Wolf.

YELLOW BELLY (BOOTH'S YELLOW JACKET). Yellow Belly was a dun stallion foaled in 1917. He was sired by Yellow Jacket by Little Rondo by Lock's Rondo and his dam was a Parke Quarter mare by Yellow Jacket by Little Rondo by Lock's Rondo. He was bred by John E. Parke of Kyle, Texas. Later he was owned by W. I. Cook of Maryneal, Texas; Walter A. Trammell of Sweetwater, Texas; Walter L. Booth of Sweetwater, Texas; and W. I. Driggers of Santa Rosa, New Mexico.

YELLOW BOY. Yellow Boy was by Chocolate by Yellow Wolf by Old Joe Bailey by Eureka and his dam was a Waggoner mare sired by Yellow Wolf by Old Joe Bailey. His second dam was by Waggoner's Rainy Day by Lone Star. He was bred by W. T. Waggoner of Fort Worth, Texas, and owned by W. H. Campbell of Gainesville, Texas.

YELLOW BOY, BURNETT'S. This Yellow Boy was a dun stallion foaled in 1920. He was by Yellow Jacket by Little Rondo by Lock's Rondo and out of Old Mary by Ben Burton by Blind Barney by Steel Dust. His second dam was Mandy by Old Dutchman by Lock's Rondo by Whalebone. He was a half brother of Yellow Bear. He was bred by W. T. Waggoner of Fort Worth, Texas, and owned by Tom L. Burnett of Fort Worth, Texas. He ate prairie dog poison and died a couple of years after Tom Burnett bought him.

YELLOW BOY, SIMS'. This Yellow Boy was a dun stallion foaled in about 1922. He was by Yellow Belly by Yellow Jacket by Little Rondo and out of a gray Cook mare. He was bred by W. I. Cook of Maryneal, Texas, and owned by Walter A. Trammell of Sweetwater, Texas, and then by John T. Sims, Jr., of Snyder, Texas. He was sometimes referred to as Sims' Yellow Jacket.

YELLOW FEVER. Yellow Fever was a dun stallion by Yellow Wolf by Old Joe Bailey by Eureka and out of a Waggoner mare. He was bred by W. T. Waggoner of Fort Worth, Texas, and owned by A. B. Wharton of Simi, California.

YELLOW GOLD. Yellow Gold was a palomino stallion by Plaudit by King Plaudit (TB) and out of a mare by Fred Litze by Old Fred by Black Ball. He was bred by Waite Phillips of the Philmont Ranch at Cimarron and owned by Ervin H. Elliston of Logan, New Mexico, and C. J. Fisher of Stanley, New Mexico.

YELLOW JACKET. This is the first Yellow Jacket as far as Quarter Horses are concerned. He was a dun stallion foaled in 1908 who lived until 1934. He was by Little Rondo by Lock's Rondo and out of Barbee Dun by Lock's Rondo. He was bred by Jim Barbee of Kyle, Texas, and later owned by John E. Parke of Kyle, Texas; W. T. Waggoner of Fort Worth, Texas; and J. Lee Bivins of Amarillo, Texas. The Waggoners bought him in 1916 or 1917 and gave him to Lee Bivins in 1924.

YELLOW JACKET. This Yellow Jacket was a dun stallion sired by Yellow Jacket by Little Rondo by Sykes' Rondo and out of a Waggoner mare by Yellow Wolf by Old Joe Bailey.

He was bred by W. T. Waggoner of Fort Worth, Texas, and owned by Mike Beetch of Lawton, Oklahoma. Later he was purchased by Tom Burnett of Fort Worth, Texas.

YELLOW JACKET, BOOTH'S, see YELLOW BELLY.

YELLOW JACKET, EAST'S. East's Yellow Jacket was by Yellow Jacket by Little Rondo by Sykes' Rondo and out of a Waggoner mare. He was bred by W. T. Waggoner of Fort Worth, Texas, and owned by T. T. East of Kingsville, Texas.

YELLOW JACKET, FUQUA'S. This stallion was a dun foaled in about 1933. He was by Blackburn by Yellow Jacket by Little Rondo. He was bred and owned by J. L. Fuqua of Clayton, New Mexico.

YELLOW JACKET, NACK'S. Nack's Yellow Jacket was by Yellow Jacket by Little Rondo by Lock's Rondo. He was owned by William Nack of Cuero, Texas, and by Walter Rebert of Christoval, Texas. He has been referred to as the Nack Horse.

YELLOW JACKET, O'CONNOR'S. O'Connor's Yellow Jacket was sired by Chicaro (TB), but his dam was a mare by Yellow Jacket by Little Rondo. He was bred by John Dial of Goliad, Texas, and owned by Jim O'Connor of Goliad, who may have been the owner of the mare when she foaled Yellow Jacket.

YELLOW JACKET, PHELPS'. Phelps' Yellow Jacket was a nineteenth-century race horse. He was sired by Copperbottom by Copperbottom by Sir Archy. He was owned and raced in 1892 by W. Phelps of Arkansas.

YELLOW JACKET, PYLE'S, see SCOTT.

YELLOW JACKET, SNYDER'S. This Yellow Jacket was by Beetch's Yellow Jacket by Yellow Jacket by Little Rondo. He was owned by Marcus Snyder of Hardin, Montana.

YELLOW JACKET, WADDELL'S. Waddell's Yellow Jacket was by Captain Costigan (TB) and out of a mare by Moss King by Big King by One-Eyed Kingfisher. He was bred by Waddell brothers of Odessa, Texas.

YELLOW STONE. Yellow Stone was a palomino stallion foaled about 1935. He was sired by Champagne by Dundee (TB) and out of Dorothy Dawson. He was bred by Coke T. Roberds of Hayden, Colorado.

YELLOW WOLF. Yellow Wolf was a dun stallion foaled in 1912 who lived until 1935. He was sired by Old Joe Bailey by Eureka by Shelby and out of Old Mary by Ben Burton by Blind Barney by Steel Dust. His second dam was Mandy by the Old Dutchman by Lock's Rondo. He was bred by Dick Baker of Weatherford, Texas, and later owned by W. T. Waggoner of Fort Worth, Texas; Tom Parrot of Throckmorton, Texas; J. M. Rickles of Woodson, Texas; Dick Shelton of Tilden, Texas; and Tom Franklin of Jordanton, Texas. Old Mary was also the dam of Yellow Bear, Yellow Boy, and Yellow Wolf.

YELLOW WOLF, ADAIR'S. This Yellow Wolf was by Yellow Wolf by Joe Bailey by Eureka and out of a Waggoner mare. He was bred by W. T. Waggoner of Fort Worth, and owned by the J. A. Ranch of Palo Duro, Texas. He was a small horse, purchased about 1930.

YELLOW WOLF, BROWN'S. This Yellow Wolf was the first owned by the Waggoner Ranch. Little is known about his breeding, except that he was said to be by Pid Hart by Shelby by Tom Driver. Waggoner bought him from the Brown brothers of Fort Worth, who bought him when he was through racing. He had been a well-known race horse around Galveston at the turn of the century. He got his name not from his color but from an Indian chief. He was seal brown in color, stood a full 15 hands, and weighed 1060 pounds.

YELLOW WOLF, BURNETT'S. Burnett's Yellow Wolf was a dun stallion sired by Yellow Wolf by Old Joe Bailey by Eureka and out of a Waggoner mare. He was bred by W. T. Waggoner of Fort Worth, and owned by Tom L. Burnett of Fort Worth.

YELLOW WOLF, GUTHRIE'S. Guthrie's Yellow Wolf was by Yellow Wolf by Old Joe Bailey by Eureka and out of a Waggoner mare. He was bred by W. T. Waggoner of Fort Worth, Texas, and owned by Rat Guthrie of Santa Anna, Texas.

YELLOW WOLF, LEWIS'. Lewis' Yellow Wolf was foaled in about 1935. He was sired by a stallion sired by Sappho by Brown King by Arch Oldham. He was owned by Martin Lewis of Cienego, New Mexico.

YELLOW WOLF, OLD. Old Yellow Wolf was a bay foaled in about 1877. He was by Whalebone by Old Billy by Shiloh and out of Paisana by Brown Dick by Cold Deck. His second dam was Belton Queen by Guinea Boar. He was bred by William B. Fleming of Belmont, Texas, and owned by T. H. King of Belmont, Texas; Joe W. Mangum of Rancho, Texas; and J. M. Brown of Giddings, Texas.

YELLOW WOLF, REYNOLDS'. Reynolds' Yellow Wolf was by Yellow Wolf by Old Joe Bailey by Eureka and out of a Waggoner mare. He was bred by W. T. Waggoner of Fort Worth, Texas, and owned by J. H. Minnick of Crowell, Texas; Frank Rhodes of Throckmorton, Texas; and the Reynolds Cattle Company of Throckmorton.

YELLOW WOLF, SCHOTT'S. Schott's Yellow Wolf was by Rainy Day by Lone Star by Gold Enamel (TB) and out of a Schott mare. He was bred by Eugene J. Schott of Riomedina, Texas, and owned by Frank Wallace of Alamogordo, New Mexico.

YELLOW WOLF, YOUNG. Young Yellow Wolf was by Old Yellow Wolf by Joe Bailey by Eureka and out of a Waggoner Quarter mare. He was bred by W. T. Waggoner of Fort Worth, Texas, and owned by R. H. Brown of Throckmorton, Texas, and the SMS Ranch of Stamford, Texas. Tom Waggoner gave this Yellow Wolf to R. H. Brown. Later R. H.'s son, R. A. Brown, sold the horse to the Swensons of the SMS Ranch.

YUCCA. This palomino stallion was sired by Spark Plug by Jack McCue by Peter McCue. He was owned by Guy Elliott of Tucumcari, New Mexico.

Z

ZAAL. Zaal was a sorrel stallion foaled in 1927. He was by Ganadore (TB) and out of Olivia by The Senator by Leadville (TB). His second dam was Little Judge by Little Steve by Pony Pete by Barney Owens. He was owned by Samuel Russell, Jr., of Middletown, Connecticut.

ZAINO (CAMERON BAY). Zaino was a dark bay stallion by Cameron by Texas Chief by Little Joe and out of Jenny by Harmon Baker by Peter McCue. He was bred by C. Manuel Benevides of Laredo, Texas.

ZANTANON. Zantanon was a dark sorrel foaled in 1917 who died in 1941. He was by Little Joe by Traveler and out of Jeanette by Billy by Big Jim. He was bred by Ott Adams of Alfred, Texas, and owned by Erasmo Flores of Nuevo Laredo, Nuevo Leon, Mexico; C. Manuel Benevides of Laredo, Texas; Byrne James of Encinal, Texas; and Alonzo Taylor of Hebbronville, Texas.

ZURICK HORSE, see STAR SHOOT.

VI

Geographical Index of Breeders*

ALABAMA (1)
  Crowell, John
    Bill Austin

ARIZONA (28)
  Bowman, Everett, Hillside
    Snooper, Sonny Boy
  Browning, J. E., Willcox
    Bally
  Dubois, Mark, Bonita
    Chico Lindo
  Gardner, C. A., Elgin
    Pop Corn
  Gardner, Mayburn, Camp Verde
    Fuzzy
  Goodyear Farms, Litchfield Park
    Crowder, Rowdy
  Kane, John E., Douglas
    Sonny Boy
  Kennedy, J. J., Bonita
    Apache Kid, Little Brother, Doc, Duke, Guinea Pig,
    Monte Cross, Red Cloud, Strawberry

*The number following the state is the total number of founda-
tion Quarter sires bred in the state. The first line of each entry
lists the name of the breeder or breeders and, if known, the address. The second line lists the foundation sires bred.

242

Logan, Charles, Tucson
　Riley
McKinney, J. T., Willcox
　Mack
Murdock, Dave, Camp Verde
　Murdock
Page, P. P., Willcox
　Wonder World
Parker, W. D., Sonoita
　Dink, Hairpin, Jake
Sands, Louis, Glendale
　Ten File
Sorrills, Roy, Nogales
　Little Ben, Scooter
Wear, W. D., Willcox
　Tony Cottontail

CALIFORNIA (22)

Adams, John, Woodland
　May Boy, Mefford, Shannon, Steam Beer, Uncle Billy
Armstrong, J. J.
　Moore
Blasingame, Lee, Fresno
　Little Confidence, Orphan Boy
Dibbler, T. B., Santa Barbara
　Dueno, Gold Maize
Hughes, Harry, Carrizo
　St. Pat
Jennings, B. W., Visalia
　Orphan's Pride
Knight, T. J., Beatrice
　Walter Overton
Liger, E. L.
　Madstone
Musick, A.
　Johnny Moore, Vanderbilt

Pacheco, Louie, Santa Maria
  Pacheco
Spencer, Homer, Potter Valley
  Duke
Winter, Theodore, Woodland, Sacramento
  Broncho, Jumbo, Millinette, Telegraph

COLORADO (59)

Anderson, B. G., Craig
  Fred
Borilla, Casimiro, Trinidad
  Primero, The Senator
Casement, Dan and Jack, Whitewater
  Balleymooney, Climax, Interrogator, Red Cloud
Crouse, Leo, Elbert
  Sir Rowdy
Dawson, Bruce, Hayden
  Booger Red
Dawson, Si, Hayden
  Bob H, Fred Litze, Old Nick
Horn, Leonard, Wolcott
  Young Peekaboo, Rex
Hubbard, R. H., Oak Creek
  Nick
Jenkinson, T. D., Glenwood Springs
  Glenwood Springs
Kurruish, R. J., Littleton
  Senator Jr.
Lamont, R. P., Larkspur
  Surprise
Leonard, Henry, Colorado Springs
  Leinster, Neel Gray, Rainmaker, St. Damian
Lindauer Brothers, Grand Valley
  Bumble Bee
McDonald, R. W., Glenwood Springs
  Yampah

Myers, Ernest, Hoehne
  Pacific
Peavy, Marshall, Steamboat Springs
  Nick S, Saladin, Si Ding, Tim
Peterson, A. E., Elbert
  Gold Coin, Mont Megellon, Spiegel
Roberds, Coke T., Hayden
  Billy Sunday, Buck Thomas, Coke T, Faithful, Frank,
  Gold Dust, Jiggs, Mose, Pony, Rusty, Sleepy Dick, Yel-
  low Stone
Savage, Ben, Steamboat Springs
  Roman Gold
Semotan, Quentin, Clark
  Chief
Spencer, Cash, Peyton
  Woodrow Wilson
Stetson, Frank, Oak Creek
  Teddy
Turner, D. B., Colorado Springs
  Falacy, La Plata, Red Boy, Red Devil, Red Lion, Red
  Vigil
Van Dyne, Riley, Fort Garland
  Butler Red
Williams, Kirk, Mancos
  Billy White, Columbus, Dutch, Silver Dick

CONNECTICUT (1)

Russell, Samuel, Jr., Middletown
  Red Magic

ILLINOIS (47)

Blakeley, Edwin, Kelbourne(?)
  Kilbourne, Menzo Shurtz
Brown, Joseph, Petersburg
  Johnnie Brown, Peter Brown

Koontz, Mr.
  Little Dan Tucker
Leavitt, J. M., San Jose
  Nelson
Owens, James, Berlin
  Reputation Jr.
Rea, Grant, Carthage
  Young Roan Dick
Stuart, Harry, Lewiston
  Barney McCoy
Wade, Robert, Plymouth
  Roan Dick, Sirock, Bob Wade
Watkins, Hugh, Walter, B. C., Oakford
  Duck Hunter, Jesse Hoover, Joe Joker, John Wilkins,
  Kendricks, Oakford, Tom D II, Trucker Miller, Walking
  John
Watkins, Sam, Elias, Tom, Petersburg
  Bay Billy Sunday, Billy Mason, Coal Oil Johnny, Cotton
  Eyed Joe, Cyclone, Dan Tucker, Diamond Joe, Dobbin,
  Harmon Baker, Hickory Bill, Hi Henry, Jodie, Pat Tuck-
  er, Peter McCue, Peters Cue, Ramsey, Running Mal-
  lard, Sam Watkins, Sealem, Sellex, Terns Trick, Tom
  Harding, Tot Lee, Wake Up Jake, Walter P, Weaver

IOWA (3)

  Cunningham, T. J., Lanesboro
    Lanesboro
  Sumners, W. M., Lineville
    Dr. Glendenning, Walter Howard

KANSAS (15)

  Casement, Dan (see Colorado)
  Day, John, Asawata
    Little Pete

Lawrence, S. E., Maple City
   Pawhuska, W. H. Ashland
Lewis, Joe, Hunnewell
   Doe Belly, Joe Lewis, Rolling Deck
Smiley, Mike, Sylvan Grove
   Guinea Pig, Johnny Corbett, Pony Pete, Printer Tom,
   Red Texas, Little Steve
Trowbridge, H. A., Wellington
   Little Danger, No Remarks, Okema

KENTUCKY (16)

Bryan, Dr.
   Alasco
Duncan, H. T.
   Gray Eagle
Edwards, W. N., Adair County
   Van Tromp
Harris, John
   Little Tiger, Old Tiger
Ross, Webb, Scott County
   Bay Printer, Flying Dutchman, Rheube, Sweet Owen,
   Viley
Sanders, Lewis, Jr.
   Weazle
Treacy, B. J., Lexington
   Kennedy, Mahogany, Morissey, O'Connell, Tom Tug

LOUISIANA (1)

Zeringue, Noah, Abbeville
   Flying Bob

MEXICO (5)

Greene Cattle Company, Cananea
   Old Biscuit, Lover, R. O. Sorrel, San Fernando Sykes,
   Son of Sykes

MICHIGAN (2)

Mathewson, J. M., Lowell
Odd Fellow, One Dime

MISSOURI (12)

Alsup brothers, Bald Knob
Mose Brimmer, Red Buck, Rondo, Young White Lightning
Berry, Joe, Mount Vernon
Cold Deck
Chote, Alex, Lockwood
Black Ball
Floyd, Nathan, Carthage
Cold Deck
Hedgepeff, John, Joplin
Barney Owens
Lillard, J. W., Richards
Marshall Ney
Owens, Bill, Smithville
Bay Cold Deck, Boanerges
Stockton, Bill, Lockwood
Slip Shoulder

MONTANA (3)

Baker, R. H., Helena
Red Buck
Kirkendall, H., Helena
Panama
Snyder, Marcus, Hardin
Grey Sis

NEBRASKA (1)

Anderson, W. M., Cody
Rancher Bank

NEW MEXICO (41)

Andes, M. E., Portales
  Jack of Diamonds, Red Wing
Bond, J. W., Ramah
  Windigo
Booth, J. S., Deming
  Texas
Brister, J. M., Lordsburg
  Lucky
Brown Brothers, Farmington
  Tex
Burns, Bob, Hope
  June Bug
Forker, H. L., Nara Visa
  Swanky
Francis, Charles, Floyd
  Dick Dillon, Shorty
Francis, J. W., Floyd
  Texas Jack
Francis, W. J., Elida
  Jack McCue
Fuqua, J. L., Clayton
  Yellow Jacket
Gallegos, Filiberto, Gallegos
  Whiskaway II
Harrington, Albert, Correo
  Red, Teddy
Hayes, A. T., Greer
  Miacho
Jenkins, J. R., Corona
  Old Jesse
Kelly, Jim and Earl, Las Vegas
  Kelly, Star Shoot
Kimble, Roy, Clayton
  Reincocas

Lee, O. M., Alamogordo
   Lee Bay, Little Trouble
Mitchell, Albert, Albert
   Mitch, Sunday
Neafus, J. C., Newkirk
   Young Chickasha Bob
Phillips, Waite, Cimarron
   Golden Lad, Monte Carlo, Yellow Gold
Saunders, H. P., Roswell
   Mud Lark, Nooblis, Robert A, Wandering Jew
Springer, Ed (CS Ranch), Cimarron
   Little Joe, Mike, Little Nick, Pat
Thomas, George, Guy
   Santa Claus
Willett, A. F., Des Moines
   Red Cedar
Williams, John, Stead
   Speedy
Zurick, J. W., Stead
   Pancho

NORTH CAROLINA (17)

Abbington, Hardiman, Bertie County
   Twickham
Alston, J. J., Halifax County
   Brinkley's Peacock, Spider
Cox, John
   Bacchus (Cox's)
Eaton, C. R., Granville County
   Garrick
Eaton, John R., Granville County
   Van Tromp
Haynes, Herbert
   Fabricus
Hunter, Tom, Edgecombe County
   Ball

Jones, Wyllie, Halifax County
  Blue Boar
McGeehee, William, Person County
  Janus
Mills, William, Granville County
  Little Bacchus
Potter, John, Granville County
  Old Bacchus
Shrewsberry, Alexander, Franklin County
  Saint Tammany
Snelling, Hugh, Granville County
  Black Snake
Williams, Governor, Graven County
  Comet
Williams, Will, Martin County
  One-Eye
Wilson, George
  Ranger

NEW YORK (3)

  Land, Robert, Long Island
    Vito
  Lowrey, Edward, Norwich
    Boanerges
  Smith, Lawrence, Smithtown
    Young Pawhuska

OKLAHOMA (63)

  Armstrong Brothers, Elk City
    Hermus
  Armstrong, Dan, Doxey
    Fear Me, Library, Red Fish, Speedy Ball
  Armstrong, Reed, Foss
    Dr. Blue Eyes, Little Man
  Axley, George, Guthrie
    Frank Johnson

Beetch, Mike, Lawton
Mike Beetch, Smokey, Gray Eagle
Blake, Coke, Pryor
Dave Mack, Dexter, Grey Wolf, Hogue Horse, Iron
Wood, Rambler, Red Devil, Red Man, Smuggler, Tramp,
Traveler, Tubal Cain
Burlingame, Milo, Cheyenne
John Wilkes
Campbell, C. B., Minco
Denver, Jeff, Minco Jimmy, Tom Campbell, Uncle
Jimmy Gray
Clark, Henry, Boise City
Nabob, Ned Oakes, Taffy
Cooper, Jess, Roosevelt
Midnight
Cooper, Keller, Elk City
Tom
Dawson, John, Talala
Muskogee Star
Doty, George, Afton
Chicken Smart
Francis, William, Elk City
Red Bird
Harrel, John A., Canute
Duck Hunter, Jack Dempsey, Red, Red Reed, Scare-
crow
Herridge, Joe, Fairfax
Little Brother II
Huggins, M. B., Clinton
Ranger II
Hurley, A. D., Canute
A. D. Reed
Kellum, Smith, Cheyenne
Old Bob Peters, Young Bob Peters
Lissley, W., Oklahoma City
Rendon

SOUTH DAKOTA (2)

7-11 Ranch, Hot Springs
Billie Sunday, July

TENNESSEE (6)

Alsup brothers (see Missouri)
Chrisman
Swayback
Clayton, H. H.
Shiloh
Harding, W. B., Nashville
John W. Norton
Hunter, Dudley
Grey Rebel
Maxwell, N. B., Wendell
Cold Deck, Paddy

TEXAS (578)

Adams, Jim, Alfred
J. D.
Adams, Ott, Alfred
Bay Brown, Bonnie Joe, Bullet, Clemente Garcia, Cotton Eyed Joe, Del Monte, Filipe, Grano de Oro, Jim Brown, Jim Wells, Pancho Villa, Sleepy Sam, Snake Bit Horse, Tocho Garcia, Zantanon
Allen, H. C., San Angelo
Sealskin
Allen, Will, Uvalde
Rose's Sykes Horse
Allred, Mr., Mineral Wells
Dan
Anson, William, Christoval
Billy Anson, Billy Anson Sorrel, Whitehead's Billy Anson, Brown Jug, Concho Colonel, Harmon Baker Jr., Harmon N, Hi Eastland, Jazz, Jim, Old Joe, Major Domo,

Bodie, A. H., Pontotoc
  Pablo
Bouldin, Clayton, Belmont
  Bill Fleming
Bowers, Aubra, Allison
  Cimarron
Brewster, William, Edenburg
  Sleepy
Brown, J. M., Giddings
  Billy Fleming, Jim Reed
Brown, Jim, Karnes City
  Karnes City Jim
Bunton, J. A., Uvalde
  Bunton Horse
Burnett, Tom, Fort Worth
  Silver Cloud
Burson, John, Silverton
  Choctaw
Butler, Emmett, Kenedy
  Ben, Sid
Campbell, W. H., Gainesville
  Silver Dollar
Canales, C., Premont
  Cirildo
Cardwell, O. W., Junction
  Barney, Dutch, Hill Top, Silver M
Castello, C. E., Woodson
  Sammy
Christian, D. W., Big Spring
  Barney L, Barney Lucas, Bobbie Lowe, Burton Brown,
  Dusty Brown, Earl Ederis, Eddie Earl, Frank Allen,
  Haliday, Hudson Jr., Jackie Boy, Lenox, Merle Lee,
  Palmistry, Rigsby, Rock and Rye, Sam Sparks, Smithy,
  Step Back, Cunningham's Traveler, Turn Back, Wan-
  dering Jew, Webb's Choice
Clegg, George, Alice
  Albert, Barefield Horse, Basil Prince, Clegg Cripple

Sorrel, Clegg Dun, Edes Horse, El Rey, George, Gotch, Henry, Joselia, Northington Horse, Red Chief, San Antonio, Streak, Sutherland, Little Texas Chief, Tom Thumb Jr., Siminoff's Uncle Jimmy Gray, Will Wright

Cook, W. I., Maryneal
Sim's Yellow Boy

Copeland, W. J., Pettus
Little Ace, Willie

Corder, J. M., Sanderson
Chocolate Drop, Gun Powder, Muy Pronto, Ned Wilson, Pedro Rico, Pickaninny, Prince Albert, Rambling Sam, Red Seal II, Ringmaster, Robin Hood, Rush, Select, Senator, Shooting Star, Skipper Delight, Starlight, Stepping On It, Tom Gay

Cowey, John, Dewville
Rambling Jack

Cowsert, J. D. and M. A., Junction
Elexa Joe, Red Devil

Cruz, Santana, Driftwood
Lone Man

Cunningham, Jack and Arron, Comanche
Dusty Brown, Gulliver

Custer, J. L., Spofford
Pure Gold, Straight Edge

Davenport, Josephine, Center Point
Hell Cat

Davis, R. C., Big Spring
Don Topaz

Davis, W. R., Sterling City
Concho, Golden Admiration

Deahl, Ed, Panhandle
Gold Dust

Dial, John, Goliad
Ace, Clamp Sorrel, Gold Wing, Mr. Rex, Little Rex, Sudden Change, Truant Boy, O'Connor's Yellow Jacket

Dixon, W. P., Flatonia
Sam Harper Jr.

DuBose, Friendly, Nueces County
  King
Dunman, R. L., Coleman
  Proctor
East, A. L., Sarita
  Mac
Evans, Dan, Stephenville
  Poncho
Evans, L. L., Brownwood
  Rayd Orr
Farish, S. P. and W. S., Berclair
  Little House
Fleming, W. B., Belmont
  Alex Gardner, Anthony, Billy Dribble, Chunky Bill, Cuadro, Little Jack, Joe Collins, Joe Murray, Old Joe, John Crowder, Pancho, Pink Reed, Red Rover, Shiloh Fleming, Whalebone, Old Yellow Wolf
Franklin, Mose, San Antonio
  Frank Gray, Tony Rogers
Fricke, Otto, Gonzales
  Guy
Fuller, P. L., Snyder
  Little Fort, Red, Selam II
Gardner, Alex, John, Charles, San Angelo
  Billy Bartlett, Brown Billy, Bulger, Chief Wilkins, Chulo Mundo, Crawford, Jim Ned, John Gardner, Little John, Muggins, Three Finger Jack, Dolan's Traveler, Little Traveler
Gates, Jack, Devine
  Cold Deck, Red Rover
Gibson, Mr., San Antonio
  Little Kid, King
Godfrey, Dick, Menard
  Jack of Diamonds
Gray, Dick, Gorman
  George Duke, Honest Dick, Willrun

Green, Grant, Uvalde
  Sykes Horse
Gunn and Poston, Austin
  Star Tex
Habey, Dick, Hondo
  Tom Mix
Haby, Martin, Nick, Sterle, Riomedina
  Black Jim, Golden Amel, Golden Streak, Jimmy Gray
  Jr., Just Right
Haley, Tom and C. R., Sweetwater
  Dash, Old Dutchman, Lock's Rondo, Shelby, Shiloh,
  White Heel
Hall, W. S., Boerne
  June Bee
Hancock, W. E., Perryton
  Jolly, Lindy
Harkey, Jim, Fort Stockton
  Dodger, Four Flush
Harkey, Leigh, Sheffield
  Little Dodger, King
Harkey, Sam, Sheffield
  Tempest
Harr, Aubra, Millett
  Maltsberger Dun
Hemphill and Walters, Mertzon
  Dark Alley
Henderson, Tom, El Dorado
  Hard Tack
Hewell brothers, Nixon
  Sun Shot
Hicks, Raymond, Bandera
  Red Buck
Holman, J. S., Sonora
  Diamond, Holman Horse, Jap, Jap Holman, Johnny,
  Keggy, Mosco, Red Wing, Ruby Davis, Top Hat, Spil-
  ler's Top Hat

House, J. W., Cameron
  Joe Butler, Jonas
Hudspeth, Roy, San Angelo
  Roy Hudspeth
Huettig, Corinne, Kyle
  Rex
Jackson, J. J., Coleman
  Greaser
J. A. Ranch, Palo Duro
  Jack Walton, J. A. McCue, Midnight II, Young Midnight, Smokey, Wilkens
Jeffries, Joe D., Clarendon
  George Morgan, John Caldwell
Jenkins, W. F., Menard
  Rob Roy
Jones, Frank, Marfa
  Jones' Ace of Hearts
Joyce, Jack, Graham
  Prince Charming
Keeling, Robert, San Angelo
  Keeling Horse
Keller, George, Erath County
  Snip
Ketchum, G. Berry, Sheffield
  Damit, Old Mineral, Red Rover
King Ranch, Kingsville
  El Venado, Hickory Switch, Sam, Toy Boy, Violin
King, Tom, Belmont
  Priest Bob, Sam
Kuykendall, Gil, Buda
  Ben Bolt
Laning, J. A., Rocksprings
  Jimmie
Lock, W. W., Kyle
  Cold Deck, Stone's Rondo, Texas Chief

Meyer, H. J., Hondo
  Show Boy
Minnick, J. H., Crowell
  Young Eagle, Frank Patton Dun, Workman Horse
Mitchell, W. B., Marfa
  Golden Grain, Roman Sappho, Sappho
Moody, W. E., Toyah
  Lonnie Grey
Moore, J. W., Mobeetie
  Judge Wilkins, Sam Watkins
Moore, W. M., San Saba
  Clover Leaf
Morris, E. E., Rocksprings
  Glory
Morris, Jim, Devine
  Little King
Morris Ranch, San Antonio
  Prince
Moss, Luke, Llano
  Kingfisher
Murray, Paul, Pandora
  Paul Murray
Nack, William, Cuero
  Billy Mangum, Joe Ratliff, Red Knight
Nasworthy, John R., San Angelo
  Little Buck, Charley Wilson, Hal Fisher, Nigger, Wall
  Paper
Neal, Luke, Gillett
  Ace of Hearts, Gotch
Newman, J. F., Sweetwater
  Booger Red, Coalie, Dr. All Good, Kid Weller, Red
  Ray, Reno Rebel
Newton, George, Del Rio
  Marion Wilson, Little Menard, Little Penny, Tormentor
Nixon, J. W., Hondo
  Billy, Rebel

Pfefferling, Henry, San Antonio
  Eddie Gray, High Ball, Jack of Diamonds, Major Speck,
  Stockley Horse, T. C. Wheat Bay, Tommie Gray
Rayburn, Bill, Hood County
  Pat
Raymond, Fred, Raymondville
  Gotch, Tuerto
Renfro, J. E. and Matt, Menard (also Mineral, Sonora,
  Fort Stockton)
  Concho Kid, Glad One, Helter, June Bug, Kinch, Moon
  Mullens, Mushmouth, Pecos Pete, Pee Wee, Red Buck,
  Tinkertoy, Rio, Tom Polk
Reuteria, Luis, Edenburg
  Turk
Reynolds Cattle Company, Fort Worth
  Rooster, Trammell
Rickles, J. M., Bridgeport
  Richard
Saenz, Anastacio, Rios
  Ace of Hearts II, Leonell, Little Pancho, Saenz
Saski, Jack, Cuero
  Ace of Diamonds
Schaffer, Dick, Pampa
  Schaffer's Ace of Hearts
Scharbauer, Clarence, Midland
  Old Salty
Schott, Eugene, Riomedina
  Ben Hur, Black Bear, Little Fox, Handsome Hiram,
  Jimmie Bell, Lone Star, Man-a-Life, Medina Sport, O
  Jimmy, Pal-o-Mine, Prince, Raindrop, Rainy Cloud,
  Rainy Day, Red Wing Sir, Twin City, Schott's Yellow
  Wolf
Seale, C. C., Baird
  Judge Welch, The Virginian
Senne, F. G., Hondo
  Black Streak

Shelts, William, Spearman
  Teddy
Shely, Will and Dow, Alfred
  Buster, Captain Joe, Dorado, Jess Parsons, Little Joe,
  Joe Shely, King, Mack, Red Bird, Texas Chief, Whale-
  bone
Sims, John T., Jr., Snyder
  Royal D
Smith, Millard, Van Horn
  Teddy
Smith, Webb, DeWitt County
  Sleepy Dick
Snyder, Marcus, Seminole
  Little Red
Southerland brothers, Eagle Lake
  Broke Shoulder
Springs, Andrew, Seguin
  Coley
Stanfield, E. Shelby, Thorp Spring
  Anti Pro, Bill Garner, Eureka, Pid Hart, Rocky Moun-
  tain Tom, Thurman
Starke, Barney, Tulia
  Old Mike
Stead, Will, Tulia
  Spark Plug, Will Stead
Steffek, C. L., Hallettsville
  Slim Jim
Sulden, Wilson, Hallettsville
  Little Dick
Sutton, R. C., Cotulla
  Tim Page
Swenson brothers, Stamford
  Swenson
Sykes, Columbus, Stockdale
  Spokane

Sykes, Crawford, Nixon
Arch Oldham Jr., Billy Cowey, Blue Eyes, Crawford Sykes, Dogie Beasley, Prince Oldham, Little Rondo, Sykes' Rondo, Allen's Sykes

Talley, Henry, Nixon
Rex Jr.

Taylor, John, Kendleton
Sam Bass

Thompson, Clyde, Moore
Midnight

Thompson, Ed, Stinnett
Sonny Boy

Tijerino, Pedro, Cuero
Johnny

Tindall, Jack, Eastland
Buck

Tinsley, J. R., Gonzales
Robert T

Tips, George, Kenedy
Sweet Dick

Trammell, Walter and Tom, Sweetwater
Young Barney Owens, Easter, George House, Grover, Jim Trammell, No Good, School Boy, Si, Little Tom, Trouble

Tullos, Emory, Charlotte
Drowsy Henry

Waddell brothers, Odessa and Kermit
Dinero, Johnnie Reed, Longfellow, Muskrat, Nigger Baby, Oddfellow II, Pete King, Powder River, Red Dennis, Waddell's Rondo, Samoset, Stand Pat, Woodpecker, Waddell's Yellow Jacket

Waggoner, W. T., Fort Worth
Apache, Chocolate, Clover, Clover Wolf, Young Dr. Mack, Eagle, Gold Dollar, Gold Nugget, Gold Standard, Harrison, Olg Wag, Keeney Horse, Rainy Day, Royal Ford Jr., Skyrocket, Spark Plug, Sparky, Tarzan, Hick-

man's Waggoner, Jackson's Waggoner, Scharbauer's Waggoner, Smith's Waggoner, Yankee Doodle, Yellow Boy, Burnett's Yellow Boy, Yellow Fever, Yellow Jacket, East's Yellow Jacket, Adair's Yellow Wolf, Burnett's Yellow Wolf, Guthrie's Yellow Wolf, Reynolds' Yellow Wolf, Young Yellow Wolf

Walling, W. P., Robert Lee
  Barney, Rattler
Walston, Frank, Menard
  Red Kite
Walters, Pleasant, Oakville
  Hondo, Pleas Walters
Wardlaw, L. B., Del Rio
  Cuter
Waring, Sam, Eden
  Master Gould, Operator, Red Seal
Watson, John, Burnet County
  Gray John
Wheat, Gus, Sonora
  Black Jack
White, G. R., Brady
  Silver Streak
Whitehead and Wardlaw, Del Rio
  Johnny Walker Horse
Wilkins, John, San Antonio
  Billy Sunday, Charley Howell, Edgar Uhl, Joe Howell, Marco San, San Antonio
Wilkinson, Arch, Menard
  King John, Walking Prince
Williams, John, San Angelo
  Sonora Harmon
Wingate, D., Devine
  Lone Star, Magician
Wisdom, E. E., San Antonio
  Jiggs

Witherspoon and Sanders, Hereford
  Straight Shot
Wood, F. T., Abilene
  John McKay
Wright, Cotton, Banquite
  Tom Thumb
Wright, W. A., Kingsbury
  Major Gray
Wright, W. T., Alice
  San Juan
Wylie, Will, Palo Duro
  Miller Boy

VIRGINIA (22)

Alexander, Mark, Mecklenburg County
  Old Veto
Allan, Fayette, Halifax County
  Nonpariel
Atkinson, John
  Janus
Bugg, Jacob, Mecklenburg County
  Buck Sorrel, Dreadnot
Burwell, Lewis, Mecklenburg County
  Phoenix
Davidson, George
  Aeolus
Goode, Robert, Mecklenburg County
  Flag of Truce
Goode, John, Mecklenburg County
  Babram, Paddy Whack, Twigg
Haskens, James, Brunswick County
  Shad
Hendrick, Obed, Halifax County
  Celer
Meade, Everett, Amelia County
  Meade's Old Celer, Cloudius

Patrick, John, Charlotte County
  Kentucky Whip
Ragland, Lipscomb, Halifax County
  Diomed
Skipwith, Sir Peton, Mecklenburg County
  Cripple
Stewart, Peter, Greensville County
  Moggy
Turpin, Thomas, Powhatan County
  Brimmer, Camden, Fleetwood

WASHINGTON (1)

Eaton, George, Yakima
  Chief

WYOMING (10)

Allison, C. A., Weston
  Jim Rix, Pearly Bills, Picarilla II, Polo King
Hersig, Mark, Cheyenne
  Moses
Moye, Earl, Arvada
  Dutch Martin, Monty, Nigger, Big Red, Starlight